Candrakīrti's Introduction to the Middle Way

OXFORD GUIDES TO PHILOSOPHY

Series Editors

Rebecca Copenhaver, Washington University, St. Louis
Christopher Shields, University of Notre Dame
Mark Timmons, University of Arizona

Advisory Board

Michael Beaney, Ursula Coope, Karen Detlefsen, Lisa Downing, Tom Hurka, Pauline Kleingeld, Robert Pasnau, Dominik Perler, Houston Smit, Allen Wood

Oxford Guides to Philosophy presents concise introductions to the most important primary texts in the history of philosophy. Written by top scholars, the volumes in the series are designed to present up-to-date scholarship in an accessible manner, in order to guide readers through these challenging texts.

Anscombe's Intention: A Guide
John Schwenkler

Kant's Doctrine of Virtue: A Guide
Mark C. Timmons

Sidgwick's The Methods of Ethics: A Guide
David Phillips

Spinoza's Ethics: A Guide
Michael LeBuffe

Bentham's Introduction to the Principles of Morals and Legislation: A Guide
Steven Sverdlik

Mary Shepherd: A Guide
Deborah Boyle

Candrakīrti's Introduction to the Middle Way: A Guide
Jan Westerhoff

Candrakīrti's Introduction to the Middle Way

A Guide

JAN WESTERHOFF

OXFORD
UNIVERSITY PRESS

OXFORD
UNIVERSITY PRESS

Oxford University Press is a department of the University of Oxford. It furthers the University's objective of excellence in research, scholarship, and education by publishing worldwide. Oxford is a registered trade mark of Oxford University Press in the UK and certain other countries.

Published in the United States of America by Oxford University Press
198 Madison Avenue, New York, NY 10016, United States of America.

CIP data is on file at the Library of Congress

ISBN 978–0–19–761234–7 (pbk.)
ISBN 978–0–19–761233–0 (hbk.)

DOI: 10.1093/oso/9780197612330.001.0001

Paperback printed by Marquis Book Printing, Canada
Hardback printed by Bridgeport National Bindery, Inc., United States of America

MIX
Paper from
responsible sources
FSC® C103567

Contents

Structural Outline of the Text

1. **The importance of compassion [1:001–1:004]**
   Obtaining the 1st bodhisattva stage [1:005–1:008]
   The perfection of generosity [1:009–1:016]
   Metaphorical description of the 1st stage [1:017]
2. **Obtaining the 2nd bodhisattva stage: The perfection of moral discipline [2:001–2:009]**
   Metaphorical description of the 2nd stage [2:010]
3. **Obtaining the 3rd bodhisattva stage [3:001]**
   The perfection of patience [3:002–3:010]
   Further qualities of the 3rd bodhisattva stage [3:011–3:012]
   Metaphorical description of the 3rd bodhisattva stage [3:013]
4. **Obtaining the 4th bodhisattva stage: The perfection of effort [4:001]**
   Further qualities of the 4th bodhisattva stage [4:002]
5. **Obtaining the 5th bodhisattva stage: The perfection of meditation [5:001]**
6. **Obtaining the 6th bodhisattva stage [6:001]**
   The perfection of wisdom [6:002]
   The source and the recipients of the teachings on emptiness [6:003–6:007]
   6a. Refutation of the four ways of causal production [6:008a]
      6a.1 Production from itself [6:008b–6:013]
      6a.2 Production from another [6:014–6:097]
         Refutation of production from another through reasoning [6:014–6:022]

Refutation of production from another through reasoning with reference to an absurd consequence [6:014–6:016]
Refutation of production from another through reasoning with reference to time [6:017–6:020]
Refutation of production from another through reasoning with reference to four alternatives [6:021]
Refutation of production from another through experience [6:022]
The two truths [6:023–6:032]
Implications of the theory of the two truths [6:033–6:042]
Avoiding eternalism and nihilism [6:033–6:034]
Avoiding the view that intrinsic natures exist at the level of either truth [6:035–6:036]
Accounting for karma [6:037–6:042]
The Yogācāra position [6:043–6:097]
Exposition of the Yogācāra position [6:043–6:047]
Refutation of the Yogācāra position through reasoning [6:048–6:083]
Example 1: Dreams [6:048–6:053]
Example 2: Floaters [6:054–6:056]
The role of karmic potentials [6:057–6:067]
The Yogācāra position is argumentatively and scripturally unsatisfactory [6:068]
Example 3: Meditative experience [6:069–6:070]
Common difficulties for all three examples [6:071]
Dependent nature and reflexive awareness [6:072–6:078]
Yogācāra and the two truths [6:079–6:083]
Why Yogācāra was taught [6:084–6:092]
Sūtras teaching Yogācāra are *sūtras* with interpretable meaning [6:094–6:097]

6a.3 Production from itself and from another [6:098]
6a.4 Production from no cause [6:099–6:103]
Intrinsic natures are mistaken projections [6:104–6:106]
Emptiness does not mean nonexistence [6:107–6:113]
Benefits of realizing dependent origination [6:114–6:119]
6b. Refutation of intrinsically existent persons [6:120–6:165]
6b.1 Refutation of the self and aggregates as different [6:121–6:125]
6b.2 Refutation of the self and aggregates as identical [6:126–6:145]
Refutation of the self and aggregates as identical by reasoning [6:127–6:131]
Refutation of the self and aggregates as identical by scripture [6:132–6:133]
Refutation of the self as the collection of aggregates: the analogy of the chariot [6:134–139]
Difficulties with mis-identifying the object of negation [6:140–6:141]
Self and aggregates are not support and supported [6:142]
The self does not possess the aggregates [6:143]
The 20 wrong views of the self [6:144–6:145]
6b.3 Refutation of the self as neither identical with the aggregates, nor different from them [6:146–6:149]
6b.4 Summarizing the view of the self [6:150]
6b.5 The analogy of the chariot [6:151–6:165]
The chariot does not exist in any of the seven ways [6:151–6:158]
The chariot exists as a mere dependent designation [6:159–6:165]
Other entities are similarly dependently designated [6:166–6:170]
Is the Madhyamaka position self-refuting? [6:171–6:178]

The 16 types of emptiness [6:179–6:218]

Condensed classification into four kinds of emptiness [6:219–6:223]

Conclusion [6:224–6:226]

7. **Obtaining the 7th bodhisattva stage [7:001]**
8. **Obtaining the 8th bodhisattva stage [8:001–8:003]**
9. **Obtaining the 9th bodhisattva stage [9:001]**
10. **Obtaining the 10th bodhisattva stage [10:001]**

    Explanation of the qualities of each bodhisattva stage in terms of its special enumerated features [11:001–11:010]

11. **Explanation of the level of Buddhahood [11:011–11:051]**

    The Buddha's knowledge [11:011–11:013]

    The Buddha's activity [11:014–11:016]

    The three bodies of the Buddha [11:017–11:027]

    The ten powers of the Buddha [11:028–11:040]

    Describing the Buddha's qualities [11:041–11:043]

    The physical embodiment of the Buddha and its activity [11:044–11:047]

    The continuity of the Buddha's teaching [11:048–11:051]

12. **Origin and uniqueness of Candrakīrti's exposition of Madhyamaka [11:052–11:056]**

Introduction

1. Preliminary remarks: Introducing Candrakīrti

The translation of Candrakīrti's name is "Glorious Moon," and if we consider the historical context of Candrakīrti's times it becomes apparent that he was indeed, like the moon, surrounded by lights in the star-studded firmament of Asian intellectual and political history at the beginning of the 7th century. Living around the years 600–650 CE,[1] his Indian contemporaries include Brahmagupta, who presented the first rules for the arithmetical manipulation of zero, as well as Dharmakīrti, one of the most influential Indian Buddhist philosophers. Looking beyond India there is Songtsen Gampo, the founder of the Tibetan Empire, the second emperor of the Tang dynasty, Taizong, in China, the multi-talented King Amshuverma of Nepal, and the famous Buddhist scholar and traveler Xuanzang visiting India in the second quarter of the 7th century.

It is fair to say that Madhyamaka (together with Yogācāra, the other main philosophical school of Mahāyāna Buddhism) was one of India's most successful intellectual exports, and an understanding of Candrakīrti's interpretation of Madhyamaka is essential for explaining how a large number of Madhyamaka philosophers subsequently understood this intellectual system. His work also constitutes a clear, comprehensive, and intellectually

[1] 530–600 CE has been proposed as an alternative date by Lindtner (1979: 90–91), but see Ruegg 1981: 71, note 228. Duerlinger (2013: 1) suggests 570–650.

Candrakīrti's Introduction to the Middle Way. Jan Westerhoff, Oxford University Press.
 DOI: 10.1093/oso/9780197612330.003.0001

audacious introduction to central Madhyamaka ideas that provides its student with a well-appointed base camp for exploring other interpretations.

1a. Candrakīrti's works

Candrakīrti's extant works include four commentaries on key Madhyamaka texts: a detailed commentary on the foundational text of the Madhyamaka school, Nāgārjuna's *Mūlamadhyamakakārikā* called the "Clear Words" (*Prasannapadā*), two commentaries on Nāgārjuna's shorter works, the "Seventy Verses on Emptiness" (*Śūnyatāsaptati*) and the "Sixty Stanzas on Reasoning" (*Yuktiṣaṣṭikā*), and a commentary on Āryadeva's "Four Hundred Verses" (*Catuḥśataka*). The most substantial among Candrakīrti's independent works is the "Introduction to the Middle Way" (*Madhyamakāvatāra*) which is the focus of our attention here. Candrakīrti also composed a detailed auto-commentary to this text, the *Madhyamakāvatārabhāṣya*. Somewhat shorter independent works include the "Seventy Stanzas on the Three Refuges" (*Triśaraṇasaptati*), "a poetic introduction to lay-Buddhists from the viewpoint of the Mahāyāna"[2] and the "Treatise on the Five Aggregates" (*Pañcaskandhaprakaraṇa*), a discussion of Abhidharma ontology from the Madhyamaka perspective.[3] Some of Candrakīrti's works are still extant in the original Sanskrit, others are preserved in Tibetan translations. As befits the centrality of Candrakīrti's thought for understanding Madhyamaka, his works have received a considerable amount of attention from Western

[2] Sorensen 1986: 9.

[3] For further information on Candrakīrti's works, see Lindtner 1979: 87–91; Potter 2017: 148–248; Eltschinger 2019. A number of later tantric works are also ascribed to Candrakīrti; if these were written by the same author as the texts just mentioned, a much longer lifespan would have to be assumed for him (as the Tibetan tradition does (Chimpa and Chattopadhyaya 1970: 199)). See Vose 2009: 30.

scholars, and practically all of them have by now been translated into European languages.[4]

1b. Candrakīrti's life

We have little reliable information about Candrakīrti's life.[5] He was a Buddhist monk, possibly from South India, and belonged to the monastic university of Nālandā, at that time one of the greatest educational institutions in the world. There he specialized in teaching and commenting on Madhyamaka texts and eventually rose to the rank of Nālandā's chancellor (*kulapāti*), a position he might have held for a decade.[6]

Some of the deeds ascribed to him in hagiographical accounts seem to be more befitting to a magician than to a monastic scholar; they include milking the picture of a cow in order to provide his fellow monks with food, animating a stone lion to scare away a hostile army, moving through walls, and throwing stone vessels without touching them.

It is worthwhile to note, though, that some of these events might play a double role in being both hagiographical transmutations

[4] For readers who would like to read other works by Candrakīrti in English translation, here are a few starting points: MacDonald 2015 presents a translation of the first chapter of the *Prasannapadā* with rich annotations. Readers who would like to read more of the *Prasannapadā* should approach Sprung's 1979 abbreviated English translation with caution (for the reasons described in de Jong 1981), and would be much better advised to consult the partial German and French translations by Schayer 1931, de Jong 1949, and May 1959. Candrakīrti's commentary on the *Yuktiṣaṣṭikā* is translated in Loizzo 2007. Lang translates the first four chapters of the commentary on the *Catuḥśataka*; Sonam's 1994 rendition of a Tibetan commentary on the same text gives some impression of Candrakīrti's commentary on the remainder of Āryadeva's work. Sorensen 1986 translates the *Triśaraṇasaptati* and Lindtner 2017 presents a summary of the *Pañcaskandhaprakaraṇa*.

[5] Loizzo 2007: 385 presents a "speculative reconstruction" of Candrakīrti's life according to which he was born in 590, died in 675, and composed his "Introduction to the Middle Way" aged 25, in 615. Loizzo 2001: 36–54 contains a good survey of the biographical information on Candrakīrti transmitted in Tibetan sources.

[6] Loizzo 2001: 42.

of more mundane events in Candrakīrti's life, and at the same time reflections of his philosophical outlook.[7] Candrakīrti's feeding the monks may be a narrative reworking of his success when being charged with the administration of Nālandā's agricultural enterprises, supervising the farming and growing of crops that provided the food for an institution of considerable size.[8] The military maneuvers with the stone lion could represent Candrakīrti's skill in deflecting the threat from the Śaivite Huṇa rulers persecuting Buddhists and attacking Buddhist monasteries.[9]

These parts of Candrakīrti's hagiography might also be taken as illustrations of his philosophical outlook, and in particular of the illusionism characteristic of Madhyamaka. If one accepts that there are no objective causal relations in the world, but that all causation only takes place at the level of conventional reality, which is a vast mind-made network of agreements between agents, one might be more inclined to accept that some particularly accomplished beings may be able to "tweak" the causal structure of the world so that milk flows from a picture, rather than from a real cow.

Candrakīrti's biographies also contain various accounts of his interactions with the lay scholar and grammarian Candragomin, often presented as a proponent of Yogācāra.[10] These, too, might be a narrative representation of Candrakīrti's highly critical stance toward this rival school of Buddhist thought, a position that is amply demonstrated by the work we are about to discuss.

[7] Traditional Buddhist historical accounts often do not perceive any gap between the events occurring in a teacher's life and their teaching (see Westerhoff 2018b: 29–31).

[8] See Geshe Kelsang Gyatso 1995: 4.

[9] Loizzo 2001: 43, note 99.

[10] We will say some more about this below on pp 16–18.

2. Looking backward: Nāgārjuna and the Madhyamaka school

2a. Nāgārjuna and Madhyamaka

The Madhyamaka school, of which Candrakīrti is one of the greatest exponents, is commonly regarded as founded in Nāgārjuna's (1st–2nd ct CE) "Fundamental Verses on the Middle Way."[11] One should not assume, however, that Nāgārjuna's aim was to start a new philosophical school dedicated to the exposition of his own original ideas. Rather, his aim was to explain the original teaching of the historical Buddha, and to do so by particular emphasis on the "Perfection of Wisdom" (*Prajñāpāramitā*) texts. Nāgārjuna's connection with these works forms a central part of his biography, and even of his name. One of the *Prajñāpāramitā* texts, the "Perfection of Wisdom in One Hundred Thousand Lines," is said to have been given by Buddha Śākyamuni to a group of snake-spirits (the *nāga*s) for safekeeping in their underwater kingdom. When the time was ripe, Nāgārjuna descended to their realm and restored it to the human world.

2b. Commentators on the "Fundamental Verses on the Middle Way"

The "Fundamental Verses on the Middle Way" are a complex and dense work, and unsurprisingly gave rise to a series of commentaries trying to unlock their contents. The earliest Indian commentaries[12]

[11] The English reference translation for this text is Siderits/Katsura 2013.

[12] There is also an older, anonymous commentary, the *Akutobhayā*, sometimes ascribed to Nāgārjuna himself. Buddhapālita's commentary depends strongly on the *Akutobhayā*, and the relation between the two texts is complex. We can put the status of their relation to one side for the time being. Westerhoff (2018b: 121–123) gives some more details.

were composed by two Madhyamaka scholars, Buddhapālita[13] (c. 470–540) and Bhāviveka[14] (c. 500–570). A key difference between the interpretative approaches of Buddhapālita and Bhāviveka lies in the methodology they recommend for explaining Nāgārjuna's arguments, that is, in the *way* in which the Mādhyamaka should defend his philosophical approach. Interestingly, this question turns out to be intricately connected with different opinions on the *content* of Madhyamaka, that is, with different views on *what* the Mādhyamika is saying.

2c. The debate between Buddhapālita and Bhāviveka

According to Buddhapālita, Nāgārjuna's arguments should be spelled out by explicating the contradictory consequences of the positions Nāgārjuna wants to reject.[15] Bhāviveka, on the other hand, suggests that when Nāgārjuna rejects a specific position we should explain this by providing an argument in accordance with the ancient Indian theory of inference that derives the negation of this position from a set of premises. Bhāviveka sees two advantages in this approach. First, it avoids that the student of Madhyamaka draws the wrong conclusion about what Nāgārjuna wants to say. For example, if Nāgārjuna's rejection of entities being substantially produced from themselves[16] is understood simply as deriving a contradiction from the claim that they are so produced, the opponent might mistakenly assume that Nāgārjuna wants to assert the opposite, that entities are substantially produced from what is other than themselves. This misunderstanding can be avoided

[13] Coghlan 2021.

[14] A partial translation is provided by Ames 2019.

[15] The refutation of a position by demonstrating that it entails a contradiction is referred to by the technical term *prasaṅga*. It differs from the familiar *reductio ad absurdum* insofar as the *reductio*, but not the *prasaṅga* licenses the acceptance of the negation of the original position.

[16] See Geshe Kelsang Gyatso 1995: 183–185.

by explicitly presenting Nāgārjuna's position as a set of theses, including the position that entities are not substantially produced from themselves and are also not substantially produced from other entities. This then leads to the second advantage of Bhāviveka's explicatory approach. If we set out Nāgārjuna's approach in terms of a set of worked-out arguments (instead of a series of contradictions drawn from positions one might hold) we will be able to present a set of theses (namely the conclusions of these arguments) that describe the core content of Madhyamaka as a philosophical position. If Madhyamaka is to be successful in debating other Buddhist and non-Buddhist schools it is advantageous to be able to say what the school's position actually is, rather than letting it appear like a dialectical sniper who is quick to fire at contradictions arising from his opponent's views, but never puts up a target of his own.

This is precisely the place where a disagreement about how we should present Madhyamaka arguments morphs into one about what Madhyamaka is actually saying. Such a phenomenon is not one we encounter regularly. Two authors might disagree about how one should explain first-order predicate calculus to students (using a tableaux method or a natural deduction framework, say) but this disagreement will not turn into one about which formulae in first-order predicate calculus actually express valid inferences. In the case of Madhyamaka, however, we have a system that does not simply present a philosophical position, but also a view of the philosophical status of this position (and a view of the philosophical status of this view, and so on all the way up the hierarchy).[17] This view might be regarded as a rejection of philosophical positions,[18] in which case we see an obvious conflict with a result of Bhāviveka's explicatory style, namely the provision of a set of theses that constitute the Madhyamaka position.

[17] Madhyamaka does not offer an alternative view of reality, but an alternative to views of reality. See McGuire 2015: 68.

[18] Or as a rejection of particular *kinds* of philosophical positions. This is a matter of considerable exegetical complexity. To begin exploring this further see Ruegg 1986; Westerhoff 2010a: 61–65.

Candrakīrti defends Buddhapālita's approach of explaining Nāgārjuna's ideas[19] in terms of contradictory consequences entailed by the assertions of his opponent against Bhāviveka's preference for explicating them in terms of arguments formulated in accordance with the ancient Indian theory of inference.[20] One of Candrakīrti's key criticisms is that in order to conduct a debate about anything, both parties must have a shared understanding of what the debate is about. If there is no common conception of the subject of the inferences to be deployed, both debaters are quite literally talking about different things. The debates we are interested in here are not debates about our day-to-day world, about whether we can infer, say, fire when we observe smoke, but concern ultimate reality. Yet the Mādhyamika's conception of universal emptiness does not allow him to postulate any entity as ultimately real. Such an entity would have to be non-empty, and Madhyakama's defense of universal emptiness implies that there is nothing non-empty. Since none of the Mādhyamika's opponents will actually agree with him that there is nothing ultimately real, and hence a shared understanding of the subject-matter of the debate cannot be achieved, the Mādhyamika responds by showing any alleged ultimately real, non-empty entity can be demonstrated to entail a contradiction.

However, explaining Nāgārjuna's thought in terms of inferences as Bhāviveka proposes would commit the Mādhyamika to agreeing with his opponent about ultimate reality, and commits him to philosophical theses (the conclusions of the inferences) he has to defend. Candrakīrti regards the first as straightforwardly impossible, and the second as fundamentally at odds with Nāgārjuna's project.

[19] Perhaps due to the fact that Candrakīrti was seen as the philosophical successor of Buddhapālita in this way, defending Buddhapālita's reading of Nāgārjuna against Bhāviveka, he was sometimes regarded as Buddhapālita's reincarnation. Nevertheless, Tibetan historians were very critical of this idea (Chimpa and Chattopadhyaya 1970: 187–188). Tibetan accounts also claim that Candrakīrti's teacher Kamalabuddhi at Nālandā was a direct disciple of Buddhapālita (Loizzo 2001: 39).

[20] Candrakīrti's criticism of Bhāviveka is mainly found in the opening sections of his *Prasannapadā*, for which see Stcherbatsky 1927: 79–212; MacDonald 2015.

The Mādhyamaka provides philosophical medicine to cure the existential suffering resulting from wrong views of reality. In doing so, he makes the contradictory consequences of these views explicit; he does not present his own views as rivals to combat them.

It is Candrakīrti's defense of Buddhapālita and criticism of Bhāviveka that launched the Prāsaṅgika school.[21] When we nowadays speak about Prāsaṅgika Madhyamaka, we refer to a way of understanding Madhyamaka based on and developing Candrakīrti's exposition of Nāgārjuna, an exposition that takes itself to be grounded in Buddhapālita's explanation of the "Fundamental Verses on the Middle Way."

3. Candrakīrti's "Introduction to the Middle Way"

The "Introduction to the Middle Way," "the most comprehensive, general description of the (Prāsaṅgika-) Madhyamaka teaching"[22] is one of Candrakīrti's earlier works and is cited both in his *Prasannapadā* and in the *Catuḥśatakaṭīkā*, works that must for this reason have been composed subsequently.

3a. The text

The Sanskrit original of the "Introduction to the Middle Way" has only resurfaced relatively recently.[23] Candrakīrti's verses of

[21] The answer to the question what precisely the philosophical differences between Prāsaṅgika and its Svātantrika opponents associated with Bhāviveka were is complex, and some further ramifications of this are discussed below on pp 21–24. For a book-length treatment of this question see Dreyfus/McClintock 2003.

[22] Tauscher 2017: 150.

[23] For some of the fascinating background of the re-discovery of Sanskrit manuscripts in Tibet see Steinkellner 2004.

the 6th chapter,[24] as well as the verses of chapters 1–5 and their autocommentary[25] have been published. An edition of the remaining verses and autocommentary is currently in preparation.[26] As such, most of the secondary literature available at present is based on the Tibetan translation of Candrakīrti's text.

This Guide is meant to be read in parallel with Candrakīrti's "Introduction to the Middle Way." I recommend in particular the translation of the 6th chapter by Siderits and Katsura[27] (the first English translation of this chapter based on the original Sanskrit) and Jinpa's[28] translation of Tsong kha pa's Tibetan commentary, which includes the translations of all of Candrakīrti's verses from Tibetan. Another useful resource is Huntington (1992) which contains a translation of all of Candrakīrti's verses, with copious extracts from his autocommentary, together with a substantial amount of philosophical discussion. A further English translation of Candrakīrti's verses can be found in Fenner (1990). Rabten (1983) provides a lucid English rendition of the verses of the 6th chapter of the "Introduction to the Middle Way."

Over the past years a number of English translations of Tibetan commentaries on the "Introduction to the Middle Way" have been published. These include Rendawa's commentary,[29] Gorampa's commentary,[30] substantial parts of the 8th Karmapa's commentary on the 6th chapter,[31] the 9th Karmapa's commentary,[32] and the commentary by Jamgön Mipham.[33] There are also three

[24] Li 2015.
[25] Lasic/Li/Macdonald 2022.
[26] Anne MacDonald at the Austrian Academy of Sciences is also presently preparing an annotated English translation of the verses of chapter 6 together with Candrakīrti's autocommentary.
[27] Siderits/Katsura 2024.
[28] Jinpa 2021.
[29] Red mda' ba gzhon nu blo gros, Stöter-Tillmann/Tashi Tsering 1997.
[30] Go rams pa bsod nams seng ge, Stöter-Tillmann/Tashi Tsering 2005.
[31] Goldfield et al. 2005.
[32] Dewar 2008.
[33] 'Jam mgon mi pham, Padmakara 2004.

contemporary Tibetan commentaries, by Geshe Kelsang Gyatso,[34] Dzogchen Pönlop Rinpoche,[35] and by Dzongsar Jamyang Khyentse Rinpoche [36] available in English translation.[37]

A very detailed discussion of verses 120–165 of chapter 6 (dealing with the refutation of a substantial self) is provided in Duerlinger.[38] This includes a translation of the relevant verses and of Candrakīrti's autocommentary on them. Further separate treatments of this section of the "Introduction to the Middle Way" may be found in Wilson (1980) and Rochard (2012). For those interested in the autocommentary on the entire text, significant portions have been translated into French and German;[39] there are also several unpublished English translations of the entire autocommentary that have been circulated in various forms.[40]

3b. Structure of the text

Candrakīrti conceives of his "Introduction to the Middle Way" as an introduction (*avatāra*) to Nāgārjuna's "Fundamental Verses on the Middle Way." Its structure, however, does not follow that of Nāgārjuna's text; instead, the "Introduction to the Middle Way" is framed by reference to a well-known map of spiritual progress, the system of the ten stages (*daśabhūmi*) or "bodhisattva stages."

[34] 1995.

[35] 1999.

[36] Trisoglio 2000.

[37] English translations of comprehensive oral commentaries by Khensur Jampa Tegchok and Geshe Jampa Gyatso were produced by the Foundation for the Preservation of the Mahāyāna Tradition but have not, I believe, been made available to the general public.

[38] 2013. See also Duerlinger 2003.

[39] La Vallée-Poussin (1907–1911) translated up to 6:165 into French; Tauscher (1981) translated 6:166–226 into German.

[40] There is one translation by George Churinoff from 1994, and another from 2020 by Fredrik Liland (presently available online at https://www2.hf.uio.no/polyglotta/index.php?page=volume&vid=1113). A published English translation is Stöter-Tillmann/Tashi Tsering 2012.

This system is described in different Mahāyāna *sutras*; Candrakīrti refers in particular to the *Daśabhūmikasūtra*,[41] as well as to Nāgārjuna's *Ratnāvalī*.[42] From a philosophical perspective, entry into the 1st bodhisattva stage is crucial as it is accompanied by a direct and non-conceptual realization of emptiness, the key concept of Madhyamaka analysis. Starting from this realization, as the bodhisattvas advance through the different stages, their abilities to help other beings increase. Some of these changes are quantitative (a 1st stage bodhisattva can produce one hundred magical emanations, while a 2nd stage bodhisattva can produce a thousand), some are qualitative (at each stage, one of the ten moral perfections the bodhisattva cultivates reaches a superior level of excellence: generosity at the first stage, moral discipline at the second, patience at the third, and so on).

Candrakīrti discusses each of these stages in the "Introduction to the Middle Way," and it is likely that its comprehensiveness, conceptualizing Nāgārjuna's discussion of emptiness from his "Fundamental Verses on the Middle Way" in an exposition covering the entire path to enlightenment[43] made it one of the most popular texts on Madhyamaka in Tibet. Even though Candrakīrti says something substantial about each bodhisattva stage, more than half of the text is taken up by his discussion of the 6th stage alone. The Sanskrit term for this stage is *abhimukhī*, a term that can be translated as "approaching," "manifest," or "directly facing." What is manifest or directly faced at this stage is emptiness; bodhisattvas acquire the ability to enter into the meditation on emptiness for long periods of time. Accordingly, the perfection bodhisattvas at this stage excel in is the perfection of wisdom (*prajñā-pāramitā*).

The "Introduction to the Middle Way" is usually divided into eleven chapters. After a brief introduction (1:1–4ab, generally

[41] Honda 1968; Carré 2004; Bhikshu Dharmamitra 2019. See also Eimer 1976: 145–157.
[42] Verses 440–460, Khensur Jampa Tegchok 2016: 351–370.
[43] See Jinpa 2021: 34.

included in the first chapter), the first ten chapters discuss one bodhisattva stage each. These are followed by a final, 11th chapter, discussing the end of the bodhisattva path, Buddhahood, closing by some comments on the origin and uniqueness of Candrakīrti's exposition of Madhyamaka.

3c. The 6th chapter

The 6th chapter is without doubt the center of gravity of Candrakīrti's work, and most of the philosophical discussions that the "Introduction to the Middle Way" is famous for can be found in it. Its 226 verses provide a systematic account of the theory of emptiness (*śūnyatā*) as it is understood by the Prāsaṅgika Madhyamaka school, frequently contrasting Madhyamaka ideas with those of its Buddhist and non-Buddhist rivals. The motivation behind this contrast is twofold. On the one hand the refutation of the philosophical opponent is the obvious aim, in order to establish the correctness of the Madhyamaka position; on the other hand the description of rival views functions as a tool for explaining the Madhyamaka view better by comparing it with rival theories attempting to account for the same philosophical problems in alternative ways.

Candrakīrti's discussion can be divided into two main parts, a general theory of emptiness (verses 1–178), and a typology of different kinds of emptiness (verses 179–226). When presenting his general account of emptiness, Candrakīrti focuses on two main groups of empty things: phenomena in general and selves in particular. The historical background for this differentiation is that the early Buddhist metaphysical tradition of the Abhidharma focused on the idea of selflessness (*anātman*) or emptiness of persons (*pudgalanairātmyā*), arguing for a reductionist account of the self against a background of fundamentally real entities, the *dharmas*. Madhyamaka takes itself to expand the notion of emptiness from persons to all entities (*dharmanairātmyā*). Now if all entities are empty, persons are empty too, and the arguments for the emptiness of *dharmas* can simply be applied to persons as well. However, Candrakīrti adds a specific discussion of the emptiness of persons, following his account of the emptiness of *dharmas*, to reflect the special status of the mistaken superimposition of a substantial self in the Buddhist soteriological enterprise. Such a superimposition is the key factor that keeps sentient beings trapped in cyclic existence and therefore deserves particular focus in order to eliminate it. For this reason Candrakīrti does not confine himself to a discussion of the emptiness of phenomena in general, but follows it with one on the emptiness of persons, his famous "sevenfold analysis" (*rnam bdun gyi rigs pa*).

Candrakīrti's treatment of the first half of his general account of emptiness (verses 1–119), a comprehensive discussion which focuses on the emptiness of phenomena, is an interesting exercise in systematic investigation and philosophical doxography rolled into one. Candrakīrti focuses on a point Nāgārjuna makes at the very beginning of his "Fundamental Verses on the Middle Way," namely that for something to exist in a substantial, non-empty manner it would have to have arisen either from itself, another thing, both, or neither. Yet since no thing can be said to have arisen in any of the four ways, the presupposition that there is anything non-empty needs to be given up. Candrakīrti examines each of the four positions, linking each one with a distinct philosophical system that he explains and refutes at the same time. The first alternative, self-production, is associated with the non-Buddhist Sāṃkhya system, while the second, production from another entity, is linked with the other main philosophical school of Mahāyāna apart from Madhyamaka: Yogācāra. Candrakīrti spends most of this section discussing these two forms of causal production (which also seem to be the intuitively most plausible ones) before he continues with short remarks on the Jains (concerned with production from both self and other) and the ancient Indian materialist school of the

Cārvākas (discussing production from neither self nor other, i.e., production without a cause).

The second half of Candrakīrti's general account of emptiness (verses 120–178) is concerned with the emptiness of the self. Candrakīrti's argument focuses on the possible relations between the self as usually conceived, an independent entity existing over and above our physical and mental features, and the physico-psychological aggregates that make up the person. In his "Fundamental Verses on the Middle Way,"[44] Nāgārjuna describes a "fivefold analysis" examining five such relations: identity and difference of the self and the aggregates, the self containing the aggregates or vice versa, and the self possessing the aggregates. The first two alternatives are again linked with specific philosophical schools; identity of self and aggregates with the Saṃmitīya branch of the Buddhist Abhidharma, difference with the non-Buddhist schools of Sāṃkhya and Vaiśeṣika. The bottom line of the argument is that if there were such a thing as a self, it would stand in one of these relations to the aggregates. Because every one of them is shown to be problematic, though, Nāgārjuna concludes that no such self could exist.

Candrakīrti expands this argument into his well-known "sevenfold analysis" by adding two more relations: the self being the mere collection of all the aggregates, and the self being an arrangement of the aggregates.

Candrakīrti's typology of different kinds of emptiness (verses 179–226) introduces three classifications of emptiness: the familiar twofold one (emptiness of persons, and emptiness of *phenomena*), an extensive sixteen-fold classification derived from the *Prajñāpāramitā* literature, and a condensed fourfold classification. The sixteen types of emptiness include items such as the emptiness of the sense-faculties and sense objects, the emptiness of emptiness, and the emptiness of time, the fourfold classification

[44] *Mūlamadhyamakakārikā* 10:14, 16:2, 22:1.

lists the emptiness of the existent, the nonexistent, intrinsic nature (*prakṛti*) and entities beyond appearances (*parabhāva*). Each of these classifications is considered to be ontologically exhaustive, but they differ in the selection of empty items they present for the philosopher's considerations.

3d. Candrakīrti and Yogācāra

Two themes that play an especially important role in Candrakīrti's exposition of Madhyamaka are his defense of the Prāsangika interpretation (following Buddhapālita) over the Svātantrika interpretation of Bhāviveka and, more generally, the defense of Madhyamaka as a whole against its main Mahāyāna rival, Yogācāra. The former, intra-Madhyamaka dispute is developed by Candrakīrti primarily in his *Prasannapadā*; we have discussed this briefly above. The latter occupies an important part of the "Introduction to the Middle Way" (verses 45–97 of chapter 6).

Accounts of Candrakīrti's life present colorful descriptions of his encounters with the Yogācārin Candragomin,[45] and it is hard not to read them as hagiographical renditions of a doxographical dispute. According to one episode related in Tāranātha's account, Candrakīrti and Candragomin debated for seven years, Candrakīrti taking the side of Madhyamaka, and Candragomin that of Yogācāra.[46] For many months, Candrakīrti presented devastating objections to Candragomin, which the latter was always able to respond to perfectly on the following day. Intrigued by this fact, Candrakīrti suspects foul play and tries to find out who is feeding the answers to his opponent. He finds Candragomin in the temple of the Avalokiteśvara at Nālandā, and sees that the stone image of the bodhisattva of compassion has come to

[45] Loizzo 2001: 182–203.
[46] Chimpa and Chattopadhyaya 1970: 205–206.

life and teaches Candragomin how to handle the debates with Candrakīrti. Somewhat surprisingly, instead of being overawed by Candragomin's ability to converse with such highly realized beings, Candrakīrti complains to Avalokiteśvara and accuses him of favoritism. As one would expect, Avalokiteśvara provides an irenic response, telling Candrakīrti that he is already blessed by Mañjuśrī, the bodhisattva of wisdom, and therefore does not require Avalokiteśvara's support, who has in consequence decided to lend a helping hand to Candragomin.

It is interesting that Tāranātha's account leaves the outcome of the debate undecided, and this provides us with a frame for interpreting the Madhyamaka-Yogācāra debate less as an intellectual competition, with one victorious and one defeated party, and more as a tool for generating a deeper understanding of the Buddha's teachings. After all, Avalokiteśvara and Mañjuśrī are equally realized bodhisattvas, and if one takes the side of Yogācāra, and one that of Madhyamaka, the image presented cannot be one of a relationship between the two systems where we simply have to settle the question which of the two is right.

Candrakīrti's criticism of Yogācāra concentrates on two points. One is to show that the Yogācāra system is haunted by a variety of logical problems, the other to argue that Yogācāra cannot be seen as a philosophical explication of the Buddha's teaching described in the *sūtras*. At least on the face of it, the latter criticism seems to be particularly difficult to bring forward, since the *Daśabhūmikasūtra*, which constitutes the conceptual frame of Candrakīrti's text and is frequently cited in his autocommentary, contains a passage that is often taken to be one of the clearest scriptural statements of a central Yogācāra idea, stating that "the three realms[47] are merely mind."[48]

[47] Together these three realms, the desire realm (*kāmadhātu*), the form realm (*rūpadhātu*), and the formless ream (*ārūpyadhātu*), constitute the entirety of the world of cyclic existence in which sentient beings may be reborn.

[48] *cittamātraṃ idaṃ yad idaṃ traidhātukam*, Honda 1968: 189; Carré 2004: 128; Bhikshu Dharmamitra 2019: 237, 598.

Candrakīrti tackles this challenge head-on and discusses the *sūtra* passage in his commentary on verse 84 of chapter 6. He argues that the proponent of Yogācāra misunderstands the point of the statement: the reference to "merely mind" does not say that there is no matter, but denies that matter (or indeed any other entity one might take to be the causal origin of the world, whether it is Sāṃkhya's *prakṛti* and *puruṣa* or the Nyāya's creator god) is ontologically fundamental. For the Mādhyamika matter still exists, but it (or, indeed, anything else) is not to be accorded ultimate ontological status.

This interpretative approach is characteristic for the use of scriptural authority in Buddhist philosophy. Candrakīrti does not criticize the authenticity or authority of the *Daśabhūmikasūtra* but argues that it has to be understood in a specific way. In particular, its pronouncements about "merely mind" are not to be taken as statements about the ultimately mental nature of reality, but should be seen as directed against specific alternative proposals that characterize *other* entities as ontologically fundamental. Using this approach, the Buddhist scholastic philosophers' explanations can still range across the entire canon of the Buddha's teachings, yet differ in the extent to which they take specific texts to describe reality at the ultimate level, while others are understood as having a more restricted meaning relative to a particular context, and are hence considered to be in need of specific interpretations.

4. Looking forward: The philosophical career of the "Introduction to the Middle Way"

4a. Candrakīrti's thought in India

Understanding the history of the reception of the "Introduction to the Middle Way" from Candrakīrti's times up to the present is far from straightforward. The main problem historians of philosophy try to solve is the reconciliation of two facts. On the one hand,

Candrakīrti is accorded an exalted role in Tibet as the central commentator on Nāgārjuna's works, as someone who has played a key role in developing the most sophisticated conceptual framework for understanding Madhyamaka in his defense of the Prāsaṅgika approach; on the other hand, his visibility in India itself is quite limited. Central Indian Madhyamaka authors like Śāntarakṣita or Kamalaśīla show no awareness of his works, and it appears as if only one commentary on the "Introduction to the Middle Way" was ever written in India.[49] If we measure the importance of a philosophical work by the amount of commentarial attention it has received,[50] it appears as if Candrakīrti's Madhyamaka interpretation was extremely popular in Tibet, but not in India. One recent scholar has argued that Candrakīrti "was in fact largely ignored in his day and for some three hundred years in both India and Tibet."[51] The claim that Candrakīrti's Madhyamaka, much like the music of Johann Sebastian Bach, was rediscovered after a period of substantial neglect is not uncontroversial, however.[52] First, the idea of a volume gathering dust for hundreds of years on an ancient Indian library shelf before it is felicitously rediscovered does not sit well with the comparatively short life of manuscripts in the Indian climate. Texts that have come down to us would have been copied in regular intervals, and it is hard to see why the copyists should have done so if they did not attach some importance to the texts' contents.[53]

[49] In addition to this massive commentary by the 12th ct Jayānanda there is also a shorter 12th ct manuscript with notes on different works by Candrakīrti, including the "Introduction to the Middle Way." This text, usually referred to as the *Lakṣaṇaṭīkā*, appears to have been authored by the Tibetan translator Dharma grags during his stay at the Indian monastery of Vikramaśīla (see Yonezawa 2013, 2014).

[50] Note, for example, that it is usually assumed that there were originally eight separate Indian commentaries on Nāgārjuna's "Fundamental Verses on the Middle Way."

[51] Vose 2009: 17.

[52] See MacDonald 2015: 3–6 for a criticism of Vose's position on Candrakīrti's lack of popularity in Indian scholasticism.

[53] Our information of the "lineage" of transmission of the "Introduction to the Middle Way" from Candrakīrti's time to the end of scholastic Buddhism in India in the 12th ct is very limited. The later Indian masters of the Madhyamaka mentioned in Tibetan sources, which link the Tibetan tradition to Candrakīrti, appear not to have left us any works on Madhyamaka in general, or on Candrakīrti in particular, and some "might

Second, that Candrakīrti's approach to Madhyamaka influenced or is mentioned by important Indian scholars such as Śāntideva (8th ct),[54] Avalokitavrata (8th ct),[55] Prajñākaramati (10th ct),[56] and Ratnākaraśānti (10th–11th ct)[57] suggests that his thought continued to be studied throughout the history of Madhyamaka in India, even though his works did not attract a large number of commentaries dedicated specifically to them. Candrakīrti must also have been sufficiently well known in India sometime between the end of the 8th and the beginning of 9th century for one of his works (a commentary on Nāgārjuna's "Sixty Verses on Reasoning") to be translated into Tibetan.[58] So while it might be too strong to speak of virtual neglect of Candrakīrti's Madhyamaka by Indian scholastic writers, the reception of his work in ancient India was certainly very different from the role it later began to play in Tibetan Buddhism.

4b. Candrakīrti's thought in Tibet

At least from the time of the great Bengali scholar Atīśa (Dīpaṅkaraśrījñāna, 982–1054),[59] who played a central role in the introduction of Buddhism to Tibet, Candrakīrti's reading of Nāgārjuna was regarded as the interpretative gold standard. Atīśa writes

even be so to speak notional figures inserted in the lineages in order to maintain the idea of the continuous and unbroken transmission of a tradition the actual history of which had become shrouded in the mists of time" (Ruegg 2000: 10, note 10).

[54] Though Śāntideva does not mention Candrakīrti by name, Śāntideva and Candrakīrti are frequently grouped together as key representatives of Prāsaṅgika Madhyamaka. Their works show an interest in similar questions (such as the refutation of Yogācāra and the rejection of the concept of reflexive awareness (*svasaṃvedana*)) (Williams 1998: xiii, 2).

[55] Nagashima 2004: 66–67.

[56] Prajñākaramati cites Candrakīrti (whom he refers to as *śāstravid*, "the knower of Nāgārjuna's "Fundamental Verses on the Middle Way" (Oldmeadow 1994: 23, note 8)) extensively in his exposition of Śāntideva's *Bodhicaryāvatāra*.

[57] Tomlinson 2019: 183.

[58] Loizzo 2007: 26.

[59] Westerhoff 2018b: 276–281; Apple 2019a.

in his "Introduction to the Two Truths": "Who has understood emptiness? Nāgārjuna, predicted by the Tathāgata, saw the absolute truth (*dharmatā-satya*), and his disciple Candrakīrti."[60] The "Introduction to the Middle Way" was translated into Tibetan later than many other Indian Madhyamaka texts. It was translated two times, first by Nag tsho tshul khrims rgyal ba (1011–1064), a student of Atīśa's, and later again by Pa tshab nyi ma grags (1055–1145).[61] Pa tshab made very important contributions to the establishment of Candrakīrti's interpretation of Madhyamaka in Tibet, both through the quality of his translations of Candrakīrti's works, and through his skill in explaining Madhyamaka thought.[62] His translation of Candrakīrti's "Clear Words" (*Prasannapadā*) in particular, the first chapter of which contains a sustained criticism of Bhāviveka's reading of Nāgārjuna, was instrumental in sharpening the conceptual distinction between Prāsaṅgika and Svātantrika in Tibetan scholasticism, a distinction that is of fundamental importance for the Tibetan classification of interpretations of Madhyamaka. From Pa tshab's times onward, all Tibetan interpretations of Madhyamaka positioned themselves in relation to Candrakīrti in some way, either developing and defending his system or constructing alternative readings of Madhyamaka in direct opposition to Candrakīrti's views.

One relatively early example of the way that questions arising from Candrakīrti's interpretation of Madhyamaka captured the Tibetan philosophical imagination is the clash between Phya pa chos kyi seng ge (1109–1169)[63] and Jayānanda[64] (12th ct). Phya pa was the 6th abbot of Gsang pu ne'u thog monastery in central Tibet, while Jayānanda, the Indian commentator on the "Introduction to the Middle Way" who is supposed to have lost the debate, held

[60] *Satyadvayāvatāra* 15, Lindtner 1981: 194; Apple 2019b: 120, 56–159.

[61] See Tauscher 1995.

[62] Lang 1989: 135; Vose 2009: 51.

[63] Tauscher 1999, 2009/2010; van der Kuijp 1978.

[64] van der Kuijp 1993.

the position of National Preceptor (國師, *guoshi*) under the Tangut emperor Renzong. Their debate revolved around a number of issues, the most prominent of which were the following:[65]

1. Can inferences constructed according to the commonly accepted system of Indian logic be used to understand emptiness? Or is one's logical toolbox restricted to the demonstration of contradictory consequences (*prasaṅga*)?
2. Do Mādhyamikas have a positive philosophical thesis?
3. Can the mind of unenlightened ordinary beings constitute an epistemic instrument to generate knowledge? In particular, can the Mādhyamikas add the epistemology of Diṅnāga and Dharmakīrti to their set of philosophical resources?
4. Is ultimate truth accessible to language and thought?
5. Do conventional truths have some form of philosophical grounding, rather than being based on the agreements of everyday practice?
6. Does a Buddha have any cognitive events appearing in his mind at all, instead of all mental activity ceasing when Buddhahood is obtained?

Candrakīrti was taken to have provided negative answers to these questions, and the resulting picture of Madhyamaka was critized by Phya pa, and defended by Jayānanda. It is easy to see how these six points could have been understood as generating difficulties for Buddhist ethics and soteriology. If the Mādhyamika cannot rely on the established canon of inferential procedures developed in the context of ancient Indian debate practices, and does not hold a positive philosophical position of his own, it is unclear how he could ever propose a soteriologically efficacious set of practices (such as the four noble truths) that should be carried out. The Mādhyamika can act as a philosophical sniper shooting holes in other peoples'

[65] See also Tauscher 2003; Jinpa 2021: 6–7.

theories, but how can he ever say anything more than what is *not* the case?

He certainly cannot avail himself of the epistemological accounts developed by Diṅnāga and Dharmakīrti, and if the mind of ordinary beings, operating within the familiar linguistic and conceptual coordinates, is irredeemably deluded, and if the ultimate cannot be accessed by language and thought, there appears to be no way of escaping the world of cyclic existence by any tools at our disposal.

Moreover, if there is no grounding for conventional truths other than the world's say-so, and if the Mādhyamika can in any case only accept the existence of any objects only insofar as they occur from the perspective of another, how could there be any solid foundations for ethical pronouncements that do not depend on majority consensus endorsing them? Finally, if nothing at all happens in a Buddha's mind, how could he ever teach unenlightened beings and describe a path to liberation they can follow?

It is interesting to see that similar concerns about reading Candrakīrti in a way that might undermine the Buddhist ethical and soteriological project were shared by one of the most influential Tibetan thinkers, Tsong kha pa (1357–1419),[66] though his response was very different from Phya pa's. Tsong kha pa set out to show that Candrakīrti's Madhyamaka did not in any way undermine the level of conventional truth that underpins Buddhist ethics and soteriology by constructing an approach incorporating Candrakīrti's Madhyamaka and the epistemological tradition of Diṅnāga and Dharmakīrti side by side.[67] Even though this conceptual marriage of Nāgārjuna and Dharmakīrti generated substantial criticism within the Tibetan scholastic tradition,[68] the political rise of the dGe lugs pa school which Tsong kha pa founded resulted

[66] Jinpa 1999: 3–28.
[67] Jinpa 2002: 9, 185.
[68] Jinpa 2019: 357–358; The Yakherds 2022a, b.

in Candrakīrti's Madhyamaka, read through Tsong kha pa, becoming the official state philosophy of Tibet.[69] Not least through its influence on the living tradition of Tibetan scholasticism,[70] Candrakīrti's philosophical ideas continue to be studied, analyzed, and debated up to the present day.

5. The nature of the present commentary

Like all philosophical classics, Candrakīrti's "Introduction to the Middle Way" is a text of such depth that a commentary could achieve almost any length, depending on how many aspects of Candrakīrti, his historical background, and the systematic ramifications of his thoughts the commentator decides to pursue. Obviously, in a volume such as this we have to be selective. The commentary in this Guide is meant for students without much previous acquaintance with Buddhist Philosophy in general, or Madhyamaka in particular, and it is mainly intended for readers with a primarily philosophical interest in Candrakīrti's work. Our focus is therefore on explaining how Candrakīrti's arguments work, what criticisms have been brought or may be brought against them, and how they might be defended. My comments concentrate on the "Introduction to the Middle Way" itself, and even though I will explain Candrakīrti's ideas in relation to his autocommentary, I will usually not say much on issues that are only discussed in the autocommentary, without appearing specifically in the verses of the root text. Explaining Candrakīrti's arguments raises various interesting subsidiary questions: what the best English equivalents of the various Sanskrit technical terms Candrakīrti uses might be, what the precise positions of Candrakīrti's opponents were and how faithfully he represented them, how the various references to other

[69] Murti 1995: 87.
[70] See e.g. The Yakherds 2022a: 230–263.

treatises and *sūtras* in Candrakīrti's autocommentary expand the points he makes in the "Introduction to the Middle Way" itself, how he relates them to the larger architecture of Buddhist thought, and how specific passages of the "Introduction to the Middle Way" were interpreted in different ways by later scholars. Such questions can only be properly discussed in a commentary much more comprehensive than the one provided here, and the following discussion will not have much to say on these, apart from the occasional brief remark. The aim of our guided tour through Candrakīrti's text is to supply the reader with a first reliable account of what Candrakīrti is saying, the arguments he marshals in support of his points, an assessment of the mechanics of these arguments, and a discussion of possible challenges. Throughout the text there will be pointers to the secondary literature for those who would like to investigate specific aspects of Candrakīrti's thought further.

For the benefit of those readers who would like a concise overview of the topics covered in Candrakīrti's "Introduction to the Middle Way," a synopsis of the entire text, providing a summary of each verse, is included at the end of the book. This is not meant as a substitute for the text itself, but hopes to equip the reader with a ready reference to the flow of ideas in Candrakīrti's work in an abbreviated and lucid manner, following the interpretation set out in the commentary presented in this volume.

The present volume does not presuppose any familiarity with Oriental languages on the side of the reader. I have therefore only provided Sanskrit and Tibetan equivalents in cases where the acquaintance with the original term for a specific concept is particularly useful when pursuing its discussion across the voluminous literature on Buddhist Studies.

Commentary

Candrakīrti's Introduction to the Middle Way. Jan Westerhoff, Oxford University Press.
© Oxford University Press 2024. DOI: 10.1093/oso/9780197612330.003.0002

Chapter 1

Section 1. The importance of compassion

Candrakīrti begins his exposition by describing the source of the different types of enlightened beings distinguished in Buddhism: *arhats*, *pratyekabuddhas*, and fully enlightened Buddhas.[1] The former, often referred to as "hearers,"[2] constitute the lowest form of enlightenment according to the Mahāyāna perspective. They hear the teachings of the Buddha, have, as a result, permanently escaped from cyclic existence, and subsequently explain their insight to others. However, they lack some of the qualities of the latter two. The *pratyekabuddhas* surpass the qualities of the *arhats* in terms of merit and wisdom, but are again found lacking when compared to the fully enlightened Buddhas. The *pratyekabuddhas*, unlike the *arhats*, have obtained enlightenment without being instructed by a teacher in their final lifetime, and without teaching the insights they have gained to others. **1:001**

Arhats and *pratyekabuddhas* come from the "mighty sages," fully enlightened Buddhas or *tathāgatas*, since it is the teaching of these Buddhas that is the basis of the realization of the other two kinds of enlightened beings. Fully enlightened Buddhas, in turn, come from the bodhisattvas, the Buddhas-to-be, since each one of them will have been a bodhisattva in a previous lifetime. Bodhisattvas, finally, have as their source three mental qualities: the compassionate mind, the non-dual mind, and the awakening mind (*bodhicitta*). Compassionate mind is the desire to protect all sentient beings from suffering. The non-dual mind refers to the bodhisattva's developing insight into emptiness, to being free of the erroneous superimposition of substantial entities, and of the mistaken belief that things do not exist at all. The awakening mind, finally, the specific characteristic feature that

[1] For more discussion of these three categories see D'Amato 2008: 539–541.

[2] *śrāvaka*.

characterizes the bodhisattva, is a mental state that combines the two, fusing great compassion with insight into emptiness.

1:002 Of these three mental states, the compassionate mind is the foremost, since it is the cause of the other two, the non-dual mind and the awakening mind. Candrakīrti therefore begins his treatise by praising compassion, which, like a seed for a plant, is the first cause of the attainment of full enlightenment. Moreover, compassion is also, like water, essential for the growing of the seed, and, like the fruit, is the enduring result of this process of cultivation. Compassion is hence essential at the beginning, middle, and end of the Buddhist path: compassion provides the initial motivation for becoming a Buddha to help all beings, compassion ensures that the bodhisattva does not abandon the path he has embarked on, though faced by an infinity of beings presenting a multitudinous display of evil conduct, and compassion ripens into continuous enlightened activity of a Buddha once liberation is obtained, producing, in turn, compassionate intentions in the minds of his disciples, like a fruit brings about further seeds.

1:003 Candrakīrti now sets out to differentiate compassion into three different types,[3] relative to the objects it is directed at. These are the compassion directed at sentient beings, the compassion directed at phenomena, and the compassion without object. Sentient beings first develop the mistaken belief in a substantially real self where there is only a rapidly changing conglomeration of physico-psychological states, and subsequently become attached to things associated with this self: *my* body, *my* mental states, *my* possessions, *my* friends, and so on. Because of this they are caught in *saṃsāra* like a pot in an endlessly turning water-wheel.[4] In his autocommentary,

[3] For further discussion of these three types see Newland 1984: 55–67, 124–143; Cabezón 1992: 24, 412, note 2.

[4] The water-wheel may have been invented in India ("one of the most important inventions which India gave to the world," Lannoy 1992: 420) and possibly inspired the idea of perpetual motion machines, a cosmic example of which was provided by *saṃsāra* ("To the Hindus the universe itself was a perpetual motion machine, and there seemed

Candrakīrti develops the analogy of the water-wheel in greater detail. As the buckets are tied to the wheel with ropes, beings are tied to *saṃsāra* by the bonds of karma. The wheel has to be set in motion by the farmer to bring up the water, and so the cycle of existence is kept turning by consciousness. The pots go all the way around from the top of the wheel to the bottom of the well, and so sentient beings go through the highest and the lowest realms of existence. As moving the buckets down is easy, but pulling them up is hard, descent into the lower realms requires no effort, while ascent to the higher realms needs dedicated practice of virtue. As the buckets form a circle, without a first and last, the twelve links of dependent origination[5] have no first or last member. And as the pots are battered against the side of the well incessantly, without ever leaving the wheel, so sentient beings are afflicted by the different kinds of suffering in beginningless cyclic existence without respite.

For these reasons the bodhisattva develops the first kind of compassion toward them, the compassion directed at sentient beings. While the first type of compassion is directed at sentient beings without further qualification, the second, compassion directed at phenomena, considers sentient beings under the specific aspect of their impermanence and momentary nature, while the third, compassion without object, is directed at sentient beings with a focus on their empty nature.

In order to illustrate the second and third type of compassion, **1:004**
compassion directed at phenomena, and compassion without object, Candrakīrti introduces the example of the reflection of the moon appearing in a pond, once the rippling of the waters has momentarily subsided. This illustrates the two key concepts of impermanence and emptiness. The image of the moon is not stable,

nothing absurd in an endless and spontaneous flow of energy," White 1962: 131). See Zin/Schlingloff 2022: 1–20.

[5] See 6:106 below. For further discussion of the twelve links of dependent origination see Geshe Sopa 1984, 1986.

but moves with the motion of the waves and will disappear completely as soon as the waters of the pond are sufficiently disturbed. Sentient beings are themselves impermanent, but also afflicted by the suffering of change, the fact that any state will sooner or later disappear and change into something else. Moreover, while it may look as if there was a substantial, self-supporting object swimming in the pond, there is really only a complex setup of causes and conditions giving rise to the illusion of something intrinsically real, while its dependent and imputed nature becomes evident once it is subjected to analysis. In the same way the bodhisattva cognizes the impermanence of each sentient being, as well as its empty nature, its being merely a conceptual imputation on the five aggregates. He sees beings as immersed in an ocean of ignorance agitated by the winds of conceptualization, appearing only as a reflection of their own good and bad karma. Realizing this, the bodhisattva's resolve to remove the suffering of all sentient beings increases.[6]

Obtaining the 1st bodhisattva stage

1:005 The bodhisattva's attainments of compassion and wisdom are structured according to a succession of ten stages (*bhūmi*).[7] These stages

[6] It is a remarkable fact about Buddhist ethics that the realization of the insubstantial nature of the object of one's compassion is not supposed to diminish, but rather to increase it. On the status of ethics in relation to virtual objects see Westerhoff 2020: 73–78; Chalmers 2022: 350–364. See also below 6:006–6:007.

[7] Each stage is associated with a specific perfection:

1. *Pramuditā*, Perfect Joy—*dāna*, generosity
2. *Vimalā*, Immaculate—*śīla*, ethics
3. *Prabhākarī*, Luminous—*kṣānti*, patience
4. *Arciṣmatī*, Radiant—*vīrya*, effort
5. *Sudurjayā*, Hard to overcome—*dhyāna*, meditation
6. *Abhimukhī*, Turned toward—*prajñā*, wisdom
7. *Dūraṅgamā*, Far Progressed—*upāya*, method
8. *Acalā*, Immovable—*praṇidhāna*, vow
9. *Sādhumatī*, Perfect Intellect—*bala*, power
10. *Dharmameghā*, Cloud of Dharma—*jñāna*, knowledge.

are not differentiated according to the nature of the insight the bodhisattva attains, but in terms of the different perceptual capacities and abilities of manifestation the bodhisattva acquires at each stage.[8] Having developed the wish to liberate all sentient beings from suffering, while seeing these very beings as empty, the practitioner obtains the first of the ten stages, called "Joyous." The aspirations that he develops at this stage correspond to those described in the prayer of the bodhisattva Samantabhadra, presented in the *Gaṇḍavyūhasūtra*, the final chapter of the *Avataṃsakasūtra*.[9] The practitioner is now to be properly described as a bodhisattva, and bearing this epithet is the first (1) of eight qualities possessed by a bodhisattva on the first stage.

1:006 In addition to bearing the epithet of a bodhisattva, the practitioner is also regarded as one born into the Buddha's lineage (2), which means that he will never practice the paths of the other realized beings, the *śrāvaka*s or *pratyekabuddha*s instead, but proceeds directly to the stage of a fully enlightened Buddha. In addition, the bodhisattva has abandoned the three fetters[10] that bind us to the cycle of rebirth: the mistaken view that the transitory collection of psycho-physical aggregates constitutes a self,[11] doubt about the efficacy of the path, and the false belief that the performance of rituals can lead to liberation (3). Comparing Buddhist practice to a journey, the first corresponds to not wanting to go (because there is no emptiness of the self to be realized), the second to doubts about being on the right road, and the last to choosing the wrong road. As a result of his realization and abandonment of obscurations the bodhisattva feels extraordinary happiness (4); it is for this reason that the 1st bodhisattva stage is called "Joyous." He also develops a

[8] Candrakīrti will discuss these in greater detail in 11:001–11:009.

[9] Cleary 1993: 1511–1518. See also Brunnhölzl 2018.

[10] *saṃyojanatraya*. See Walshe 1995: 484; La Vallée Poussin 1988–1990: 3: 839. We also find a list of ten fetters (*saṃyojana, kun tu sbyor ba*) beginning with the three fetters mentioned here; see Bhikkhu Bodhi 2000: 1565–1566.

[11] *satkāyadṛṣṭi*. See below, 6:120, 6:127, 6:145.

specific set of abilities at this stage, including the ability to make a hundred world-systems tremble (5).[12]

1:007 After obtaining the first stage the bodhisattva does not remain at this level of realization, but obtains successively higher stages (6). He cannot fall back into an ordinary state below the 1st bodhisattva stage (7) and is no longer an ordinary being (8), but has a status analogous to that of a stream-enterer on the path of the *śrāvaka*. The stream-enterer constitutes the first step of realization on the route to *arhat*ship; he is regarded as having abandoned the three fetters, thereby obtaining a state in which he will become an *arhat* in at most seven lifetimes. As such, this condition is irreversible; the stream-enterer cannot ever return to the group of ordinary, non-realized beings. In the same way, once the bodhisattva has reached the 1st bodhisattva stage he is set on the course toward becoming a fully enlightened Buddha and can never leave this path.

1:008 Immediately after having achieved the 1st bodhisattva stage the practitioner surpasses the *arhat*s and *pratyekabuddha*s in terms of merit accumulated which, by the power of his great compassion, continuously increases. It is only when reaching the 7th bodhisattva stage, however, that he also surpasses them in terms of insight into emptiness. This implies that the insight into emptiness achieved by the *arhat*s and *pratyekabuddha*s is the very same as that of very advanced Mahāyāna practitioners. In particular, Candrakīrti does not claim that *arhat*s and *pratyekabuddha*s have the same realization of the emptiness of persons as the bodhisattvas, but fail to realize the emptiness of phenomena, since for him the realization of

[12] See 11:001–11:003. The meaning of this ability is not entirely clear. Huntington (1992: 220, note 10) notes: "The Tibetan *gyo bar nus par gyur ba* is quite clear in itself, but it does not seem to concur with the Sanskrit *parijātaśaktiḥ*. The Sanskrit, however, is obscure, and there is no adequate evidence about its meaning or the reason for the Tibetan translation." The idea of "trembling" or "causing to move" can be understood in a very direct sense (earthquakes (*bhūmikampa*) act as *omina* in Indian mythology and are, for example, associated with major events in the life of the historical Buddha), or, more indirectly, in terms of the ability to influence. Dzogchen Pönlop Rinpoche (1999: 51) interprets this quality as the ability to "communicate the power of their mind, or the power of their wisdom, in 100 different worlds".

the two kinds of emptiness are intrinsically linked.[13] Candrakīrti notes, however, that this significant overlap of the bodhisattva's realization of emptiness with that of the *arhat*s and *pratyekabuddha*s does not make the Mahāyāna superfluous as a separate stream of the Buddha's teaching. The reason for this is that the Mahāyāna teaches other things besides emptiness (such as the idea of a bodhisattva, the perfections, great compassion, and so forth), and that it presents the teachings of emptiness in much greater detail than the texts addressed to *arhat*s and *pratyekabuddha*s.

This verse has generated a considerable amount of commentarial attention. This is not only due to the fact that it addresses the differentiation between the Mahāyāna and the vehicle of the *arhat*s and *pratyekabuddha*s, but since it has important systematic implications for understanding what precisely the realization of emptiness is a realization of, and how there could be a differentiation between different levels within the realization of emptiness. The reader is encouraged to consult the major Tibetan commentators for a thorough discussion of this important point.

The perfection of generosity

The ten perfections, the virtues associated with the bodhisattva **1:009**
path, generosity, moral discipline, patience, effort, meditation, wisdom, method, vow, power, and knowledge, are discussed in many Mahāyāna scriptures, including the *Daśabhūmikasūtra*. Even though the bodhisattva practices each of these simultaneously, and even though the insight into the nature or reality underlying them is the same at every stage, each of the ten stages is associated with the mastery of a particular perfection. On the 1st stage the bodhisattva

[13] If the *arhats* did not realize emptiness, Candrakīrti points out, "they would not even realize the selflessness of the person, because imputation of a self relies on observing the aggregates." See also Jinpa 2021: 93.

achieves the highest degree of the perfection of generosity, being willing to give his possessions, and even his body,[14] to any beings who might benefit from it. Though one may not be able to perceive all of the extraordinary qualities of the bodhisattva, those which cannot be perceived directly, like his insight into emptiness, may be inferred, as fire is inferred from the presence of smoke. It is only in the presence of the realization of emptiness that such extraordinary generosity, as it is observed in the case of the bodhisattva, fusing insight into the nature of reality with ethical perfection, could manifest.

1:010 Candrakīrti continues his discussion of the ethical quality of generosity, though he now focuses on the generosity practiced by ordinary beings, not the extraordinary generosity of the bodhisattva. Buddhist ethical theory assumes a karmic link between the possession of wealth or material resources and the practice of generosity; the latter is the karmic seed that ripens as the former. As happiness is very difficult to achieve for most beings without a basic level of resources in terms of food, drink, clothing, shelter, and so on, which alleviate the suffering arising from hunger, thirst, exposure, etc., the Buddha taught generosity at the very outset of his teaching, even before teaching moral discipline. This is because its result will equip beings with the qualities needed to engage in practices leading to the final eradication of suffering. The practice of generosity by itself will not lead to liberation from cyclic existence, it simply leads to somewhat more pleasant states within cyclic existence. Nevertheless, the karmic fruit it generates can, if used wisely, provide a stable basis for a practice that not merely ameliorates some of the symptoms, but eliminates the disease, leading ultimately to liberation from *saṃsāra*.

1:011 Generosity will still produce karmic seeds for prosperity even if only pursued for purely selfish aims. Those who are not, like the bodhisattvas, motivated by the selfless desire to help other beings, but give material or other goods for the wholly selfish reason that

[14] For further discussion of this motif in Indian Buddhist literature see Ohnuma 1998.

they want to acquire the karmic potential for gaining wealth in the future will still enjoy the fruit of their generous conduct. As such, even when practiced without a compassionate motivation, the effects of generosity will be able to ameliorate the kind of suffering that arises from a lack of material resources.

Not only does ordinary generosity generate wealth which helps to dispel some kinds of suffering, it can also set a being on the path to enlightenment if, as a result of his accumulated karmic merit, he meets a teacher who teaches him not only about obtaining a better status in cyclic existence, but also about how to leave cyclic existence behind altogether, by practicing the path of the *arhat*s and *pratyekabuddha*s. As such, generosity has benefits in worldly terms, by generating the potential for wealth, but also in terms that go beyond the world of *saṃsāra*, by facilitating the entry into the path to liberation. 1:012

A key difference between ordinary generosity and the generosity of a bodhisattva is that for the former, positive karmic results will only arrive at some time in the future, and the giver might feel regret about the loss of the item just given. The bodhisattva, on the other hand, experiences great joy as a karmic fruit of generosity at the very moment of giving, since the aim of his generosity is not his own subsequent benefit, but the welfare of the recipient of the generosity at the moment of giving. As results of his generosity become immediately apparent, the bodhisattva is more inclined to practice generosity continuously, and as such accumulates merit much faster through his practice than ordinary beings. 1:013

The preceding discussion entails that practicing the perfection of generosity is of fundamental importance for non-bodhisattvas, since it prepares their entry into the path to liberation, as well as for bodhisattvas, since it generates the merit that lets them advance further on the bodhisattva path. For this reason the Buddha taught generosity as the first among the perfections.

Candrakīrti points out that the joy the bodhisattva experiences when being asked for anything exceeds even the joy of obtaining *nirvāṇa*, and that the joy experienced when the bodhisattva then 1:014

acts on the request is even greater. As such, bodhisattvas on the first stage feel neither physical nor mental pain as a result of their generosity, even when this involves giving away their bodies.

1:015 Mahāyāna practitioners below the 1st bodhisattva stage do experience physical pain if their generosity leads them to cut off parts of their own body and so forth. However, while ordinary beings would be held back by this, those on the Mahāyāna path are not, since they use the pain they experience to remind them of how beings in the lower realms, such as the hell realms, suffer continuously, and are subject to much more intense suffering than they presently feel. This motivates them to bring the suffering of all beings to an end even more quickly.

1:016 The distinction between the perfection of generosity conceived of in mundane and supramundane terms is that the former conceives of the three relata of the relation of giving, the donor, the recipient, and the object given, as substantially existent, while the latter does not. The bodhisattva who practices the supramundane perfection of giving knows that all three relata are dependently arisen and hence empty. As a consequence he does not experience any attachment to the object given, to the receiver, or to himself as the giver. A similar differentiation between the mundane and the supramundane applies to all perfections, not just to the perfection of generosity.

Metaphorical description of the 1st stage

1:017 Candrakīrti concludes the discussion of the 1st bodhisattva stage by comparing the joy the bodhisattva experiences at this stage to the moonstone, which Indian mythology considers to originate from rays of moon-light. Like a gem, this joy abides in the bodhisattva's mind, beautifying it, and dispelling by its light the multiple obscurations abandoned on the path of seeing.[15]

[15] *darśanamārga*, the third of the five paths (*pañcamārga*) to enlightenment. On these see Obermiller 1998: 13–24; Padmakara 2010: 215–216, 219–222.

Chapter 2

Section 2. Obtaining the 2nd bodhisattva stage: The perfection of moral discipline

The virtue associated with the 2nd bodhisattva stage is the perfec- 2:001
tion of moral discipline. The bodhisattva's mind is free of desire, anger, and mistaken views, and due to these three failing to act as mental motivating factors he does not engage in any wrong physical or verbal acts: killing, stealing, sexual misconduct, lying, divisive speech, harsh speech, or idle gossip. Instead, he practices the ten virtuous actions: three belonging to the mind (absence of attachment, loving kindness, and right view), three belonging to the body (cherishing life, giving, and a virtuous form of conducting sexual relations), and four belonging to speech (speaking truly, speaking so as to reconcile the divided, speaking kindly and elegantly, and speaking in a focused manner about important matters). The bodhisattva practices such virtuous behavior in all states of mind he might find himself in, including dreams.

While the ten virtuous actions are also practiced by the 2:002
bodhisattvas on the 1st stage, the bodhisattvas on the 2nd stage achieves an even higher level of ethical perfection. Having likened the minds of the bodhisattvas at the 1st stage to the moonstone, Candrakīrti compares those on the 2nd stage to the moon itself as it shines on a clear autumn night.[1] In Indian culture the light of the moon is traditionally associated with coolness, and Candrakīrti relates the etymology of the Sanskrit term for moral discipline, *śīla*, to the term for coolness, *śīta*, indicating that moral discipline cools the fire of the passions. Like the moon, the bodhisattva at the 2nd stage is also, due to his perfection of moral discipline, endowed with a special glow or radiance.

[1] See below p. 218, note 22.

2:003 As was observed for acts of giving,[2] any instance of moral discipline involves three elements, in this case the acting subject, the action itself (either as carrying out a virtuous action, or as abstaining from a non-virtuous one), and the object toward which the action is directed. While moral actions are meritorious independently of how these "three spheres" are understood, the perfection of moral discipline pursued by the practitioner on the 2nd bodhisattva stage sees agent, action, and object of action as equally dependently originated and empty. The purity of this moral discipline is characterized by the absence of the dualistic distinction between substantial existence and complete nonexistence with regard to the three elements involved in each moral action.

2:004 Moral discipline produces synergetic effects when joined with generosity. While the latter will produce pleasant effects in future lives, those who do not practice moral discipline at the same time will experience these pleasant effects in some of the lower realms, as a pampered pet, say, or as an affluent ghost. Such circumstances will make it difficult to practice further generosity; one will be like an investor who spends the interest together with all the capital, and is unable to generate any further revenue. The positive karmic seeds having been reaped in the form of pleasant experiences, no seeds of the same nature are sown. If we practice generosity and moral discipline together, however, we will reap the karmic benefits of giving, and be reborn in states where it is easy to perpetuate generosity, setting in motion a virtuous circle creating more and more positive karma.

2:005 Once one is born in one of the lower realms (the realms of animals, hungry ghosts, or hell beings) one is likely to find oneself at the mercy of others (as animals relative to their owners, hell-beings relative to hell-guardians, etc.), robbing one of the freedom to make virtuous choices accumulating positive karma. Like a defeated warrior, bound and thrown into a deep abyss, one will be unable to raise

[2] See 1:016.

oneself up again, eventually cycling around the lower realms again and again, propelled by the force of negative karma accumulated in forms of rebirth dominated by ignorance, greed, and fear. This underlines the necessity to practice the perfections of generosity and moral discipline now, while born in human form, to set in motion a process accumulating positive karma that first ensures birth in the higher realms, and ultimately liberation from cyclic existence altogether.

In the sequence of perfections the Buddha taught the perfection 2:006
of moral discipline following directly after the perfection of generosity. The reason for this is that if the fruits of generosity are enjoyed in a future life, while one has been reborn in a lower realm because of moral failures, these fruits, once enjoyed, will not return. Yet if rebirth in a higher realm ensues, because of the practice of moral discipline, this rebirth functions like a field, which can be cultivated by the fruits of previous generosity, in order to practice further generosity, thereby generating a continuous yield of good karma.

The practice of moral discipline is an essential ingredient of 2:007
the path to any goal; whether one desires ordinary happiness in *saṃsāra*, pursues the paths of the *arhat* or the *pratyekabuddha*, or whether one strives, via the path of the bodhisattva, for the complete liberation of a fully enlightened Buddha, in all cases one will avoid the ten non-virtuous actions and practice their opposites, the ten virtuous actions. As anyone attempting to move upward in or out of cyclic existence practices moral discipline it constitutes a necessary condition for advancing toward these goals. It does not, however, act as a sole condition, as other perfections contribute to these goals as well.[3]

Candrakīrti points out that the bodhisattvas on the 2nd 2:008
stage, excelling in the perfection of wisdom, do not mix with the unvirtuous, as the pure ocean will expel a corpse thrown into

[3] Jinpa 2021: 124.

it,[4] and as fortune and misfortune cannot be simultaneously present in one place. Continuous ethical training has prepared the bodhisattva's mind in such a way that it naturally disassociates itself from any mental states incompatible with the practice of moral discipline.

2:009 Echoing a point made before,[5] Candrakīrti differentiates between mundane and supramundane moral discipline. The former is based on the idea of an agent restraining from a specific action, where the action itself and the object the action is directed toward are conceived of as existing substantially. The latter does not presuppose that these "three spheres" exist with an intrinsic nature. Supramundane moral discipline is practiced by bodhisattvas on the path of seeing and above.[6]

Metaphorical description of the 2nd stage

2:010 Candrakīrti concludes the second chapter by a poetic description of the 2nd bodhisattva stage. Continuing with the lunar theme,[7] this stage is likened to the moon, giving rise to the bodhisattva who is therefore described as a "moon-born son of the victorious Buddha." The 2nd bodhisattva stage is compared to the moon in three respects. As the moon is an adornment of the world, yet beyond it, the 2nd stage and the bodhisattvas on it are not confined by the chains that bind cyclic existence, but are still active within it, and are the glory of cyclic existence, due to the perfections they

[4] In the *Uposathasutta* (*Aṅguttara Nikāya* 8:19, Bhikkhu Bodhi 2012: 1142–1144) the Buddha refers to eight extraordinary qualities (*acchariyā abbhutā dhammā*) of the ocean, in order to illustrate eight similarly extraordinary features of his teaching and the rules for the monastic community. The third of these is the fact that the ocean does not absorb impure substances such as corpses thrown into it, but expels them by washing them up on its shore. In the same way, the comparison describes, will the monastic community expel any member who does not follow the rules of monastic discipline.

[5] See 1:016, 2:003.

[6] See above, p. 36, note 15.

[7] See 2:002, 11:054.

embody. As the white radiance of the moon is free from stains, the 2nd bodhisattva stage bears the name "immaculate," since the bodhisattva is free from any blemish associated with the ten non-virtuous actions. And as the cooling light of the autumn moon dispels the heat of the day, the bodhisattva's activities remove the mental suffering of sentient beings which result from morally deficient actions.

Chapter 3

Section 3. Obtaining the 3rd bodhisattva stage

3:001 Candrakīrti explains that the 3rd bodhisattva stage bears the name "luminous" since the fire of wisdom the bodhisattva develops at this stage burns away all objects of knowledge, producing a light with the essence of peace. The bodhisattva's insight into emptiness refutes any notion of intrinsic nature objects might be considered to have; at the same time it also dissolves the idea of a subject with an intrinsic nature that apprehends these objects. In this way the duality between subject and object and the obscurations embodied by this are pacified.

Candrakīrti also notes that a copper-like glow, similar to the sun, appears to the bodhisattva at this stage. His autocommentary does not expand on this further; there are various ways in which this statement might be interpreted. It may be understood in the most literal sense as a visual phenomenon that appears to bodhisattvas at a specific level of realization; there are other examples where the appearance of specific visual experiences is considered to mark progress along levels of meditative training.[1] More metaphorically, this reference to the sun (following Candrakīrti's mention of the moon in the preceding verse) could be read as referring to the light of full enlightenment. As the copper-colored dawn announces the rising of the sun, the 3rd bodhisattva stage announces the realization of the state of the fully enlightened Buddha the bodhisattva will obtain at the end of his path. Finally, and more specifically, some commentators[2] take the reference to the copper-colored glow to refer in particular to post-meditative states of 3rd stage

[1] Such as the various signs (*nimitta*) marking the process of training in *śamatha* meditation (see Ñyāṇamoli 1976: 1:129–130).
[2] Jinpa 2021: 129; Padmakara 2004: 156.

bodhisattvas. When absorbed in the meditation on emptiness, the duality between external objects and internal subjects as substantially real has completely disappeared for them. Once they leave the meditative state, the shining light that obliterates this distinction recedes, and duality reappears, but the bodhisattva's perception is accompanied by an "afterglow" of the realization of emptiness. In this sense the reference to the copper-colored glow would indicate that the insight into emptiness is no longer tied to specific mental exercises the bodhisattva performs, but pervades more and more of his cognitive life.

The perfection of patience

The moral quality particularly associated with the 3rd bodhisattva stage is the perfection of patience. At this stage the bodhisattva has developed his patience to such an extent that even if someone were to cut their body part by part for no reason at all, they would develop no anger, but only patience toward such a being. This patience is motivated by the bodhisattva's great compassion, since he is mindful of the extremely painful consequences such actions will cause for the perpetrator, who will, as a karmic consequence, experience much greater suffering than the bodhisattva experiences. **3:002**

The bodhisattva's patience does not simply flow from his compassion, but also from his wisdom, constituted by his insight into emptiness. He realizes at the experiential level that all constituents of the harmful action directed at him,[3] the perpetrator, the victim, and the act itself, with its specific temporal and qualitative characteristics, are without intrinsic nature and insubstantial like a reflection. This realization undercuts any anger the bodhisattva may have felt, which relies on the substantial existence of the **3:003**

[3] The "three spheres"; see 1:016, 2:003, 2:009.

person harmed, the one who causes the harm, and the action that connects them. Realizing the illusion-like nature of all three the bodhisattva is able to practice the perfection of patience instead of anger.

3:004 Patience is a virtue that should also be practiced by those who have not reached the heights of realization of the 3rd stage bodhisattva, characterized by great compassion and insight into emptiness. Candrakīrti points out that those who cannot yet practice patience motivated in the way highly realized bodhisattvas do should at least realize that anger is a profoundly irrational response to harm inflicted on one. First, in addition to the physical and mental suffering we are already undergoing as a result of the injury, we *add* more mental suffering in the form of unpleasant, angry mental states. Unsurprisingly, this does not reduce the suffering we already felt, but increases our overall amount of suffering. In addition, while being utterly ineffective in alleviating present, painful states of mind, the danger of anger lies in habituating the mind into generating anger in the future, thereby increasing the likelihood of more suffering in future situations which may be exacerbated by approaching them with an angry state of mind. Hence, the practitioner should realize that both from a short-term and a long-term perspective anger is an unhelpful and harmful response to any condition we perceive as an injury.

3:005 In addition, it is irrational to feel anger toward someone harming us, as the pain we experience from their hand is nothing but the maturation of negative karma we have ourselves generated in the past. Once these karmic seeds have matured in the relevant experiences their power is exhausted, and they cannot produce further suffering for us in the future, such as being reborn in a lower realm. As such we should feel great relief at the experience of pain, as when taking the final portion of an unpleasant medicine that will cure our disease once and for all, or as when a doctor applies a sharp instrument to permanently cure a painful condition. The last thing we should want to do is create more potential for similar experiences in the future by acting angrily toward the person who has harmed us.

The accumulation and the ripening of karmic potentials cannot 3:006
be understood in an isolated manner, but necessarily involves other members of the network of dependent origination. First, the ripening of a karmic potential can be obstructed by the presence of other karmic potential.[4] The manner in which a specific karmic potential present in one's mental continuum produces an effect does not simply depend on this potential, but also on what other potentials are present at the same time. Second, the force of the karmic potential produced by a certain action depends not simply on the agent, but also on the object of the action. Anger developed toward highly realized beings, such as bodhisattvas, is taken to have considerably stronger consequences than anger directed toward ordinary beings.[5]

Since anger is particularly potent in preventing the maturation of positive karmic seeds, and as anger directed at highly realized beings will produce disastrous karmic consequences, we have an especially strong reason to practice patience and to strive to avoid angry states of mind at all cost.

The karmic consequences of anger in this and future lives in- 3:007
clude physical unattractiveness, being surrounded by the morally
debased, and being unable to tell right from wrong. Choosing non- 3:008
virtuous over virtuous actions will then swiftly lead to rebirth in the lower realms in future lives. Generating the perfection of patience, on the other hand, leads to a beautiful appearance, the esteem of holy beings, and to proficiency in moral choices, resulting in rebirth in the human or divine realm, by allowing us to exhaust negative karma accumulated in the past.

[4] Candrakīrti uses the term *'joms* (possibly translating the Sanskrit *pratihan*) which can mean both "to destroy" and "to suppress." Whether the karmic potentials produced by anger fully destroy those produced by generosity, or merely strongly suppress their manifestation is a contentious point.

[5] See Śāntideva's *Bodhicaryāvatāra* 1:34, 6:1; Crosby/Skilton 1995: 8, 50.

3:009 Realizing the benefits of patience and the disadvantages of anger, all beings, ordinary beings and bodhisattvas,[6] should practice patience.

3:010 Candrakīrti notes about the perfection of patience what he has already stressed concerning the previous two perfections, those of generosity and moral discipline,[7] namely that this perfection remains mundane as long as it involves a distinction between agent, object, and action, between the person who acts patiently, the person one has patience toward, and the act of patience as entities with intrinsic natures. This applies even if the resulting positive karmic potential is dedicated toward enlightenment. The supramundane form of the perfection of patience, attained by the bodhisattvas at the 3rd stage, on the other hand, is free from the distinction between the "three spheres."[8] This latter form of patience might be identified with patience arising in specific meditative states in which the distinctions between agent, object, and action no longer appear, while the mundane form of patience corresponds to the form of patience practiced outside of meditative states, when the appearance of the distinction reasserts itself.

Further qualities of the 3rd bodhisattva stage

3:011 Bodhisattvas at the third stage are characterized by other abilities apart from the perfection of patience. These include proficiencies in a set of three quartets of important meditative states,[9] attainments including the four absorptions of the form realm,[10] the four

[6] Candrakīrti describes the practice of patience by bodhisattvas in 3:002–3:003 and that by ordinary beings in 3:004–3:008.

[7] See 1:016, 2:003, 2:009.

[8] See 3:003.

[9] For more information on these quartets, see Kelsang Gyatso 1995: 99–114; Brasington 2015; and below, 6:207.

[10] *rūpāvacaradhyāna*. For further discussion of these different states see Dayal 1932: 225–236; Catherine 2011; Lamotte 1944–1980: 3:1209–1238; Gelongma Karma Migme Chödrön: 3:992–1018.

formless absorptions, and the four immeasurables, loving kindness, compassion, empathetic joy, and equanimity.[11] The bodhisattvas also achieve a range of supernormal powers,[12] including the ability to create magical emanations,[13] to hear beyond the range of normal perception, to read the minds of others, to remember their own former births,[14] and to know the karmic potential of all sentient beings. They have completely exhausted the "three poisons" of attachment, aversion, and ignorance in their own mind and are able to overcome attachment in the minds of others.

Candrakīrti notes that the first three of the six perfections, gen- **3:012**
erosity, moral discipline, and patience, being comparatively easy to practice outside of a monastic setting, are recommended by the Buddhas to bodhisattvas who are laypeople,[15] while the practice of the remaining three, effort, meditation, and wisdom, are primarily recommended to ordained bodhisattvas, though it is not to be assumed that all perfections cannot be practiced equally by all bodhisattvas.

In addition, the first three perfections contribute to the accumulation of merit necessary to eventually obtain the physical body of a Buddha, characterized by all the marks of physical perfection usually associated with it.[16] During the course of their training bodhisattvas have to complete two sets of practices to achieve full Buddhahood. The first is the accumulation of merit; the second, the accumulation of knowledge, generates the Buddha's "absolute" body or *dharmakāya*[17] and is brought about by the perfections of

[11] *apramāṇa*. also known as the "divine abodes" (*brahmavihāra*). On these see Dalai Lama/Thubten Chodron 2020: 3–47.

[12] *Abhijñā*. For further discussion of the five types of supernatural powers mentioned by Candrakīrti see MacDonald 2009: 135, note 7.

[13] **ṛddhi, rdzu 'phrul.*

[14] **purvanivāsānusmṛti, sngan gyi gnas rjes su drang pa.*

[15] See also Nāgārjuna's *Ratnāvalī* 4:99 (Khensur Jampa Tegchok 2016: 325).

[16] On this see Powers 2008.

[17] On the idea of the different "bodies" of a Buddha distinguished in Mahāyāna Buddhology see Conze 1962: 172–173, 232–234; and below, 11:014, 11:017.

meditation and wisdom, while the perfection of effort contributes to both accumulations.

Metaphorical description of the 3rd bodhisattva stage

3:013 Having eliminated the mental darkness of defilements in their own minds by the sun-like nature of the "luminous" 3rd bodhisattva stage, the bodhisattvas set out to similarly eliminate defilements in all other beings. Despite the intensity of their intention the bodhisattvas are, however, completely free of anger toward other beings less accomplished than they are, due to the perfection of patience cultivated at this stage.

Chapter 4

Section 4. Obtaining the 4th bodhisattva stage: The perfection of effort

The 4th bodhisattva stage is characterized by the perfection of effort. Effort is enthusiasm for virtuous actions and as such brings about every good quality, facilitating the attainment of those not yet attained and enhancing those already attained. This perfection is said to "blaze forth" at the 4th bodhisattva stage, hence it is given the name "radiant." It links the first three perfections of generosity, moral discipline, and patience, recommended primarily for lay bodhisattvas and the cause of the accumulation of merit, with the final two perfections, meditation and wisdom, the cause of the accumulation of knowledge, because it brings about both accumulations equally. 4:001

Further qualities of the 4th bodhisattva stage

The copper-light glow referred to in 3:001 is replaced by an even brighter light on this 4th "radiant" bodhisattva stage. This light results from the cultivation of the 37 factors of enlightenment,[1] a set of seven lists of doctrinal concepts taken to comprise the entire Buddhist path. As a result, any sense of self has now completely vanished[2] for the bodhisattva. 4:002

[1] *bodhipākṣikā dharmāḥ*, referred to again in 6:208. They include the four foundations of mindfulness (*smṛtyupasthāna*), the four right efforts or abandonments (*samyakpradhāna*), the four bases of miraculous powers (*ṛddhipāda*), the five faculties (*indriya*), the five powers (*bala*), the seven limbs of enlightenment (*bodhyaṅga*), and the noble eightfold path (*āryāṣṭāṅgamārga*). A detailed discussion of these may be found in Gethin 2001; see also Eimer 1976: 42–51; Lamotte 1944–1980: 3: 1119–1207; Gelongma Karma Migme Chödrön 3:924–991; Geshe Kelsang Gyatso 1995: 120–125; Dalai Lama/ Thubten Chodron 2019: 413–460.

[2] This does not have to entail that all the cognitive obscurations (*jñeyāvaraṇa, shes bya'i sgrib pa*) underlying the sense of self have also vanished at this stage. Commentators disagree on how comprehensive the bodhisattva's abandonment of the sense of self at the 4th stage is.

Chapter 5

Section 5. Obtaining the 5th bodhisattva stage: The perfection of meditation

5:001 The 5th bodhisattva stage is called "hard to overcome" because at this stage the bodhisattva cannot be overcome by *devaputra*, the Māra of attachment dwelling in all realms of the world.

The deity Māra, well-known as the antagonist of the historical Buddha, is intent on preventing practitioners from achieving enlightenment.[1] Four types of Māra are distinguished in the scholastic literature,[2] the Māra of the aggregates, the Māra of afflictions, the Māra of the Lord of Death, and the divine son of Māra. The Buddhist understanding includes conceptualizing some of the Māras as individual agents (in the case of *devaputramāra*),[3] as impersonal processes (in the case of Māra of the Lord of Death), as well treating them as personifications of afflicted mental states of unenlightened beings. According to the last understanding the Māra of the aggregates refers to our misconception of the aggregates as constituting a substantial self, the Māra of afflictions to the forces of aversion, attachment, and ignorance in our mind, the Māra of the Lord of Death to our fear of change and dying, and *devaputra*, the divine son of Māra, to our craving for pleasures of the senses.

Candrakīrti's autocommentary points out that the 5th stage bodhisattva also cannot be overcome by other Māras subservient to *devaputra*, the Māra of attachment. This might be taken to refer to the other three kinds of Māra, indicating that the bodhisattva has achieved a level of realization where his progress cannot be impeded by grasping at the aggregates as the self, by mental afflictions, or by the fear of death.

[1] See Nichols 2010b.
[2] Nichols 2010a: 14, note 16.
[3] See Geshe Kelsang Gyatso 1995: 128.

The quality particularly associated with the 5th stage is the perfection of meditation; it provides the bodhisattva with a mastery of the subtle nature of the four noble truths. The four noble truths, as well as any other truths there may be are subsumed under the two truths which, Candrakīrti points out, are the only truths there are. The 1st, 2nd, and 4th noble truths, the truth of suffering, the origin of suffering, and the path leading to the cessation of suffering, belong to conventional truth, while the 3rd noble truth, the truth of the cessation of suffering, belongs to the ultimate truth. The system of the four noble truths is taught in order to indicate the cause and effect of what is to be rejected, and of what is to be adopted. Afflictions are to be rejected; their cause is explained in the 2nd noble truth, the truth of the origin of suffering, their effect is described in the 1st noble truth, the truth of suffering. What is to be adopted is the purification of the afflictions; its cause is provided by the 4th noble truth, the path leading to the cessation of suffering, and its effect is indicated in the 3rd noble truth, the cessation of suffering.

Chapter 6

Section 6. Obtaining the 6th bodhisattva stage

6:001 Candrakīrti begins his account of the 6th bodhisattva stage, called "turned toward" or "directly facing" (*abhimukhī*), by describing the qualities of the practitioners at this level.[1] They are characterized by three properties: they turn toward the qualities of a perfect Buddha, they realize dependent origination (*pratītyasamutpāda*), and they obtain cessation.

The first means that they have moved considerably closer to the obtainment of Buddhahood than the bodhisattvas on the previous five stages. The reason for this is the second property, the realization of dependent origination. In a very general way, dependent origination is characterized by the Buddha as the fact that "when this exists, that comes to be; with the arising of this, that arises. When this does not exist, that does not come to be; with the cessation of this, that ceases."[2] In Madhyamaka, more specifically, dependent origination is equated with the notion of emptiness.[3] One way of conceiving of dependent origination is by understanding it as the opposite of Humean supervenience, "the doctrine that all there is to the world is a vast mosaic of local matters of particular fact, just one little thing and then another."[4] To pursue Lewis's example, if you take out any piece of the mosaic, it will retain its color; if Humean supervenience did not hold, and the color of each piece was not simply a 'local matter' its color might change

[1] Compare also the characterization of the 6th stage in Nāgārjuna's *Ratnāvalī* 5:51–52 (Khensur Jampa Tegchok 2016: 362–365).

[2] Bhikkhu Bodhi 2000: 552, *imasmiṃ sati idaṃ hoti. imassuppādā idaṃ uppajjati. imasmiṃ asati idaṃ na hoti. Imassa nirodhā idaṃ nirujjhati*, Nidānasaṃyutta, Saṃyutta Nikāya 2:21, PTS S ii 28.

[3] *Mūlamadhyamakakārikā* 24:18. See Siderits/Katsura 2013: 277–278.

[4] Lewis 1986: ix. See also Weatherson 2015.

when separated from its neighbors.[5] Dependent origination holds that the world does not simply consist of an array of individuals each of which has its properties simply by itself, but that things are connected by a network of dependence relations.[6] Even though dependent origination is a specific view of how dependence relations are distributed in the world, it is not simply promoted here as a correct philosophical position. In addition to simply *rationally assenting* to it, and to its associated position of universal emptiness, on the basis of arguments such as those Candrakīrti will present later on in the work, the bodhisattva at the 6th stage also *realizes* it. The difference between rational assent and realization is that only the latter affects specific automatic default ways of cognizing and conceptualizing the world.

This is indicated by the third property, cessation (*nirodha*) that bodhisattvas are said to obtain at this stage. Cessation is obviously not the cessation of suffering described in the 3rd of the four noble truths (*nirodha-satya*), and hence liberation from cyclic existence but a specific meditative state[7] attained through the perfection of meditation (*dhyāna-pāramitā*) achieved at the previous bodhisattva stage. This state is characterized by a shift in perception of the world that removes the differentiation between cognition and object cognized, one of the key features of the conventional reality

[5] An example where this actually happens (at least as far as *perceived* color is concerned) is the Rubik's cube color illusion (Seckel 2004: 72).

[6] Note that dependent origination does not have to amount to the stronger claim that everything depends on *everything* else (an understanding implied by the *Avamtaṃsakasūtra*'s image of Indra's net, an arrangement of jewels where each jewel reflects every other jewel (Cleary 1993: 925; 1983: 37–38)), but may simply be construed as saying that everything depends on *some other* thing,

[7] The Buddhist commentarial literature differentiates various meditative states characterized in terms of "cessation." See for example Kelsang Gyatso 1995: 142–145; Lusthaus 2002: 123–159. Siderits/Katsura 2024 argue that Candrakīrti use of the term *nirodha* (*'gog pa*) refers to a meditative state called *nirodhasamāpatti* (*'gog pa'i snyoms 'jug*) characterized by the absence of all mental activity (see Conze 1962: 113–116, 236). The source of this is unclear, and the idea of the bodhisattva acquiring a specific new manner of perception, rather than the absence of perception, appears more plausible.

in which we live our lives.[8] Instead, the bodhisattva sees subjects and objects to be essentially equivalent to reflections. Rather than perceiving objects through a pane of glass, with the subject at the other side, the bodhisattva sees objects as equivalent to reflections in the glass,[9] undermining the default presumption that there is any more to these objects than just their appearance (simultaneously, it should be pointed out, undermining the presumed substantiality of the perceiving subject).

The perfection of wisdom

6:002 Candrakīrti noted in the previous verse that through having realized dependent origination and obtained cessation, the bodhisattva is said to abide in wisdom (*prajñā*). Wisdom plays a fundamental role in the Buddhist moral architecture of the six perfections (*pāramitā*). This is nicely illustrated by the arched gateway (*toraṇa*) that surrounds representations of the Buddha in Tibetan art.[10] It consists of six kinds of beings stacked together in an arch, representing the six perfections of generosity (*dāna*), moral discipline (*śīla*), patience (*kṣānti*), effort (*vīrya*), meditation (*dhyāna*), and wisdom. The basis of the arch, which props up the entire structure, is a pair of lions, representing wisdom. In the Mahāyāna texts we also find a lists of ten perfections which adds four more to this list of ten. This scheme of ten is then aligned with the ten bodhisattva stages,[11] the perfection of wisdom being associated with the 6th stage, the stage discussed in the present chapter.

[8] Candrakīrti characterizes conventional truth in terms of the opposition of *jñāna* and *jñeya* (May 1959: 226).

[9] Mikyö Dorje (Goldfield et al. 2005: 16–18) points out that bodhisattvas at the 6th stage do not simply see phenomena as similar to reflections (*gzugs brnyan dang 'dra ba*) but not even as equivalent to reflections (*gzugs brnyan dang mtshungs pa*), meaning the emptiness of phenomena is here no longer conceptualized through a simile, but that the reflection-like nature of things is realized directly.

[10] Beer 1999: 88–90.

[11] See above, p. 30, note 7.

Candrakīrti argues that the other perfections are in need of the perfection of wisdom to allow them to carry out their soteriological function. This is not because the other perfections are inert (as the blind men in Candrakīrti's simile are not lame), but because their abilities need to be directed in a specific direction to achieve the goal of enlightenment. In itself the practice of generosity, for example, is efficacious to the extent that the associated intentions will generate positive karma which will mature in pleasant experiences at a later stage. But the mere accumulation of positive karma will not produce any soteriological result. The first five perfections need to operate in tandem with the perfection of wisdom in order to bring about the possibility of liberation from the cycle of rebirth. The perfection of wisdom conceived of in terms of the realization of dependent arising as described in 6:001 entails a shift in the perception and conceptualization of the world, a different form of comportment free from the view of a substantially real subject around which the rest of the world of external objects and other beings revolves. This fundamentally changes the nature of actions expressing the other five perfections in such a way that they differ in an important way before and after obtaining the 6th bodhisattva stage.[12] It is only after they have changed through the realization of dependent arising that they can become instruments directly efficacious for obtaining the goal of enlightenment.

The source and the recipients of the teachings on emptiness

At this point the question arises how Candrakīrti will present this transformative realization to his audience. He dismisses the idea that one could simply do so by explaining relevant Buddhist *sūtra*s, such as the Perfection of Wisdom *sūtra*s or the *Daśabhūmikasūtra*, **6:003**

[12] See Garfield 2015: 308.

which constitutes the structural basis of Candrakīrti's present work. The reason for this is that the intent of these texts is difficult to ascertain, and that in any case somebody like him would not be able to explain the way things are on the basis of these works. Candrakīrti therefore bases his exposition on the works of Nāgārjuna who, resting on claims made by the relevant scriptures, described a set of arguments that could be employed to understand the idea of universal emptiness (which is equated with that of dependent origination).[13]

To establish the authority of Nāgārjuna, Candrakīrti quotes a passage from the *Laṅkāvatārasūtra* predicting the life and work of Nāgārjuna.[14] It is especially interesting to note that Nāgārjuna is described there as having attained the 1st bodhisattva stage, an attainment associated with a direct realization of emptiness.[15] As such, Nāgārjuna does not only have theoretical, but also direct knowledge of emptiness and can therefore be relied on as an authoritative source when it comes to explaining it.

6:004 Having argued that the teaching he is going to deliver, an explanation of the theory of emptiness based on Nāgārjuna's exposition, is suitable for achieving the intended result, a direct and
6:005 experiential realization of emptiness as experienced on the 6th bodhisattva stage, Candrakīrti now considers the suitability of the student. This is essential, for the efficacy of any teaching to bring about its intended result does not just depend on intrinsic qualities of the instruction, but also on the properties of the student. If

[13] Edward Conze (1953: 117) notes about the Perfection of Wisdom *sūtras* that "they do not develop their doctrine by reasoned argumentation but rely entirely on simple dogmatic affirmation. As *sūtras*, these works are held to be the word of the Buddha himself, and his authority is thought to be sufficient support for their veracity and truth. By a division of labor, the Buddhists left reasoned argumentation to another class of works, called *śāstras*. It is in the *śāstras* of the Mādhyamika school, from Nāgārjuna onward, that we must seek for anything in the nature of philosophical argumentation."

[14] 10:165–166, Vaidya 1963: 118; Suzuki 1932: 239–240.

[15] This realization presumably needs to be understood as a first glimpse of the more thorough realization of the emptiness at the 6th bodhisattva stage (see Dzogchen Pönlop Rinpoche 1999: 6,1: 5–6).

the student is not fully prepared he will in the best case waste his time trying to master instructions he cannot understand, and in the worst case achieve detrimental results by misunderstanding the teaching.

In his autocommentary Candrakīrti focuses in particular on the nihilistic misunderstanding of emptiness that treats universal emptiness as synonymous with universal nonexistence. What precisely this nihilistic misapprehension amounts to is a complex question,[16] though it is clear that one of the main worries of the Madhyamaka authors is that emptiness could be misconceived as an overall denial of the everyday world of conventional reality, and in particular of the law of karma and the existence of rebirth. Given the central role these play in Buddhist ethics, their denial, it is feared, would lead to the dissolution of all ethical standards, thereby immersing sentient beings more and more in cyclic existence instead of releasing them from it.

The warnings against the dire consequences of misunderstanding emptiness we find in Madhyamaka texts[17] as well as Candrakīrti's emphasis on the suitability of the student in the present verses show that the point of studying the theory of emptiness is not just to defend a specific philosophical theory. If engaging with the theory of emptiness was fundamentally the same as engaging with, say, forms of ontological anti-foundationalism as we find them studied in contemporary Western metaphysics[18] the only risk of misunderstanding it would be to end up with a wrong philosophical view—hardly something that would ordinarily be a cause of great concern.

[16] For some discussion of this question see Westerhoff 2016.

[17] See, for instance, Nāgārjuna's *Mūlamadhyamakakārikā* 24:11 (Siderits/Katsura 2013: 274) and Āryadeva's *Catuḥśataka* 12:12 (Lang 1986: 114; Geshe Sonam Rinchen 1994: 244–245), as well as Khensur Jampa Tegchok 2016: 46–48. Note that the dual of the nihilistic misreading of emptiness regards it as an (ultimately) true philosophical theory—another mistaken interpretation to be avoided (see *Mūlamadhyamakakārikā* 13:8 (Siderits/Katsura 2013: 145–146) and Candrakīrti's *Prasannapadā* on this verse (Schayer 1931: 38)).

[18] On which see Westerhoff 2020, chapter 3.

It is only because the realization of emptiness is taken to be the egress from the existential suffering of *saṃsāra*, "from which there is no other door,"[19] mistaking it for something that it is not means walking straight into the wall, with all the painful consequences this entails.

Candrakīrti lists specific physical signs indicating that the student is a suitable recipient for the teachings of emptiness that are about to follow, though we might not want to assume the contrapositive, that is, to stop reading when the signs are not present.[20] The key point Candrakīrti wants to stress here is that for the teachings of emptiness to exercise their soteriological efficacy, authoritative instructions need to come together with properly prepared students.

6:006 One might suspect that the realization of emptiness and the resulting ability of seeing the world as essentially equivalent to reflections discussed in relation to 6:001 would undermine the
6:007 role of ethical practices in the bodhisattva's training, "as heat undermines cold."[21] After all, what is the value of engaging in ethical behavior such as giving if the recipient, the gift, and the giver, too, lack any ontologically fundamental status? If the furniture of the world is not substantially real, how could it support the existence of real ethical value?[22] Yet Candrakīrti argues that far from undermining ethical practices, any glimpse of a realization of emptiness that one might obtain leads to an intensive cultivation of ethical qualities. Why this is the case is a complex matter, and in fact the relationship between ethics and emptiness in Madhyamaka is a topic of considerable depth.[23] While there is much more to be said on the compatibility (and in fact mutual presupposition) of ethics

[19] As noted in Āryadeva's *Catuḥśataka* 12:13; Lang 1986: 114; Geshe Sonam Rinchen 1994: 245.

[20] See e.g. Jinpa 2021: 164; Dzogchen Pönlop Rinpoche 1999: 6,1: 20.

[21] Jinpa 2021: 166.

[22] See Button 2013: 174.

[23] For some discussion see The Cowherds 2015; and Westerhoff 2020: 73–78.

and emptiness, in the present context Candrakīrti presents a purely prudential reason for why someone who has gained a first understanding of emptiness should practice the moral perfections. It is formulated in the Buddhist framework of karma and rebirth, and claims that a suitable student who has encountered this teaching puts such great value on learning more about the emptiness which he has just begun to realize that he will do everything possible to ensure he can continue studying it in future lifetimes. According to traditional Buddhist beliefs, practicing ethical behavior is a necessary condition for being reborn in the kind of environments where one can study at all, so the aspiring student practices ethics. Being able to study also requires some material wealth, so he practices giving. And since other perfections too generate the best surrounding for the study of emptiness, he practices them as well.[24]

The "stage of delight" Candrakīrti refers to in 6:007 is the first of the 10 bodhisattva stages. This shows that despite the fact that Candrakīrti speaks about 6th stage bodhisattvas and hence highly advanced practitioners who have directly realized emptiness, this is not his audience. He addresses students below the 1st bodhisattva stage who might have some theoretical conception of emptiness, but no realization at the experiential level. Since the majority of readers of this book will probably belong to this group, this is comforting news.

6a. Refutation of the four ways of causal production

Linking the "Introduction to the Middle Way" once more with the *Daśabhūmikasūtra*, Candrakīrti's commentary introduces a **6:008**

[24] The predicates 'lofty' (*udāra*) and 'profound' (*gambhīra*) used by Candrakīrti also link up this verse with the joint cultivation of emptiness and ethical perfection (especially the perfection of compassion (*karuṇā*)), as the latter is often used to characterize teachings on emptiness, and the former to describe teachings on compassion. See Thurman 1984: note 3, 187–188.

quotation from this text in order to launch his ensuing explanation of the notion of emptiness. The *Daśabhūmikasūtra* notes that the bodhisattva entering the 6th bodhisattva stage sees all things as being equivalent in certain respects.[25] This list includes being equivalent in being without characteristics, in being primordially pure, and in being like an illusion, but Candrakīrti focuses on all things being equally unproduced, arguing that on the basis of this all the other equivalences between things can be easily explained.

In line with Candrakīrti's intent to set out the teaching of Nāgārjuna mentioned in 6:003, this additionally links Candrakīrti's exposition with Nāgārjuna's in his "Fundamental Verses on the Middle Way." Nāgārjuna's exposition also begins by examining the impossibility of anything being produced, and Candrakīrti quotes the first verse of Nāgārjuna's work[26] here, lining up the starting points of their explanations of emptiness.

Both Nāgārjuna and Candrakīrti distinguish four ways in which a thing might be produced. It could be produced

1. from itself,
2. from another thing,
3. from both itself and another thing, or
4. neither from itself nor from another thing.

Since these four possibilities are jointly exhaustive, if we are able to show that none of the four ways of production is plausible we have established the *Daśabhūmikasūtra*'s characterization of all things being equally unproduced.

Candrakīrti immediately moves on to examining the first possibility, that things are produced from themselves. It is important to note that despite the exhaustive scope of this list, the different positions it contains are not simply to be understood as different

[25] See Honda 1968: 186–187.
[26] Siderits/Katsura 2013: 18–19.

coordinates in logical space, but are associated with specific proponents occupying this space. The idea of causal self-production is associated with the Sāṃkhya, possibly the oldest school of classical Indian philosophy. The dates of its mythical founder, the sage Kapila,[27] are, as so often, unclear, but he, and some central Sāṃkhya concepts are already mentioned in the *Śvetāśvatara Upaniṣad* (3rd ct BCE).[28] Buddhism's engagement with Sāṃkhya appears to go back to the former's very beginning[29] and continues throughout the history of Buddhist scholasticism.[30] This demonstrates the continued appeal of the Sāṃkhya system as a rival philosophical theory that was both relatively widespread and of sufficient systematic appeal[31] to justify detailed Buddhist critiques.[32]

Sāṃkhya is a non-theistic[33] metaphysical dualism that assumes the existence of two fundamental categories, *puruṣa*, a kind of pure, un-individualized consciousness, and *prakṛti*, a material substance that evolves into the world we perceive around us. With *puruṣa* as a catalyst, *prakṛti* in its primordial form (*mūlaprakṛti*) generates out of itself a sequence of twenty-three principles or *tattvas* that become increasingly more concrete, beginning with entities like the intellect (*buddhi*) or self-consciousness (*ahaṃkāra*) and ending with the sense-organs and material substances like water and earth. The

[27] Larson 1979: 139. Īśvarakṛṣṇa's *Sāṃkhyakārikā* (pre-6th ct CE) is usually considered as the textual basis of the classical form of the Sāṃkhya system.

[28] Larson 1979: 101–102; Olivelle 1998: 427, 625, note 2.

[29] Aśvaghoṣa's *Buddhacarita* (2nd ct CE) describes the historical Buddha as rejecting a form of the Sāṃkhya system (Kent 1982). See also Jakubczak 2012.

[30] Kapila is referred to in Nāgārjuna's *Vaidalyaprakaraṇa* (Westerhoff 2018a: 64–67); Sāṃkhya positions are discussed, for example, in Asaṅga's *Yogācārabhūmi* (Mikogami 1969), Vasubhandu's *Abhidharmakośabhāṣya* (Bronkhorst 1997, see also Takakusu 1904), Bhāviveka's *Madhyamakahṛdayakārikā* (Honda 1967; Qvarnström 2012), and Śāntideva's *Bodhicaryāvatāra* (9: 60–67, 126b–137, Crosby/Skilton 1995: 121–122, 128–129, 185–186, 188).

[31] Perrett 2001: 11–12 argues that Sāṃkhya's conceptualization of all mental states typically discussed in Western philosophy as evolutes of *prakṛti* renders it compatible with the computational theory of mind.

[32] See, however, Osto 2018 for an argument for "strong structural homologies" between Sāṃkhya and Abhidharma Buddhism. Nicholson 2017: 600–601 sees "clear affinities" between Sāṃkhya and Buddhism; see also Larson 1979: 92–93.

[33] Garbe 1894: 191–195.

details of this evolutionary process leading from the mental to the material need not concern us here; the key point is that the entirety of the world we perceive through our senses is contained *in nuce* within *prakṛti*, which, as a fundamental cause, contains all these effects within it as potentialities. This idea of the pre-existence of the effect in the cause (*satkāryavāda*)[34] is the focus of Candrakīrti's critique.

This is a good place to reflect briefly on Candrakīrti's take on the different rival schools of thought, Buddhist and non-Buddhist, which he discusses in the "Introduction to the Middle Way." One important question to consider is the extent to which Candrakīrti's presentation of their systems is one they themselves would endorse. Discussing this question in a way that does justice to the complexity of the intellectual systems of Candrakīrti's opponents means to dive into the world of Indian intellectual history rather more deeply than we can in the context of this introductory presentation. It is worthwhile to keep in mind, though, that the presentation of alternative views in Buddhist philosophical texts usually plays a double role. One is the refutation of philosophical opponents, and to gauge the success of this the question of whether we are presented with a faithful summary of a rival position or with a conveniently constructed straw man is important. However, the defense of his specific interpretation of Madhyamaka against all rivals is not Candrakīrti's only, and perhaps not even his primary goal. His main objective is to present his students with a route to the direct realization of emptiness. In this context the 'rival views' can be understood in a second sense, namely as misinterpretations of Madhyamaka (and, more generally, of the teachings of the Buddha) that students might develop on their way toward an understanding of emptiness. Understood in this way, the most important thing about a philosophical theory like, say, causation from itself is not whether a particular proponent of a

[34] See Bronkhorst 1999; Mikogami 1969; Larson 1979 165, note 20.

specific school of classical Indian thought really held that view, but that the student of Madhyamaka might mistakenly regard this as a plausible philosophical position that presents a conceptually stable alternative to the theory of universal emptiness. Candrakīrti's refutation can therefore be seen as having an additional pedagogical role, independent of whether or not it constitutes a faithful representation of the views of alternative philosophical accounts. If we are concerned that a specific rival view discussed by Candrakīrti is either not held by the opponent it is attributed to, or a misunderstanding of a different view they do hold, it is important to consider whether the discussion of this opposing view might not play another role in addition to an exchange of fire in an ancient Indian philosophical conflict. It may point out a location in conceptual space that the student of Madhyamaka might initially find attractive, even though it turns out, on closer analysis, to be intrinsically problematic.

6a.1 Production from itself

Taking up the first possibility, Candrakīrti notes that there is something evidently curious about the idea that things are self-produced.[35] Production, after all, is the bringing into existence of something that does not yet exist, as a rice-seed might produce a rice-shoot. But if the rice-shoot was self-produced, it would already exist at the time of its production, so there would be no point in its being produced again. If the evolution of the Sāṃkhya *tattva*s from *prakṛti* is to be understood as a temporal sequence it is unclear why it happens in the first place: after all, whatever the sequence brings about is already there before the sequence even starts. If

[35] It is important to differentiate self-production in the sense discussed here from self-*re*production, such as the reproduction of amoebae by binary fission, or the self-reproduction of self-reproducing automata (von Neumann 1966). In these cases one entity produces a second entity that might share all properties with the first one, apart from its spatio-temporal location. As identical entities need to share *all* their properties the two cannot be identical, as the notion of self-production examined here demands.

their evolution is not a temporal sequence,[36] on the other hand, we might wonder to which extent it could provide us with a model of causal production.

Apart from the fact that production of an effect such as a rice-shoot would be pointless if self-production is maintained, the rice-shoot would also in some sense produce itself again. Yet it is hard to make out in what sense this would be, as the rice-shoot does not seem to continuously duplicate, producing more and more copies of itself that are also somehow identical with it.

6:009 Moreover, as self-causation would also apply to the seed, this would continue to self-produce, since its cause (namely the seed itself) is always present. But as the seed needs to disappear for the sprout to arise (for the seed turns into the sprout), there would be no time at which the sprout could come into existence from the seed. *Sprouts could never be produced from seeds.* This is the first peculiar consequence of self-production Candrakīrti describes in this verse.

The second consequence concerns the permanence of seeds. Once the seed has been brought about, what is needed for its production (the seed itself) is already there, so its production can just continue. The production of seeds would never stop. Nothing could ever terminate such a causal chain, because that would involve intervening somewhere in the chain, making sure that despite the presence of the cause, the effect will not arise. But self-production means that the cause *is* the effect, and therefore once the cause is present, the effect is too. There is no possibility of ever breaking the causal chain. *Nothing could ever terminate the continued production of seeds.*

In a world in which causality means self-production, there can be no causally mediated change, since the effect will never be different

[36] As suggested by Burley 2007: 109: "the order they [i.e., the *tattvas*] are enumerated in represents, not the temporal sequence of their emergence, but the relations of conditionality, or dependence, between them."

from the cause. Every member of a causal chain will be exactly the same as all its other members.

A position the opponent might take here in response is that a seed is really a succession of very brief seed-moments, one happening after another, and each moment causing its successor moment. So the seed-moment at t_1 causes the seed-moment at t_2, and since each is a seed-moment, we might regard this as a form of self-causation. However, the two seed-moments might not be *exactly* identical. The preceding one might be a little bit different form the succeeding one, and so, over time, we get from a seed to a sprout. Self-causation hence does not have to rule out causally mediated change.

Candrakīrti's next verse begins by responding to this proposal, pointing out that the suggested combination of self-causation and change does not work. The position Candrakīrti is concerned with when discussing causal production from itself is not one in which cause and effect are very similar, but one in which they are identical. Identical things need to share all their properties. If every step in the chain of seed-moments is identical to its successor, there is no change. If it is different, there is no self-causation. **6:010**

If the seed changed its qualities when turning into a sprout, turning green, altering its shape, and so on, it is unclear how we could still speak of the same entity being present. Unless we deny the indiscernibility of identicals, objects that are one and the same should share all the same properties.

An alternative to this sequential idea of reconciling self-causation and change would be to think of the causal change of a seed into a sprout as a transformation of an underlying, persistent entity. This would reflect the Sāṃkhya idea of the manifest world appearing to our senses as a transformation of the underlying *prakṛti*. The difficulty with this suggestion is that once we abstract from all the qualities of the underlying, persistent entity, a kind of fundamental, transcendent Play-doh (as we have to, since no quality of any transformation-stage, being impermanent, could be one of its qualities), it is hard to see what the nature (*tattva*) of this entity is. It would have to be beyond the reach of any of our perceptions, and hence looks—to the extent to which we can make sense of it at all—much more like a theoretical fiction than the fundamental rock-bottom of reality. Moreover, if we assume that the justification for postulating theoretical fictions flows from the explanatory work they do[37] it is unclear why we need this qualityless entity in the first place. It seems to be motivated directly by the assumption of self-causation, and self-causation, in turn, is not the only way in which we could account for causal regularities in the world.

6:011 Candrakīrti continues the discussion of the question of whether cause and effect could have the same fundamental nature, despite displaying different surface properties. If cause and effect were fundamentally the same entity,[38] even though the properties they exhibit are distinct, like an actor wearing two different costumes, or like two names with the same reference,[39] we should either perceive both, or perceive neither. Whenever we do not perceive the cause (because that has already vanished) we should also not perceive the effect. This is manifestly not the case, since we perceive sprouts without perceiving the seeds that brought them about. On the other

[37] See Westerhoff 2020: 57–61.

[38] One might object here that as for Sāṃkhya seed and sprout are both fundamentally *prakṛti*, for the Mādhyamika too, they have the same fundamental nature, namely emptiness (*śūnyatā*). The difference, however, is that while both seed and sprout (like all entities) have the property of being empty, that is, failing to be entities terminating a chain of ontological dependence, there is no common property of emptiness such that all entities stand in an instantiation relation with it. Speaking about the emptiness of all things is merely an abbreviated way of referring to each object's failure to exhibit an intrinsic nature or *svabhāva* mistakenly projected onto it. This failure is not a property things instantiate, but a mere absence. That my desk and drawer fail to contain any pink elephants is not a property each instantiates. See Jinpa 2021: 617–618, note 373.

[39] When you stand in visual contact with the evening star, you also stand in visual contact with the same heavenly body otherwise described as the morning star. When you fail to stand in visual contact with the evening star, you are also not standing in visual contact with the heavenly body otherwise described as the morning star. Since there is only one star with two different names, you cannot be in causal contact with the star labeled with one name, but not in causal contact with the star labeled with the other name.

hand, whenever we do perceive the effect, we should also perceive the cause. For the reason just given that is not the case either.

Our usual, everyday understanding of causation is that when we perceive a certain effect (a sprout, an explosion, a bowl of yogurt) its cause (the seed, the spark, a bowl of milk) are past and have already gone out of existence.[40] Therefore, in addition to the conceptual difficulties with philosophical theories of self-causation described in verses 6:008–6:010, the notion of self-causation also conflicts with the ordinary, common-sense view of the world, for if the cause no longer exists when the effect does, because they are fundamentally the same entity, the effect should not exist either. 6:012

One might object that such a conflict between the everyday understanding of a concept and its philosophical analysis is not necessarily a problem, and it would indeed be unreasonable to expect that all of the properties we pre-reflectively ascribe to a given concept will be preserved. This is especially true in the context of Buddhist philosophy, which usually emphasizes how radically mistaken the common-sense view of the world really is. In the light of this Buddhist skepticism toward common sense, one might wonder what the point of stressing that self-causation does not cohere with our day-to-day understanding of the causal relation is.

There is a general and a more specific answer to this worry. First of all, when presenting a philosophical analysis of an everyday concept it would be reasonable to expect that the analyzed concept shares at least the core characteristics of the everyday concept. If it does not, we might wonder whether the analysis presented is really an analysis of the original concept, or rather an analysis of something else. In the present case, one might argue that the cause's having ceased once the effect has arisen is such a core characteristic of how we ordinarily understand causation, yet it does not apply to the example of self-causation.

[40] The argument presupposes a form of presentism according to which the past no longer exists. Candrakīrti will take up the question of whether or not cause and effect can ever be simultaneous below in verse 6:017.

More specifically, the point raised is connected with the debate between the Prāsaṅgika and the Svātantrika interpretation of Madhyamaka. For the Prāsaṅgika, entities or relations conceived in terms of intrinsic nature (*svabhāva*) are not just simply rejected at the ultimate level, but also at the conventional level. In his autocommentary Candrakīrti points out that the first (and by extension, we need to understand, also the remaining three) ways of causal production refuted by Nāgārjuna are not simply refuted at the level of ultimate reality, and hence aimed at specific philosophical theories that purport to describe this ultimate reality, but are also refuted at the level of conventional, everyday reality. The four ways of causal production all include reference to intrinsic natures, since they presuppose the existence of a causal relation 'out there' in the world, independent of human interests and concerns. As a consequence it is important for Candrakīrti to point out that one way his Prāsaṅgika interpretation differs from Bhāviveka's Svātantrika reading is by stressing that the four ways of causal production (even though all Mādhyamikas agree on their rejection at the ultimate level) cannot be taken seriously *even at the conventional level*. It is therefore important for Candrakīrti to emphasize that in the case of self-causation we encounter a direct conflict with our ordinary, everyday understanding of what the causal relation amounts to.

6:013 In addition, the idea of self-causation entails that producer and produced (such as father and son) or agent and action (such as our visual system and the process of seeing) would be the same. However, examining the world around us, it is evident that such entities are distinct; father and son have different properties and can exist without one another. As such, the idea of causal self-production seems to contradict the manifest image of reality.

This concludes Candrakīrti's examination of the first of the four ways of causal production.[41] Altogether Candrakīrti has presented

[41] The Madhyamaka rejection of self-causation is sometimes used as an opportunity to introduce the different interpretative approaches of Buddhapālita, Bhāviveka, and

us with seven arguments against self-production, arguing that if cause and effect were identical

1. production would be pointless (6:008b),
2. the effect could never be produced (6:009),
3. production would be endless (6:009),
4. cause and effect would have the same qualities (6:010),
5. we would always observe either both cause and effect, or neither (6:011),
6. this would contradict the conventional understanding of causation (6:012),
7. actor and agent, and producer and produced would be identical. (6:013).

6a.2 Production from another
Refutation of production from another through reasoning

Refutation of production from another through reasoning with reference to an absurd consequence Candrakīrti now moves on to the second way of causal production, production from another thing. This, it appears, is intuitively much more reasonable than causal self-production. Seed and sprout are, after all, different entities, so it is more plausible to assume that an entity with one nature can be causally related to a distinct entity with another nature. Moreover, in the Buddhist analysis of causation found, for example, in the Abhidharṃa, reference is made to difference kinds of causal factors, which are considered to bring about the effect.[42] So it appears that there is not only philosophical, but also scriptural support for production from another thing. 6:014

Candrakīrti. See Geshe Kelsang Gyatso 1995: 183–185 for a brief account, as well as Ames 2003.

[42] Candrakīrti discusses some of these theories in his *bhāṣya*. For some brief discussion of the background of Buddhist theories of causation see Siderits 2022, chapter 5; for a detailed account of causation as explained in the Sarvāstivāda Abhidharma see Dhammajoti 2009, chapters 6 and 7.

However, Candrakīrti does not consider production from another to be a satisfactory analysis of causation either. The problem he discusses in this verse is that while the supposition of causal self-production faced difficulties with differentiating cause and effect, production from another faces the difficulty of bringing two distinct entities into a single causal relation. It is important to realize that the notion of distinctness between cause and effect the opponent has in mind here is much more substantial than mere non-identity. It entails that the two entities considered differ by their intrinsic natures, and that therefore there is no dependence relation between them. A rice seed causes a rice sprout, but a barley seed and a wheat seed do not. Yet when conceived according to this understanding of distinctness, the rice seed is as much a distinct entity from the rice sprout as the barley and wheat seeds are. If causation is a relation between such intrinsically distinct, independent entities, why does it only connect some distinct entities (such as rice seed and rice sprout) but not others (such as barley seed and rice sprout)? There does not seem to be anything in the individual entities that makes one more likely to causally link up with another, since any such potential for linkage would conflict with the strong independence assumed to hold between them. We appear to face the absurd consequence that everything could be causally produced by anything.

6:015 The opponent responds by arguing that there are, in fact, more conditions that a cause-and-effect pair must satisfy, and that not any two entities chosen at random can be considered to be such a pair. An effect is something that has the "capacity to be produced" by a cause, which means that the cause has the potential to bring about the effect, though it can still fail to be identical with it. Despite this non-identity, cause and effect form part of a continuum of causal change (with a rice seed turning into a rice sprout, turning into a rice plant, producing more rice seeds, and so on) supported by the cause's intrinsic potential. Causation only takes place within such continua, not across them (this is why the initial part of the rice continuum is never followed by a later part of the barley continuum); in addition, the continua constitute an ordered succession (despite being part of the same continuum, a rice sprout at time t_1 cannot cause a rice seed at an earlier time t_0).

In his autocommentary Candrakīrti raises the worry that the opponent has to accept it as a brute fact that rice seed and rice sprout belong to one continuum, while rice seed and barley sprout do not. The opponent cannot refer to anything in these entities, since any such thing would undermine the strong notion of their distinctness assumed here. If it is part of *x*'s nature to bring about *y*, the natures of *x* and *y* cannot be wholly separable. Talk about continua seems to be nothing more than a complicated way of saying that *a* causes *b* rather than *c* because *a* causes *b* rather than *c*, without providing any reason, as the opponent set out to do, why not everything causes everything else.

In addition to the explanatory vacuity of the idea of the co- **6:016**
continuity of cause and effect, one might also wonder whether it does not undermine the opponent's own point. If the existence of a causal relation between two entities means that they must be integrated into a specific continuum, and integrated into it in a specific order, does this not bring with it a kind of dependence relation between causal relata that the proponent of causation from another wants to deny? In this verse Candrakīrti points out that the strong sense of distinctness the opponent has in mind will undermine all references to potentials and continua.

Barley seeds do not produce rice sprouts, lack the potential to produce them, do not belong to the rice-production continuum, and do not resemble rice seeds because they are distinct from rice sprouts, in the strong sense of distinctness presupposed here. However, if rice seeds are supposed to be as strongly distinct from rice sprouts as the opponent proposes, they too would be characterized by these four negative properties.

They too would not stand in an existential dependence relation with rice sprouts (as the strong sense of distinctness assumed here is incompatible with existential dependence), lack potential (if something has the potential to produce something else, it cannot be wholly distinct from it), lack co-continuity (linkage in a common continuum means that two entities are connected in some way and are therefore not wholly independent), and lack resemblance (if two things resemble each other, one could not exist in a lonely state without the other, as strong distinctness would demand, while keeping the resemblance relation intact). As such there seems to be no systematic reason for claiming that a causal relation holds between rice seeds and rice sprouts, but not between barley seeds and rice sprouts.

6:017 **Refutation of production from another through reasoning with reference to time** Once the effect has come into existence, the cause has ceased (as once we have a sprout, there is no seed anymore). Candrakīrti argues that we can only make sense of the relations of identity and distinctness holding between coexistent things, so that cause and effect cannot be properly regarded as distinct.

Again, it is important to be clear that ordinary distinctness in the sense of non-identity is not what Candrakīrti has in mind.[43] A solution to the equation $7/5 = x$ does not exist in the natural numbers, yet it seems to be reasonable to argue that x is not identical, and hence different from 2, despite x and 2 not being coexistent things. Candrakīrti is concerned with difference relations that form part of an entity's intrinsic nature, so that it would be part of *a*'s intrinsic

[43] There might be an issue here even about ordinary identity, if we think that identity and difference relations only obtain between members of our ontology. We may be able to say that *a* was different from *b* if *b* existed, but as *b* does not exist its identity relation to *a* is indeterminate.
Candrakīrti's presentist presupposition according to which the past does not exist, together with the restriction of the existence of relations to coexistent things, raises the question how we can conceptually or linguistically relate to nonexistent entities, e.g., how we could think or speak about the past. See Siderits/Katsura 2024 commenting on 6:017.

nature to be different from *b*.[44] But given that *a*'s intrinsic nature exists whenever *a* exists, and that it essentially involves reference to *b*, *b* would have to exist at the same time.[45] This immediately shows that if *a* and *b* are such that when one exists, the other does not (as is assumed in the case of seed and sprout) they cannot be distinct in this stronger sense.

The opponent responds not by objecting to the presentist presup- 6:018
position of the argument in the previous verse, or to the principle
that existent and nonexistent entities cannot be linked by relations, 6:019
but by suggesting that cause and effect may be simultaneous,[46] so that both could exist in the present moment, and be linked by the strong relation of distinctness discussed above. For example, as one arm of a pair of scales (which we have to assume to be perfectly rigid) goes up (the cause) the other one goes down (the effect). There is no time difference between these two events, and hence, the opponent suggests, we could also have the seed ceasing to exist *at the very same moment* the sprout arises.

Candrakīrti responds to this by pointing out that whether or not the action of the pair of scales really exemplifies simultaneous causation, it is not a good model for the seed-sprout case being discussed. In the case of the pair of scales we have one arm and its property (up) at some moment in time, and the other arm and its property (down) existing at the same moment. Yet while the rice seed is in front of us, the rice sprout is future, and does not presently exist, and when there is the rice sprout, the seed has gone. To make sense of causation from another we would have to make sense of a nonexistent entity standing in the relation of simultaneity with an existent entity, and the example of the pair of scales does not show us how this could be done.

[44] Nāgārjuna points out in *Mūlamadhyamakakārikā* 1:3 (which Candrakīrti quotes in his commentary on this verse) that the absence of intrinsic nature (*svabhāva*) also entails the absence of extrinsic nature (*parabhāva*).

[45] As pointed out by Tsong kha pa (Jinpa 2021: 215).

[46] For further discussion of the problem of simultaneous causation in Buddhism see Westerhoff 2009: 120–121; 2018b: 67–70.

Candrakīrti would have no problem with understanding the cessation of a cause and the origination of an effect as two temporally spread-out processes happening at the same time, as when we rearrange a lego structure (the cause) into a different shape (the effect). However, in these cases we are dealing with partite entities which are, given the Buddhist's mereological reductionism,[47] not ultimately real. Candrakīrti's discussion is concerned here with causal relations between entities that could be deemed ultimately real.

The opponent also suggests the possibility that seeds and sprouts as agents might not be simultaneous, but that their actions (ceasing as one, and arising as another) are. This would make sense in an ontology where actions and their underlying substances belong to different fundamental categories (such as *karma* and *dravya* in the Vaiśeṣika system)[48] and might therefore come apart.[49] Candrakīrti, however, does not believe that we can make sense of agentless activity in this way.[50]

6:020 Assuming the opponent accepts that since seed and sprout do not exist at the same time, they cannot be regarded as distinct, can he still argue for the distinctness of causes and effects that are simultaneous? The example considered here is the content of some perceptual act (the effect), which the Sarvāstivāda Abhidharma considers to exist simultaneously with whatever external object caused it, mediated by the relevant sense-organ.[51] Yet once we consider them to be simultaneous, it is unclear how they could actually stand in a causal relation, to the extent that causation is considered to be the *bringing about* of something that is not already there. If the mental content is already in the mind, how did the external object

[47] For more on which see Siderits 2007: 105–111.

[48] For brief introductions to the Vaiśeṣika ontology see Ganeri 2001, chapter 3, and Torella 2011: 57–75.

[49] Siderits/Katsura 2024 in their commentary on this verse suggest that Candrakīrti in fact has the Sarvāstivāda theory in mind here.

[50] Of course Buddhist philosophy regards activity as agentless in general, insofar as there is no substantial self. But this is a position according to which neither agent nor action is fundamentally real, not one that claims both are and happen to exist separately.

[51] Dhammajoti 2003: 42–43; 2007: 94–96.

make it be there?[52] If, one the other hand, the mental content is not already there we are back in the same situation we faced with the non-simultaneous seed and sprout.

Refutation of production from another through reasoning with 6:021
reference to four alternatives The discussion now moves from the temporal relations between distinct causes and effects to the question of existence. Suppose a specific cause exists. What would the existential status of an effect that is different from it be? If the effect *exists*, just like its cause does, the effect is already there, and so there is nothing for the cause to bring about—Candrakīrti already raised this point in 6:008. If the effect *does not exist*, however, the causal relation lacks a second relatum. This once more raises the problem of how an existent thing could be related to one that does not exist that was discussed in relation to identity and difference relations in 6:017, with the added complication that the causal relation appears to require that its relata are spatio-temporal entities.

If the effect *both exists and fails to exist* it would be a contradictory entity, and since contradictory entities are impossible, no cause could bring them about either. But as existence and nonexistence are not just mutually exclusive, but also jointly exhaustive, making sense of the effect being *neither existent nor nonexistent* is also exceedingly difficult to do. Since these are all the effect's existential possibilities, and all are ruled out, we need to re-examine the assumptions that led to this difficulty in the first place. Candrakīrti identifies the assumption that cause and effect are distinct as the source of the problem.

Refutation of production from another through experience At 6:022
this point the opponent responds that it is not in fact necessary to

[52] The same point is made in Śāntideva's *Bodhicaryāvatāra* 9:104 (Crosby/Skilton 1995: 125–126). See Khenchen Kunzang Pelden 1999: 97.

establish causation from another inferentially by setting out to refute arguments against it. Given that causation from another is the default assumption behind our ordinary thinking about causation, this should be sufficient for establishing its truth. We only need to resort to inference when trying to find out hidden phenomena that are not open to direct inspection. However, that cause and effect are distinct can simply be observed by looking at the world. Moreover, there is intersubjective agreement on the matter: most people we are going to ask about this will say that cause and effect are distinct. There is therefore no need for inference to help us decide a question that is already settled by perception.

The two truths

6:023 To appeal to ordinary perception and intersubjective consensus only makes sense, however, if we can assume these are generally accurate. Candrakīrti does not[53] and instead introduces the idea of the two truths. According to this, all things have a double character, their ultimate way of existence when they are correctly seen, and their conventional way of existence when they are seen in a mistaken manner.[54] The first corresponds to the perspective of enlightened beings, the latter to that of ordinary beings, though neither exists substantially. This latter point distinguishes the Madhyamaka conception of the two truths from the earlier Abhidharma understanding, according to which ultimately real entities, the *dharma*s, exist substantially and intrinsically.[55]

Candrakīrti's autocommentary on this verse is quite brief, but commentators often use it as an opportunity to introduce more wide-ranging discussions of this central Madhyamaka notion.

[53] Unlike other schools of classical Indian thought, Buddhist philosophy is quite pessimistic about the accuracy of untrained, common-sensical conceptions of the world (see Westerhoff 2018b: 261–263).

[54] The Sanskrit term *satya* ("truth") has a broad semantic range that can cover both statements (when they are true) and things (when they exist). For some discussion of this see The Cowherds 2013: 9–11.

[55] See Siderits 2007, chapter 6, in particular 111–113.

Two questions immediately arise in this context. First, should the two truths be understood ontologically, as two different kinds of things,[56] or epistemologically, as two different ways of seeing one thing? Second, if conventional truth is mistaken, how can we tell conventional truth from conventional falsity? Candrakīrti discusses the second question in the following two verses.

Even though most of the beliefs ordinary beings have about the 6:024
world belong to conventional truth, we can still differentiate between sense-faculties generating these beliefs that operate nor- 6:025
mally, and those that do not. If I look up at the sky and subsequently
believe there to be one moon, I believe a conventional truth. If I
suffer from double vision and believe there to be two, I believe a
conventional falsity.[57]

In addition to internal conditions that render sense-faculties unreliable there are also external conditions that are prone to generate conventionally false beliefs. These include illusion-inducing situations, as when we might see a mirage in a desert or watch a magician's performance, or take hallucinogenic drugs, as well as mistakes in reasoning we are likely to make as the result of external influence on our brain. If internal and external impairments are absent our epistemic faculties will produce beliefs that are conventionally true; if they are compromised in the way just described they will generate conventionally false beliefs.

Candrakīrti also includes mistaken philosophical views under this group of external impairments. This means that there are certain philosophical positions that can be demonstrated to be deficient even at the level of conventional truth (as we can demonstrate at the level of conventional truth that someone with double vision

[56] See Jinpa 2021: 223; Thakchoe 2004 for more discussion of this point.

[57] Though Candrakīrti spells this out further by reference to perceptual impairments, this notion of conventional falsity would also cover mistakes in reasoning we are prone to make (such as affirming the consequent, the quantifier-shift fallacy, mistaking correlation for causation, probabilistic fallacies such as the base-rate fallacy, the gambler's fallacy, and so on).

does not see accurately), and, conversely, that there are conventionally true philosophical positions. Unfortunately, being convinced by a such a position (such as Madhyamaka) will not make one enlightened, for that one also has to eliminate the underlying conceptualizing default mechanisms that generate deficient philosophical views in the first place.

6:026 Mistaken philosophical views (Candrakīrti's autocommentary refers specifically to the Sāṃkhya theory) are not just unsatisfactory because of the underlying ignorance that affects *all* positions at the level of conventional reality, but these views in particular do not even succeed in providing a conventionally satisfactory account of the manifest image of the world. Candrakīrti compares their defenders to someone trying to climb a tree who lets go of the lower branch (the way the world ordinarily appears) before having properly grasped any higher branch (a more sophisticated conventionally true account of the world)—he will inevitably fall from the tree. Like mirages and similar illusions, such philosophical positions cannot even be taken seriously in the context of ordinary worldly transactions, let alone be understood as providing us with an account of the fundamental nature of reality.

6:027 Reaffirming his skepticism about the accuracy of ordinary perceptions introduced in 6:023, Candrakīrti points out that the perceptions of ordinary beings relate to meditatively trained perceptions of the enlightened beings as perceptions by sufferers from visual impairments relate to those of healthy people. When they deliver different results, the former can never override the latter. Because of this, appealing to the fact that ordinary people take cause and effect to be distinct cannot be regarded as having any probative force.

6:028 Conventional truth is the product of delusion; together with desire and aversion this is one of the three poisons that keep sentient beings trapped in the cycle of rebirth. As such it conceals the real, empty nature of reality and, in doing so, generates a set of conventional truths about this concealing entity, and a set of fabricated entities that these truths are about.

If we envisage the conventional truth like a decorative fire screen in front of an open fireplace, the figures on the screen (Dido and Aeneas, say) would correspond to the fabricated entities, and true statements about their relations (Dido standing to the right of Aeneas) to the conventional truth. While these figures appear as entities in their own right, and appear to stand in relations to one another, it is essential to be aware that the whole arrangement has been constructed not to reveal something (such as the real spatial relation between Dido and Aeneas), but to conceal (namely the empty cavity of the fireplace).

In his autocommentary Candrakīrti adds that what appears as real for ordinary beings (tables and chairs, but not mirages and delusions—these are conventionally unreal), does not appear in this way to more advanced meditators, such as beings on the various bodhisattva stages. To these, the tables and chairs will appear as dependent, illusion-like, and hence as merely conventional. For fully enlightened Buddhas, even these illusion-like appearances have ceased, they have brought any cognitive activity fully to an end.[58] In the Madhyamaka system, what is real and what is not is not an absolute distinction, but depends on a perceiver's epistemic status: what is real from the perspective of an inferior epistemic status might not be real (and might not even appear) relative to a superior epistemic perspective.

Turning to ultimate truth, Candrakīrti notes that it is inexpress- 6:029
ible and not an object of knowledge. How is it still possible to explain it? Consider the problem of explaining four-dimensional space to three-dimensional creatures like us.[59] Since we live in a three-dimensional space we cannot simply do so by showing them

[58] See Dunne (1996) and Arnold (2005: 204) for different interpretations of the passage where Candrakīrti makes this point.
[59] Abbott 1998.

a four-dimensional object. A more promising approach is to describe to them two-dimensional creatures living on a plane, and to show how the difficulties the two-dimensional beings have in comprehending our familiar three-dimensional objects are just the same we have in trying to comprehend four-dimensional objects.

Candrakīrti uses a similar approach by introducing the example of vitreous floaters,[60] an ophthalmic condition where the patient sees illusory hair-like objects against a white background. A situation where we try to convince a sufferer from floaters that there are no hairs in their clean bowl is analogous, Candrakīrti argues, to that of an enlightened being trying to convince us of the emptiness of phenomena. Not seeing any hair, such a being might say "there are no hairs in your bowl," without being ontologically committed to the existence of hairs. Even though intrinsically existent entities do not appear to a Buddha he may still refer to them in order to help beings suffering from their mistaken appearance. We should note, however, that there is considerable scope for interpretation in trying to understand how precisely the example of the floaters is to be cashed out. Is it that *nothing at all* appears to a Buddha's mind? Or do things still appear, but without the erroneous superimposition of intrinsic nature that ordinary beings see? This question raised a considerable account of discussion among Candrakīrti's Tibetan interpreters.[61]

6:030 The reason why ordinary perception cannot be considered accurate is that the entire Buddhist soteriology is based on the idea that a crucial aspect of the Buddha's enlightenment is a particular way of seeing the world that differs radically from the way ordinary beings perceive it. We do not accept that untrained perception is as accurate as trained perception in other contexts (we prefer the jeweler's judgment about the quality of a diamond to that of someone with

[60] *timira*, often erroneously translated as "cataracts." See MacDonald 2015: 2:111–112, note 228.

[61] See Jinpa 2021: 16; The Yakherds 2021a: 159, note 46, Dzogchen Pönlop Rinpoche 1999: 6: 1: 215 for more discussion.

no experience with gems), analogously we would not want to equate the validity of ordinary ways of looking at the world with that of a Buddha's perspective.

Clearly this point is not going to convince those skeptical about the Buddhist worldview in the first place, but for those who accept that becoming enlightened entails acquiring a different kind of cognitive access to the world, assuming that ordinary, untrained perception sees the world as it really is makes it difficult to understand what the Buddha's particular insight might have consisted of. As such, it is essential for the Buddhist understanding of epistemology to differentiate the essentially correct way the Buddhas see the world, which leads to liberation, and the essentially incorrect (though for all practical purposes generally useful) way ordinary beings see it, which perpetuates cyclic existence.

Conventional statements are not able to refute ultimate **6:031**
statements, but conventional statements can refute mistaken conventional renderings of ultimate statements.

If someone tried to justify stealing your car by arguing that cars do not really exist, being conceptual superimpositions on rapidly changing conglomerates of fundamental particles, you could successfully rebut this by appealing to the conventional conceptions of cars, ownership, and so on, fixed, for example, in a code of law. If I argue that nobody is responsible for their actions because there are no substantial selves, you could prove me to be wrong by pointing out the conventions about personal identity that underpin our ethical and judiciary systems.

Such conventional statements could not, however, refute mereological reductionism or the non-self theory at the ultimate level. As conventional assertions are shot through with mistaken conceptual superimpositions, they cannot undermine assertions not subject to such superimpositions.[62] In this verse Candrakīrti

[62] For more discussion of the "semantic insulation" between conventional and ultimate truth see Siderits 2009, 2015, chapter 4, 2017.

notes specifically that ordinary cognition is not reliable in any way when concerned with ultimate reality. This statement is frequently referred to in the commentarial literature when assessing the Madhyamaka conception of epistemology in general, and the Prāsaṅgika theory of knowledge in particular. This is a complex and interesting issue which, unfortunately, we will not be able to treat here in any more detail.[63]

6:032 We have just seen that conventional truth cannot refute ultimate truth, and, in the context of the present argument the ultimate truth Candrakīrti is concerned with is the negation of the four different kinds of causation. In this specific context his discussion is concerned with the negation of cause and effect being distinct. But in addition to the fact that the belief in the distinctness of cause and effect is not able to refute the Madhyamaka rejection of all four types of causal production, it is not even the case that ordinary people believe, in their conventional thinking about causality, that cause and effect are distinct (contrary to what the opponent proposed in 6:022). "Being distinct" is understood here, again,[64] not as two entities being non-identical, but as them being distinct in their intrinsic natures. Yet a man who claims "I fathered this boy" will not consider the cause (the sperm) and the effect (the son) to be intrinsically distinct in this way, since there would otherwise be no fundamental difference between their relation, and the relation between the man's sperm and any other entity.

Hence the Candrakīrti argues that production from another (and, extending the argument, intrinsic nature in general)[65] is not simply absent at the level of ultimate reality, but also fails to exist at the conventional level.[66] Ordinary people conceive of causation as

[63] For further discussion see Jinpa 2021: 254–255, Thakchoe 2010: 114, 2011, 2013.
[64] See 6:017.
[65] See Ames 1982: 162.
[66] See Jinpa 2021: 257.

mere conditionality,[67] but not in terms of any of the four ways of causal production.[68]

Implications of the theory of the two truths

Avoiding eternalism and nihilism Adopting the view of mere conditionality at the level of conventional truth, where cause and effect lack intrinsic natures and relate to each other "like seeds and sprouts in a dream," means abandoning the idea that cause and effect are substantially either distinct or identical. In this way, absurd views of annihilation and permanence are avoided. 6:033

If cause and effect were distinct, since when the effect exists, the cause has to have ceased, cause and effect would be entirely unrelated entities. Only in the case of an existent and a nonexistent entity can we be sure that they are entirely unrelated.[69] When we have two existent entities, the existence of one might somehow rule out the existence of the other, as fire excludes the existence of ice etc. But if cause and effect are entirely unrelated, instead of a causal continuity of qualitatively related entities we would have a succession of entirely different ones, like live wild ox followed by a dead cow at a later time, instead of a live ox followed by a dead ox. As such, it would be unclear how we could speak of a causal continuum of causes and effects.

On the other hand, if cause and effect were the same, the cause would continue to exist when the effect has come to be, somehow continuously present next to the effect. This fails to account for the fact that causation does not just entail the addition of new phenomena, but also the cessation or at least transformation of what is already there. Any plausible account of causation must avoid these two positions of annihilation and permanence.[70]

[67] Compare the *bhāṣya* on 6:114 and Williams 1980: 26; Magee 2008: 37–38.
[68] Ngawang Samten/Garfield 2006: 70.
[69] See above, 6:017.
[70] Compare Nāgārjuna's *Mūlamadhyamakakārikā* 18:10.

6:034 **Avoiding the view that intrinsic natures exist at the level of either truth** For the Mādhyamika, establishing the theory of emptiness is not just an attempt at establishing a correct philosophical account of the world, but is directed at achieving a cognitive shift, a change in our default comportment toward the world at the experiential level. This shift is supposed to bring about the cessation of existential suffering which, as the third noble truth, constitutes the heart of the Buddhist path. This might lead one to believe that the realization of emptiness brings about a change in the world, destroying the substantial existence of things like a hammer breaks a pot of clay, replacing them by an empty nature. Doing so would be a mistake. For Madhyamaka, the intrinsic nature (*svabhāva*) of entities that emptiness negates was never real in the first place, but only existed as a mistaken superimposition on things that were already empty. As such, the realization of emptiness does not change the world, but the way the world presents itself to us. If the causal relation linked up entities existing by intrinsic nature, the realization of emptiness, as long as it is considered to present an accurate picture of the world, would indeed have to remove these intrinsic natures. But since the realization of emptiness does no such thing (a claim for which Candrakīrti presents scriptural support), causation between entities with intrinsic natures (which is the main object of the present discussion) cannot be maintained.

6:035 It is easy to mistake the Madhyamaka theory of the two truths for one postulating an appearance/reality divide where an ultimate reality is to be discovered behind the conventional reality obscuring it. This is not Candrakīrti's position, who instead argues that once the world around us has been properly analyzed, no entities existing with intrinsic natures can be found to exist. All that can be found is the fact that things do not arise from themselves, others, etc., in a substantial way (which Candrakīrti describes as their ultimate nature), but there is no ontologically free-standing rock-bottom layer of reality (fundamental particles, mathematical structures, foundational consciousness—whatever our favorite ontology might suggest) to be discovered. It is therefore pointless to analyze any of the things around us in order to find the reality behind the appearances. If by this 'reality' we mean mind-independent, self-sufficient entities endowed with intrinsic natures we are never going to find anything. Hence "analysis should not be carried out" with regard to things in the world. The analysis Candrakīrti has in mind here is one looking for an object's ultimate ground of being; it does not refer to analysis at the conventional level when trying to find out whether planets move in circles or ellipses, how biological traits are inherited, or when Nālandā university was founded.[71]

Another way to misunderstand the two truths would be to hold that the above arguments have shown that there cannot be causal production from itself, from others, and so on, at the level of ultimately truth, but that it can exist at the level of conventional truth. Candrakīrti, however, holds that his refutation of the four types of causal productions applies at both levels of truth. In his autocommentary he qualifies this statement by pointing out that causal production *with intrinsic characteristics* (*svalakṣaṇa*) does not obtain at either level of truth. This qualification is essential, for Candrakīrti certainly does not want to say that there is no causation whatsoever, after all, he has just introduced the notion of 'mere conditionality' in his comments on 6:032 as the ordinary view of causality, and pointed out in his remarks on 6:034 that when left unanalyzed, the ordinary understanding of causation is to be maintained. **6:036**

Candrakīrti's point appears to be that even moving the four kinds of causal production from the ultimate to the conventional level will not dissolve the problems they face.[72] This strategy sometimes works in other contexts. Surprised to see a snake at dusk in

[71] For a discussion of possible tensions between Madhyamaka non-analysis and scientific analysis of the conventional see Tillemans 2013.

[72] See Kelsang Gyatso 1995: 213.

an Irish garden (there are no snakes in Ireland), your host points out that you are looking at a garden hose. The cognitive dissonance is dissolved by moving the snake from the level of reality to that of a mere appearance. Yet if some alleged phenomenon is actually inconsistent,[73] moving it to another level of reality (assuming, of course, that conventional truth is consistent) is not going to solve the underlying problem.

6:037 But if causation is not grounded in the intrinsic characteristics of causes and effects, why is it that specific causes produce specific effects? Why do we perceive one thing rather than another, if all
6:038 things are equally insubstantial?

Candrakīrti responds by introducing the example of a face's reflection in a mirror. How to spell out this example, however, is not straightforward. When trying to understand Candrakīrti's point, note that the mirror-reflection will appear in a specific place, though there is no face present in that space. What is there, on the other hand, does not have the intrinsic characteristics of a face (it does not consist of its specific kind of matter, is not spatial, etc). The mirror 'produces' a face without a face being there. There can therefore be cases of causation where cause and effect are not connected by their specific qualities, one possessing a potential, and one being the realization of such a potential. A polished metal surface and a face do not have much to do with one another, and the commentaries make it clear that the mirror example is to be understood as just one exemplar of illusory perceptions such as mirages, echoes, and so on. Hot sand and oases, caves and sounds can stand in causal relations without there being anything 'in the things' that links them. Yet phenomena do not simply arise randomly, we do not see manifestations of faces in opaque surfaces, say. This re-emphasizes Candrakīrti's point that there is the

[73] As the four kinds of causation are deemed to be; consider Candrakīrti's earlier argument that self-causation means that causal production could never stop, yet we never observe perpetual production.

appearance of causal regularity in the world, but that digging for the foundations of this regularity will be ultimately fruitless, since nothing substantial (*prakṛti*) exists at the level of either truth.

Causation without foundation does not imply the absence of causation, however, just as while there is no face in the mirror, the reflection is not nonexistent. With causation understood in this way, the ideas of annihilation and permanence are avoided as well. There is no intrinsic nature of the cause that is annihilated when the effect arises (involving, for example, the seed's potential to produce the sprout), nor is there anything that remains permanent throughout the causal development of cause and effect (as when some underlying substance is re-arranged from seed-appearance to sprout-appearance) since such underlying ontological foundations that undergird causal regularities are wholly nonexistent.

Accounting for karma One of the advantages of accounting for causation without underlying ontological foundations, and without resorting to notions of annihililation or permanence, is that it solves the problem of how the Buddhists should explain the existence of karmic causality. The relevant parties in this discussion all accept the principle of momentariness (no entity lasts longer than a temporally unextended moment, nothing has any temporal 'thickness') and presentism (past and future entities do not exist). It is then not straightforward to explain how my present\ intention will produce a karmic result in five minutes or five years. If the karmic impulse still existed at the time, it would have to be permanent (or at least non-momentary), and if it was completely annihilated, as everything that exists now, including all mental and physical states, will be nonexistent in the next moment, it is unclear how it could still produce its specific result. Buddhist philosophers have developed a variety of theories to account for this, but Candrakīrti's Madhyamaka does not have to engage with these. He does not 6:039

have to explain how a perished karmic potential could suddenly become active years later, since something that has never arisen also cannot perish. Discussing the arising and ceasing of entities with intrinsic nature presupposes that we refer to ultimately real things. Karmic causation (like other causation) clearly obtains, but the quest to identify the unique mechanism at the ultimate level of reality that makes it obtain is futile, since such an ultimate level, conceived as a collection of fundamentally real entities with intrinsic natures, does not exist.

6:040 The opponent worries how a past entity, like a karmic potential that is past and therefore wholly nonexistent, could now, in the present, produce an effect. Candrakīrti points out that when something is present, it is not the fact that the entity is substantially real that enables it to have effects: present, insubstantial entities can have effects, too, and so can past insubstantial entities. Concerns about how the temporal status of an entity might affect its ability to be causally active are therefore misplaced. Candrakīrti illustrates this with the example of someone who dreams of a beautiful woman and, when waking up, still feels desire for her. The woman is insubstantial both during the dream and after the dream; at no time was there any real woman present. Yet the woman is able to produce real effects (in the example, specific unwholesome mental states, such as desire and attachment) both when she is present during the dream, and when she is absent, in the waking state after the dream. In the same way, an instance of karmic potential, such as an intentional state can, though existing without intrinsic nature and hence being empty, be causally active when it exists, and also a long time after its existence.

6:041 However, if we follow this example, and assume that a past, insubstantial entity like a woman seen in a dream can produce an effect in the present we are faced with the problem that the woman will be past, and hence nonexistent, one minute after the dream, but will be similarly past five days after the dream. So why does the illusory woman not continue to produce desire and attachment continuously after the dream, since her ontological status as a past entity will never change?[74]

Candrakīrti returns to the example of vitreous floaters from 6:029, pointing out that even though the participants in a causal relation might be insubstantial, this does not imply that the relationship is entirely arbitrary. The hairs 'produced' from floaters are not real hairs, but that does not imply that the floaters could just as well bring about nonexistent apples or oranges, instead of nonexistent hairs. As there is a regularity to the illusions the sufferer from floaters experiences, so there is a regularity about when an illusory woman seen in a dream produces an effect, and when she does not. Likewise, instances of karma are all identical in their empty, insubstantial status (and therefore neither substantially present nor substantially absent), yet each one brings about a particular, specific result. While the *realization* of the insubstantial nature of karma will bring about liberation, a mere conceptual analysis that ends up denying karmic regularities will have the opposite effect. For those at the level of conventional reality, wholesome actions bring about pleasant states, while unwholesome actions bring about unpleasant states. Beyond this, there is no more point in trying to determine the precise ontological structure at the fundamental level of reality that makes this all happen than there is with other instances of causality,[75] such as sprouts arising from seeds. **6:042**

[74] As we recall from the discussion of 6:009, a cause that does not change should forever produce its effect.

[75] It is interesting to compare this point to the situation in quantum physics (Bitbol 2019: 94–95): "[Q]uantum physics is persistently averse to metaphysical interpretation. Despite many half-successful attempts of providing it with a so-called realist interpretation, quantum physics still relies on Bohr's and Heisenberg's initial remark according to which no unified picture of the atomic and subatomic domain can be derived from it. According to these founding fathers of quantum mechanics, their theory is no 'view' of the microworld, but rather a mathematical symbolism intended to predict probabilistically the outcome of experiments performed at the microscale using macroscopic devices."

The Yogācāra position

6:043 **Exposition of the Yogācāra position** Even though Candrakīrti's analysis is opposed to all such ontological structures, one he focuses on in particular in the present discussion is the Yogācāra's foundational consciousness (*ālayavijñāna*). Yogācāra postulates this as the fundamental level of reality from which all entities and experiences arise. Our intentions deposit karmic 'seeds' in the foundational consciousness, at a later time, these seeds will ripen into specific experiences. Like everything else, the foundational consciousness is momentary, but each time the foundational consciousness at moment t_i generates its successor-moment at t_{i+1}, this successor will also contain a copy of all the seeds. By this mechanism the Yogācārin explains how past karmic causes can bring about present karmic effects.

As I suggested elsewhere,[76] the trajectory of Buddhist philosophical development may be understood as influenced by three centers of gravity: philosophical arguments, scriptural support, and meditative experience. At this stage in the text the second of these comes into view, for Candrakīrti's opponent points out that the Buddhist scriptures themselves refer to the foundational consciousness, and as such Buddhist philosophy has a strong reason to incorporate this notion into its explication of karma. Candrakīrti responds by pointing out that such references are mere propaedeutic devices (*neyārtha*); as a physics teacher might explain some-
6:044 thing by means of Newtonian concepts she knows to be false from a relativistic perspective, the Buddha will refer to mechanisms like the foundational consciousness in order to instruct disciples who would not otherwise understand the theory of karmic causality. The Buddha refers to a variety of other ideas in his teachings, such as, for example, the reality of the person, the existence of things other than persons and so on, yet none of these are to be understood as describing the fundamental structure of reality. They are

[76] Westerhoff 2018b: 4–9.

all simply expository devices designed to explain specific points to particular audiences.

The discussion of the feasibility of the second of the four kinds of causation, causation from another, now focuses more specifically on Yogācāra as one prominent example of causation conceived of in this way. To this end some of the key Yogācāra ideas are introduced. According to the Yogācāra perspective, when bodhisattvas have reached the 6th bodhisattva stage they realize (through an argument to be explained shortly) that only mental, but no material entities exist. This rejection of a mind-independent world of objects 'out there' also undermines the idea of a substantial subject 'in here'. As such, for the Yogācārin the entire world, which is ordinarily understood as divided up into distinct subjects that individually perceive a shared world of objects, is simply a causal flow of exclusively mental phenomena lacking any owners. 6:045

The Yogācāra mechanism of world-generation[77] is spelled out by a familiar aquatic metaphor. As waves appear on the surface of a great ocean stirred by wind, appearing as separate phenomena, even though they are of the same substance as the ocean, the foundational consciousness, which contains all karmic seeds ever produced by all beings, gives rise to the phenomenal world by its own potential. This world *appears* to be non-mental in parts, but is in fact wholly mental. 6:046

In the three nature (*trisvabhāva*) theory of Yogācāra, the foundational consciousness is equated with the dependent nature (*paratantra-svabhāva*), in distinction to the imputed nature (*parikalpita-svabhāva*), the appearance of material objects that do not in fact exist, and the perfected nature (*pariniṣpanna-svabhāva*), the absence of the imputed in the dependent nature.[78] In this 6:047

[77] In his autocommentary Candrakīrti compares the Yogācāra account of creation with the theistic one, noting that the key difference is that for Yogācāra the universal creator, the foundational consciousness is not permanent.

[78] For further discussion of the three nature theory see Westerhoff 2018b: 182–184; Garfield 2002.

foundationalist structure an ultimately real entity, the dependent nature, is postulated as the ground of all appearances. Statements about emptiness in the Buddhist *sūtras* can then be interpreted not as the denial of the ultimate reality of anything (as is done in Madhyamaka), but as the absence of reality in some entities (the imputed nature) combined with its simultaneous presence elsewhere (in the dependent nature).

To the two points that Candrakīrti has already made in this verse and the preceding ones (that the dependent nature does not rely on any objects external to it, but produces everything from the potential present within it, and that it is ultimately real) he adds a third: that the dependent nature's "intrinsic nature is to be utterly beyond all hypostatization." From the Yogācāra perspective, our conceptual and linguistic practices are wholly penetrated by our ordinary view of the world, including the split into the subject 'in here' and objects 'out there'. Because these practices belong to the realm of the illusory imputed nature we cannot use them to spell out the illusion's basis, the dependent nature. The dependent nature is empty of the conceptual and linguistic shadows cast onto it, which constitute the imputed nature, but this notion of emptiness (which, according to Yogācāra, is emptiness properly understood) does not undermine the existential status of the dependent nature.

Refutation of the Yogācāra position through reasoning

6:048 **Example 1: Dreams** To explain the presence of perceptual content without reference to external objects perceived, the Yogācārin frequently uses the example of dreams. Someone asleep in a tiny room can dream of a herd of elephants, animals of a size that would never fit inside the room. So there can be instances of perception-like events involving elephants without any elephants being present.

The dream example relies on accepting an ontological divide between the unreal dream object and the real dreaming mind. However, for the Mādhyamika there is no justification for such a divide in terms of reality. Because neither the dream-object nor the dreamer has been produced through any of the four ways of causation, from itself, from another, both, or neither, they are equally empty. But this means that the Yogācārin's example is dialectically ineffective. To play a role in a debate an example must be accepted by both parties, and be understood in the same way. This is not the case with the dream example.

But, the Yogācārin responds, the dreaming mind must be real, 6:049
otherwise, how could its contents, the various element of the dream, be recalled when awake? The continuity between dream mind and waking mind demonstrates the real existence of the former. But if the ability to remember "I dreamt about an elephant" is sufficient to establish the reality of the possessor of the dream-perceptions, the dreaming mind, why is it not *also* sufficient to establish the reality of the object dreamed about, the elephant, given that both the dreamer and the elephant feature in the experience remembered? The Yogācāra opponent seems to be forced to choose between either accepting both dreamer and dream-elephant to be real (which contradicts his denial of external objects) or to consider them both to be equally unreal (which contradicts the ontological divide between real representation and unreal object he wants to establish).

The opponent might point out in reply that the dream-elephant 6:050
cannot be real, since sense-perception does not operate in dreams. Whatever visual impressions of elephants we have during dreams, they are not caused by light-waves bouncing off a pachyderm, then hitting our retina. Rather, in a dream we are exclusively in contact with mental things, and our subjective awareness of them makes it hard to label the mental episodes experienced as unreal. These experiences we then unknowingly project outward, taking them to be perceptions of external, material objects. The same, the Yogācārin argues, is taking place in waking life. Here, too, our epistemic faculties only connect us with mental things, some of which are treated as if they were caused by external, material phenomena.

6:051 Perceptual processes appear to take place in dreams just as in waking life. When we dream about seeing an elephant, a sense-organ, such as the eye in the dream, causally interacts with some dream-object, producing a visual perception as a result. From the Yogācāra perspective the first two, being material objects, are unreal, but the third, the mental episode, is real. This not only raises the question why one of the three is ontologically privileged (why is not everything that takes place in the frame of a dream on a par when it comes to its mode of existence?), it also leaves open how real and unreal phenomena are supposed to interact. If an instance of visual perception existentially depends on sense-organ and object, would we not expect that the unreality of the last two also implies the unreality of the first? This is what Candrakīrti does say. From the Madhyamaka perspective, dream-eye, dream-object, and dream-perception[79] are all equally unreal.

6:052 The unreality of sense-organs, objects, and perceptions carries over to the waking state. None of the three exists with intrinsic nature, and the relation between dream state and waking state mirrors
6:053 that between waking state and awakened state. As the three are present within the dream, but disappear in the waking state so the sense-organs, objects, and perceptions of the waking state will disappear in the awakened state of enlightenment. All three are either present within the relevant framework (the dream, the conventional reality of the waking world) or absent, once we move out of that framework. But there is no ontological difference *inside* a given framework, such that some (perceptions) are real, while others (their external objects) are unreal.

6:054 **Example 2: Floaters** Given that the dream example seems to be problematic as an example illustrating the Yogācāra idea of objectless perception, the opponent switches to the case of vitreous floaters we first met in 6:029. As one afflicted by floaters will see hairs where

[79] As the autocommentary makes clear, this includes the five sense-consciousnesses as well as the mental consciousness that apprehends mental objects.

there are none, mistaking phenomena intrinsic to the eye for external things, so, the Yogācārin argues, an unenlightened being will perceive external material entities where there are none, projecting subjective inner phenomena to an imaginary objective outside. Candrakīrti responds that this example too fails to establish an ontological divide between the real perceptions and the unreal objects. From the perspective of one suffering from floaters, both the hair-perceptions and the hairs they represent are real, while from the point of view of one with healthy vision, neither the hairs nor the perception of the hairs exist.

Moreover, if the example of the floaters really provided an ex- 6:055
ample of perception in the absence of objects perceived, the illusory hairs should appear to one with healthy vision as well. This is because perception of hairs must be coming from somewhere, and for the Yogācārin it arises from a fundamentally real consciousness, in the absence of any external hairs. Yet both conditions are fulfilled in one with and in one without floaters; both possess a fundamentally real consciousness, and for both external hairs are absent. One might worry here that this misrepresents the Yogācārin's position, for he does not assert that the illusory hairs *just* arise from consciousness, but from consciousness together with an ophthalmic condition that superimposes itself like a grid on consciousness itself. But for this to work, the ophthalmic condition must be something external to consciousness, in which case the illusory hairs would be a joint product of consciousness and something external to it. This is not what the Yogācārin wants to say. One way for him to respond is to move the ophthalmic conditions into consciousness, so that it is no longer regarded as external, while at the same time assuming that it is not present in all streams of consciousness: only those that have it will experience the illusory hairs.

The Yogācārin makes this point by referring to karmic 6:056
potentials[80] in different mental continua. My past intentions

80 Variously referred to as powers (*śakti*), traces (*vāsanā*), or seeds (*bīja*).

deposited such potentials in my mind and, once the conditions are right, these will mature in the form of perceptual experiences. One suffering from floaters will have potentials present in their mind that ripen as hair-perceptions in an otherwise clear bowl, while those with healthy vision lack these potentials.

6:057 **The role of karmic potentials** Candrakīrti is not impressed by this suggestion because he is critical of the very idea of karmic potential as understood by the Yogācārin. He points out that there cannot be a potential for a *present* cognitive episode, since such an episode already exists. A cause is supposed to bring about its effect, and as such, assuming them to be simultaneous is problematic (see 6:020 above). Nor can we sensibly refer to a potential for a *future* cognitive episode, for how are we going to distinguish the potential for it from all the other karmic potentials? We cannot indicate a group of potentials as potentials for cognitive episode *c* if *c* does not exist. If we refer to "the potential to bring about *c*" we do not refer to anything at all. To try to differentiate potentials by nonexistent cognitive attitudes is as pointless as trying to differentiate barren women by their children.

6:058 The opponent may point out that we can in fact refer to future nonexistents to pick out specific present existents. If the king asks his cook to bring the rice for tonight's dinner, this dinner does not exist yet. Nevertheless, the cook will be able to fulfill the king's command by determining which rice-grains have the *potential* for being tonight's dinner. In the same way, the Yogācārin argues, we can determine which karmic seeds constitute the *potential* for producing the experience of illusory hairs, even if this cognitive episode does not exist yet.

The Mādhyamaka agrees that even presupposing nonexistents can specify existents, the implications of this presupposition actually undermine the opponent's point. The cook faces a problem: since tonight's dinner does not exist yet, how can the property 'being the rice for tonight's dinner' identify one of the many subsets of grains of rice in the granary? Even if we assume, somewhat implausibly, that one of these subsets of grains of rice already bears that property, the cook has no epistemic access to it. He solves the problem by picking out some rice, thereby helping to bring about the entity referred to by the king's description. The property of the rice-grains and the cook's actions exist in a mutually dependent manner. There was no prior fact, had by some subset of the rice-grains all alone, specifying that *it* would constitute the rice for the future dinner. Returning to the Yogācārin's original point, this implies that karmic potentials and cognitive episodes also exist in a mutually dependent manner. But this is incompatible with the Yogācāra idea that consciousness (and the cognitive episodes that constitute part of it) exists as an intrinsic, fundamental reality independent of anything else.

6:059

The difficulties the Mādhyamikas raised so far concern the relation between present karmic potentials and future cognitive episodes. But the same problem does not arise if we consider present cognitive episodes which, unlike future entities, exist. Can the Yogācārin argue that these have arisen from past karmic potentials? The Yogācārin considers a mental continuum to consist of a succession of distinct mental moments, each of which possesses its own intrinsic nature. But, as Candrakīrti has already noted in 6:014, linking up intrinsically distinct entities into a causal relation is fraught with difficulties. There is not anything in the nature of one mind-moment that makes it the cause of another mind-moment, otherwise the nature of one would involve that of the other, and they could not be intrinsically distinct. But then *any* mind-moment should be able to link up causally with *any other* mind-moment. Independent of the absurdity of believing that everything is caused by everything else, this also undermines the point the Yogācārin has set out to prove, namely that *specific* karmic potentials give rise to *specific* subsequent cognitive episodes.

6:060 Faced with this criticism the Yogācārin does not retract his view that distinct mind-moments are intrinsically distinct but argues that they all belong to one continuum. This explains why only spe-
6:061 cific mind-moments cause specific other ones—mind-moments only cause other mind-moments in the same continuum. However, this raises the question why only some intrinsically distinct entities, like the potential for seeing illusory hairs and the cognitive episode of seeing them, are joined in a continuum, while other entities that might be deemed intrinsically distinct, such as Alice and Bob, are not joined in a continuum. If they were so joined, Alice's thoughts would cause Bob's actions, and vice versa, but this is not the case. The opponent's claim that just some entities form continua, while others do not, seems somewhat *ad hoc*. Moreover, it is not clear what kind of justification he could appeal to. There certainly could not be any features individually possessed by members of some sets of intrinsically distinct entities but not by others, which make the members of the former set form a continuum, since this would contradict the assumption that the entities are intrinsically distinct in the first place.

Of course neither the Mādhyamika nor the Yogācārin considers Alice and Bob to be intrinsically distinct. Both are just convenient designators for rapidly changing conglomerates of mental and physical phenomena. But this then shows that the Yogācārin has the order of explanation wrong: we don't refer to unified continua to explain why only some things cause other things (e.g., why Alice's eating causes Alice to be full, but not Bob), rather, the network of causal relations is there first, and continua like persons are practically useful ways of referring to specific sub-networks, such as Alice or Bob. Within the context of Buddhist no-self theory we cannot refer to unified continua such as persons to explain why only some mind-moments cause other mind-moments.

6:062 Candrakīrti's Yogācāra opponent now continues with the explanation of his position, noticing first that what we regard as sense-perception is really no such thing. Focusing on the visual sense,

he points out that there is a more or less continuous succession of karmic potentials ripening in the form of visual experiences. These potentials have been deposited in our foundational consciousness as the result of intentional actions at earlier times. We ordinarily think that experiences are caused by a sensory organ, the eye, in causal contact with an external object. In fact, however, the eyes, as well as all other sensory organs, are purely mental entities, though they are mistakenly regarded as material. The tripartite model of
perception we find in the Abhidharma, comprising sensory organ, 6:063
external object, and sensory cognitive episodes, is replaced by a bipartite one in Yogācāra, consisting of the karmic potentials in the foundational consciousness and of the cognitive episodes these potentials bring about.

In addition to the first part of the tripartite model, the second part, the external object, is also wholly mental. Cognitive episodes arise from past karmic potentials without any involvement of external objects. In his autocommentary Candrakīrti presents two examples, a red flower, and a transparent crystal appearing red because it has been placed on a red cloth. The red flower gains its color from its own nature, the genetic information present in its seed. The crystal gains its red color from an object external to it, the cloth, which shines through the crystal.

For the Yogācārin the former, not the latter, provides a model for how cognitive episodes arise. An episode of perceiving something red has its specific content due to its own nature, which is the karmic potential 'planted' in the mind that is responsible for its ripening. Despite external objects lacking, nevertheless such cognitive episodes are misrepresented by ordinary beings as representations of external objects, objects which function like the red cloth shining through the 'crystal' of the cognitive episode.

As such, while perception in a dream is not the same as percep- 6:064
tion when awake, the two kinds of perception work in analogous ways. Potentials internal to the mind ripen and produce cognitive

episodes. These episodes are, however, not understood as having their source in other mental things, but the supposed causes of these episodes are projected outward, and are imagined as external objects producing these cognitive episodes.

The dream-example was already discussed in 6:048–6:053. In both places the example is taken to support an ontological bifurcation of the participants in the perceptual process, the idea that some of them are real, while some are unreal. In the earlier discussion the focus was on the reality of cognitive episode, here it is on the unreality of its object.

6:065 Candrakīrti objects by noting that if visual cognitive episodes can arise during dreams, while the eyes are not operating, simply due to the ripening of the appropriate karmic potentials, it remains unclear why blind people do not experience visual episodes in the same manner. When the right potential matures, would they not be able to see, when awake, in the same way that we see in dreams?

6:066 The Yogācārin argues that both sighted and blind people have the
karmic potential for visual cognitive episodes, but that in the case
of blind people these potentials only ripen when asleep, so that they
have visual appearances in dreams, but not when awake. This, however, Candrakīrti argues, cannot work. The Yogācāra theory sets
out to explain all our experience in terms of entities it considers to
be ultimately real, namely the foundational consciousness and the
6:067 karmic potentials it contains. Yet dreaming or waking is not part
of what is ultimately real. This does not mean that the Yogācārin cannot distinguish between dreaming and waking; the differentiation between these states is possible from a Yogācāra perspective by reference to the continuity and coherence of our experiences. However, since neither dreaming nor waking is ultimately real, they cannot be considered to 'switch on' or 'switch off' the manifestation of ultimately real karmic potentials in blind people such that they only ripen in one state. For the opponent it must remain an unexplained brute fact why the blind person's karmic potentials for visual experience ripen only in dreams, but not in the waking state.

If this is the case, Candrakīrti asks, can the Mādhyamaka not say that blind people do not have visual experiences when awake (which the opponent agrees with) because their eyes do not function, and that their visual experiences in dreams are due to other factors, but not due to the ripening of karmic potentials? Dialectically they seem to be in the same situation, with an unexplained feature their respective theories cannot account for. The Yogācārin cannot explain (referring to karmic potentials) why visual experiences only arise in one state, and not in the other, the Mādhyamaka cannot explain (without referring to karmic potentials) why visual experiences arise in a dream. However, the situation is not a stalemate, since the Mādhyamika can in fact explain why visual experiences arise in a dream without referring to karmic potentials: they arise due to previous interaction between our sense-faculties and external objects in the waking state (in the state of the congenitally blind this would presumably have to be extended to experiences in past lives). This renders sensory organs, external objects, and sensory cognitive episodes in a dream all false or unreal, unlike in the case of Yogācāra, where the first two are regarded as unreal, and the last one as real.

The Yogācāra position is argumentatively and scripturally unsatisfactory Candrakīrti sums up his criticism of the Yogācāra position by arguing that their position is both systematically and scripturally unsatisfactory. It is systematically unsatisfactory since their arguments are simply re-stating their thesis. If, for example, the Yogācārin continues to use the dream-example when faced with the opposing position that cognitive episodes in a dream are caused by prior waking perceptions, arguing that they are produced by the ripening of karmic potentials, he is simply repeating an essential Yogācāra claim without providing any independent argumentative support for it. 6:068

The Yogācāra position is scripturally unsatisfactory since the Buddha repeatedly stated that emptiness is not to be conceived of as one ultimately real thing being empty of another (as the Yogācārin takes the dependent nature to be empty of the imputed nature), but as the absence of ultimate reality in any thing.

6:069 **Example 3: Meditative experience** However, if the examples of dreams and vitreous floaters are problematic and if the Mādhyamika is right in regarding objectless perception as impossible, how can we make sense of specific experiences achieved through meditative training? The opponent refers here to the practice of meditation on the impure (*aśubha-bhāvanā*). This meditation practice, often considered as directed toward the elimination of feelings of desire undermining meditative concentration, focuses on the unattractive aspects of human bodies and decaying corpses. As one advances in the mastery of this practice, visual cognitive episodes of corpses similar to actual perceptions will appear to the practitioner.[81] As there is no actual corpse present, is this not an example of objectless perception?

Candrakīrti accepts the possibility of such meditatively induced cognitive episodes, but responds that it constitutes an example of a mental exercise involving the unreal and is therefore unable to provide a model for the account of perception the Yogācārin wants to defend. Because the cognitive episodes of corpses are intentionally cooked up, the perception, the object perceived, and the perceiving consciousness in this case are all unproduced. Candrakīrti here presumably does not understand "unproduced" as "not substantially real," since the perceiving consciousness is substantially real for the Yogācārin. Rather, his point is that perception of corpses here is a self-induced hallucination, based on the teacher's instructions, rather than an objectively induced cognitive episode. Despite the Yogācāra denial of external objects, it considers cognitive episodes to have causes that are objective to the extent that they are outside

[81] *Visuddhimagga* 6:65–66 (Ñyāṇamoli 1976: 1: 196).

of our immediate control. While I myself generate future karmic potentials, the potentials already present will ripen into perceptions independent of my wishing them to do so. But the perception of corpses resulting from the meditation on the impure, involving the specific intention to generate particular cognitive episodes is not like this, and so it cannot illustrate the account of perception the Yogācārin has in mind.

On the other hand, if the example of the meditatively generated corpse-perceptions functioned in the way in which Yogācāra understands perception, then other people should be able to see the corpses too. Yogācāra accepts intersubjectively observable objects (brought about by sufficiently similar karmic potentials in different mind-streams), yet these cognitive episodes of corpses resulting from mastery of the meditation on the impure are not intersubjectively observable. While every meditator properly engaging in these practices will obtain the same result, and will hence obtain cognitive episodes of visually perceiving corpses, they will not perceive the same corpse. On the other hand, when the Yogācārin and the Mādhyamika both look at the tree in the quad, they will see the same tree. The simultaneous ripening of karmic potentials in their mind-streams generates cognitive impressions sufficiently similar to act as the basis of intersubjective agreement. The cognitive impressions generated by individual meditative endeavors, on the other hand, are not similar enough to let us assume that different meditators on the impure perceive the same corpse. If they were, we would no longer be dealing with the result of mental exercises involving the unreal, but with perceptions of real objects, as when different people watch the same play on stage. 6:070

Common difficulties for all three examples Candrakīrti then points out that there is a common problem for all of the Yogācāra examples, whether it is the case of vitreous floaters or specific versions of the claim that different organisms experience 6:071

the world differently.[82] They all set out to declare the antecedent of the perception-percept relation to be real, and the consequent to be unreal. However, as the two are existentially dependent on one another, as the Mādhyamika argues, we cannot have one without the other. We cannot ground the perception in the percept (as the realist would like to do), and we cannot ground the percept in the perception (as the Yogācārin would like to do). In particular, we cannot have representational cognitive episodes without something that they represent. If representation intrinsically involves some of the represented's structure being mirrored in the representation, the representation being what it is will inevitably involve the represented. So one would either have to say that because there is nothing represented, there are also no representations (a point hard to maintain given that our perceptions appear to represent the world), or that both exist, but in a non-fundamental, mutually dependent manner. The Mādhyamika embraces the second alternative.

6:072 **Dependent nature and reflexive awareness** Another problem for the Yogācāra position is the epistemological status of the basis of all appearances it alone considers to be ultimately real, the dependent nature. This dependent nature is free of the distinction between observing subject and observed object characterizing our usual conceptualization of the world. But then, if there is such a thing as the dependent nature, how could we know it? It could not be known by anything other than the dependent nature since, *ex hypothesi*, there is nothing other. But it also could not be known by the dependent nature itself, since things cannot operate on themselves, as an acrobat cannot climb on her own

[82] In the Indian context this is usually phrased in terms of the example of a cup of water appearing like ambrosia to the gods, like molten metal to hell beings, and so on. For a contemporary incarnation of this idea see von Uexküll 1928: 2–3; Buchanan 2008: 13. The example gives rise to considerable discussion in Tibetan scholasticism. See, for example, The Yakherds 2021a: 280–291.

shoulders.[83] Hence the dependent nature would be necessarily unknowable, and to accept the existence of things that can never be cognized does not seem to cohere well with Yogācāra's criticism of cognition-independent, external objects.

Candrakīrti denies that the mind can be reflexively self-aware, to which the Yogācārin replies that the dependent nature can indeed know itself, since there are cases of objects operating on themselves, as e.g. a lamp illuminates a room, and also illuminates itself. Moreover, we know that the mind is capable of operating on itself from the fact that there is memory. If you and I remember a lunar eclipse we both saw, the content of my memory cannot just be the eclipse, because this would then also be the only content of your memory, so that the contents would be the same. But my memory is not identical with your memory. Rather, I remember the eclipse-as-seen-by-me, and you remember it as-seen-by-you. But since a memory can only be a memory of what really happened, this implies that when seeing the eclipse we did not just experience it, but also our unique way of apprehending it. This means that our mind was both directed at the external content *and* at its own manner of representing this content. This latter function cannot be performed by a second mind-moment being aware of the first one, because we otherwise would also have to postulate a third being aware of the second, and so on, all the way up to an infinite regress.[84] If our mind was pursuing an infinite sequence of cognitions of an ever higher order all based around an eclipse, say, it could never move on to the cognition of anything else, another star, for example, but would be forever stuck in a never-ending series of 'cognitions of' based on some initial cognition. The only way to avoid this is if consciousness was in some way able to split up into different sequences, one stream 6:073

[83] Compare here Candrakīrti's discussion of this 'anti-reflexivity principle' in his *Prasannapadā* (MacDonald 2015: 2: 237–238).

[84] Moreover, assuming momentariness, by the time the second mind-moment becomes aware of the first, the first mind-moment has already passed out of existence, so that it would be unclear what the second mind-moment actually apprehends.

following ever higher order perceptions based on the eclipse-perception, another following ever higher order perceptions based on the star-perception, and so on. However, all contestants in this debate agree that there is only a single stream of consciousness, and though it may appear to us as if there are several things happening in our mind at the same time (simultaneously tasting *and* seeing the coffee, for example), we are simply misled by a quick succession of mental events, as when a needle pierces a hundred lotus petals in one instant:[85] the event might seem instantaneous, even though it is composed of a large number of shorter sub-events. Hence, in order to avoid the infinite regress the mind must be considered as reflexively aware of itself, thereby resolving the question how we can have epistemic access to the dependent nature.

This argument, however, will only be convincing if reflexive awareness is the *only* way of explaining the existence of memory, which Candrakīrti denies. He points out that "the unestablished does not at all serve the purpose of establishing" since memory understood in terms of reflexive awareness is itself contentious. As long as it, rather than memory understood in terms of alternative mechanisms generating it, has not been demonstrated, it cannot be used to establish reflexive awareness as its cause. Candrakīrti will present his own account of memory in 6:075.

6:074 Not only does Candrakīrti deny that reflexive awareness is the best explanation of memory (so that the existence of the latter would support the existence of the former), he also argues that it cannot, in fact, explain memory at all. Let us assume that every moment of consciousness is simultaneously directed at its object and at itself. Still, a given moment of consciousness and a later moment that remembers it are distinct entities, and in the present context of discussing production from another, these two moments have to be regarded as intrinsically distinct. That means that nothing about the nature of one can in any way involve anything about the nature

[85] See Chakrabarti 2020: 148.

of the other. But in this case there is no more of a connection between my memory m' and the earlier, reflexively aware cognition m that is now remembered than there is between m' and any other cognitive episode n of mine. Moreover, there is no more of a connection between Alice's cognitive episode c at t_1 and its memory c' at t_2 than there is between Bob's cognitive episode d at t_1 and its memory d' at t_2. Assuming reflexive awareness does nothing toward explaining why there is a specific link between m and m', but not between n and m', and why there is a specific link between c and c', but not between c and d'.

Arguing that the specific link results from the fact that c and c' belong to Alice's continuum, while d and d' belong to Bob's does not help here, since for the Buddhist there is nothing more to a mental continuum than a causally connected sequence of mind-moments.[86] However, making sense of an ultimately real causal connection between intrinsically distinct entities is just as difficult[87] as making sense of a mnemonic connection.

If reflexive awareness is not able to explain memory this does, 6:075
of course, raise the question of how the Mādhyamika is going to explain it. Candrakīrti agrees that in everyday life, and hence at the level of conventional reality, we accept the identity of the one who remembers the lunar eclipse today with the one who saw it yesterday. Since the Mādhyamika does not endorse the existence of entities with intrinsic nature he also does not face the problem mentioned in the preceding verse, namely that of claiming the memory episode and the remembered episode to be intrinsically different. Agreeing to the ordinary conception of memory, however, does not imply accepting reflexive awareness as conventionally real. This is because the reason why reflexive awareness is introduced here in the first place is to provide an ontological foundation of an everyday phenomenon, specifying what

[86] Compare the discussion of 6:061.
[87] Compare the discussion of 6:017.

memory *really* is (namely a specific manifestation of the operation of reflexive awareness). But the Mādhyamika considers these kinds of attempts to analyze the conventions of everyday life as problematic, since such conventions are based on phenomena that are wholly deceptive. We can participate in the conventions of everyday life without analysis, but when we analyze them we find only emptiness. There is no justification for introducing a group of entities (even at the level of conventional reality) that is supposed to constitute the ultimate nature of conventional practices.[88]

6:076 If the opponent is not able to support the existence of reflexive awareness the epistemic status of the Yogācārin's dependent nature remains unresolved. How would we ever have any epistemic access to this entity which is supposed to be the only fundamentally real one? Moreover, if the dependent nature was somehow able to perceive itself the perceiver, perception, and perceived object (and, more generally, any agent, action, and object of action) should all be identical,[89] a position that is hard to align with the way the world appears to us and with the way it is usually conceptualized in, for example, grammatical analysis[90] which regards agent, action, and object as three distinct entities.

6:077 In the discussion beginning with 6:008b, Candrakīrti has argued that no entities with intrinsic nature could be caused by themselves, or by other things. The dependent nature, as a supposed bearer of intrinsic existence, therefore has to be unproduced. He also pointed out[91] that in the absence of reflexive awareness it must

[88] That is not to say that there is no justification for introducing a group of entities that explain how conventionally real things work. The Madhyamaka criticism does not apply to explanations of *how things function*, as opposed to explanations of *what things really are*. Arguably a significant amount of scientific explanations belong to the former, and not to the latter type.

[89] This is the position taken by Diṅnāga in his *Pramāṇasamuccaya* 1:10 (Hattori 1968: 29, 106).

[90] For more on the discussion of the philosophical uses of the Indian *kāraka* system see Salvini 2008: 39–63.

[91] 6:073–6:076.

be unknowable, since there is no route of epistemic access to it. But this raises the question why the Yogācārin is happy to accept one example of an epistemically inaccessible entity, but not others, including contradictory entities such as the sons of barren women. If there is no general problem about admitting objects that transcend all conceptualizations, are ineffable by nature, and only to be cognized by enlightened beings into our ontology, there seem to be no limits to what kinds of entities one might be able to include in one's account of reality at the most fundamental level.[92]

If the Mādhyamika is successful in his rejection of non-causal, epistemically inaccessible entities, however, the dependent nature can no longer be considered to be the unique fundamental basis from which the entire observed world emerges. And once this is removed from the Yogācāra system, everything else will disappear as well. It is because the Yogācārin is so concerned with finding a substantial basis of all appearance that the entire world of appearances is undermined in the end, since every attempt to establish the existence of entities existing by intrinsic nature that could function as such a basis will end up in failure. As a result the Yogācārin does not successfully account for either the ultimate or the conventional truth. As for the former, the entity supposed to fill this place, dependent nature, is beset by problems described in the preceding arguments. As for the latter, not only is the imputed nature (*parikalpita-svabhāva*) with its division of the world into an internal subject and external objects fully nonexistent from the Yogācāra perspective, also, once the dependent nature is challenged, it is impossible to establish the existence of anything other than it within the confines of the Yogācāra system. Moreover, if both truths prove to be nonexistent in this way it is difficult to see how this theory could still account for key Buddhist concepts such as karmic causality, since it would **6:078**

[92] See Westerhoff 2020: 58–61, 219, note 84.

be impossible to locate them either at the level of ultimate or at the level of conventional truth. This form of nihilism, which undermines the notion of karma, is incompatible with Buddhist soteriology and hence cannot provide the basis for the path to enlightenment.

6:079 **Yogācāra and the two truths** Without a proper understanding of the two truths as taught by Nāgārjuna there can be no prog-
6:080 ress along the Buddhist path, since they specify, in terms of the ultimate truth, the aim to be attained, and in terms of the conventional truth the means employed in order to reach this aim. But if one is unable to satisfactorily account for either truth, as Candrakīrti takes the Yogācārin to be, enlightenment will be out of reach.

6:081 The Yogācārin now criticizes Candrakīrti by claiming that the Madhyamaka analysis in terms of analyzing causation that we have witnessed so far in this chapter would, if accepted, not only refute the Yogācāra's concept of a dependent nature, but the Mādhyamika's concept of conventional truth as well. If the entities accepted by the Yogācārin are refuted since the Mādhyamika demonstrates their emptiness, the opponent could simply take any entity the Mādhyamika accepts as conventionally real and refute its existence by showing it to be empty too.

Candrakīrti uses this to as an opportunity to say more about the Madhyamaka conception of conventional truth. He points out that he does not accept entities postulated by the Yogācārins, such as the dependent nature, even at the level of conventional truth. For the Yogācārin, the dependent nature comes with the property of being perceptible to the Buddha's mind, which, given the authoritativeness of a Buddha's cognitions, also endows it with ultimate reality.

The Mādhyamika, however, does not accept conventionally real entities that could also be established by an enlightened mind. Instead, he accepts conventionally real entities because they play a role in the context of ordinary worldly conventions,[93] facilitating communication with people using these conventions, which allows the Mādhyamika to help them to progress along the path to enlightenment. As such, demonstrating the emptiness of any of these is not a problem for the Mādhyamika, since their emptiness does not conflict with their ability to produce effects.[94]

In order to underline the fact that for the Mādhyamika, acceptance of conventionally real entities is not due to the nature of these entities themselves, but is due to the attitude other beings have toward them, Candrakīrti refers to a group of highly realized Buddhist practitioners, the *arhat*s. For these, conventional reality consisting of categories essential to the Abhidharma ontology such as matter and the remaining four psychological constituents of a person no longer exists. After death these *arhat*s enter into a peaceful state in which such entities no longer appear. Accordingly, in the company of *arhat*s the Mādhyamika would not appeal to the existence of conventionally real physical and psychological entities such as the five aggregates that make up a person. But ordinary beings are not *arhat*s, and for this reason matter and mind appear to them. As such, the Mādhyamika agrees with them and accepts their ontology, not because it can make any claim to mirroring the world's fundamental reality, but in order to communicate with beings navigating within the confines of a framework of entities they imagine to be real. **6:082**

It is the Yogācārin, not the Mādhyamika, who pursues a project of revisionist metaphysics. He argues that the imputed nature, which includes central elements of our everyday conception of the world, such as external material objects, does not exist at all. This, Candrakīrti points out, has two important consequences. First, the dispute is one the Yogācārin should have with proponents of the **6:083**

[93] See above, p.85, note 71.
[94] See Nāgārjuna's *Vigrahavyāvartanī* 22 (Westerhoff 2010a: 27, 47–48).

ordinary perception of the world, not with Mādhyamikas, since it is the claims of the former about a mind-independent world of external objects that the Yogācārin wants to refute. Second, the resolution of this dispute is of limited interest to Madhyamaka. If the Yogācārin succeeds in his revisionist project and establishes an idealist metaphysics based on the dependent nature as community consensus, the Mādhyamika will accept this as the conventional truth. And if he is unsuccessful, the Mādhyamika will accept the ordinary account of the world, including its postulation of mind-independent matter as conventional truth. For the Mādhyamika, conventional truth incorporates the way ordinary beings see the world, and *how exactly* ordinary beings see the world is of minor importance from a philosophical perspective, though it is of course important from the perspective of the beings that live within the framework of the unenlightened perspective on the world. Those truths which are pragmatically successful within this framework constitute conventional truth. When referring to conventional truth the Mādhyamika does not accept ordinary beings' view of the world because it would in some way correspond to the way the world is, but simply as a tool to communicate with these beings.

6:084 **Why Yogācāra was taught** Buddhist philosophy is shaped not simply by a contest of arguments, but also by the desire to have the conclusions of one's arguments cohere with the assertions found in the Buddha's teachings. As such, the Yogācārin points out, the Mādhyamika's respect for the way ordinary beings see the world should be outweighed by their respect for the philosophical positions described in the autoritative *sūtras*. One of these, the *Daśabhūmikasūtra*, he argues, clearly supports the Yogācāra position by describing the world as merely mind.[95] Yet Candrakīrti claims that such pronouncements were not made in order to present ultimately true ontological theories, but to refute

[95] See above, p. 17.

the specific misunderstandings of those who might believe that the world arises from something other than mind, a permanent creator such as a substantial self or a divine agent. On this understanding the word 'merely' in the phrase 'merely mind' does not specifically exclude external entities, as when the Yogācārin denies the existence of the imputed nature, but is targeted more generally at other generating principles that could have been considered to give rise to the world as it appears to us. While the mind is thus taken to be the sole creator of the whole world, including the external objects, it is not to be taken ontologically seriously. In his autocommentary Candrakīrti gives the example of a blue mosaic floor that is so beautifully made it appears like a pool of water. Yet when someone tries to scoop up the water and moves a clay pot into the surface of the 'water,' the pot will break. As the mosaic floor provides a specific appearance, and fulfills a specific purpose, but is a representation not to be mistaken for the real thing, the idea of the merely mental nature of the world will appear in a specific way, once the world has been analyzed by Yogācāra arguments. It will fulfill a specific purpose in excluding other possible sources of the phenomenal world, but remains a propaedeutic device, and is not to be mistaken for an
ultimately real ground of reality. 6:085

Another of the *sūtra*s central for Yogācāra, the *Laṅkāvatārasūtra*, also points out that whatever entities other philosophical schools consider to be the origin of the world—substantial selves, material particles, the *prakṛti* of the Sāṃkhya school, a creator god—all finally reduce to mind.[96] Again, Candrakīrti notes that the Buddha did not teach this *sūtra* in order to establish an ultimately true ontological theory, but in order to refute supposedly ultimately true ontological theories of rival schools proposing generative principles other than mind that bring about the world. All of these
schools (and, Candrakīrti notes, some Buddhists as well) postulate 6:086

[96] *Laṅkāvatārasūtra*, 2:137; Lindtner 1992: 263; Suzuki 1932, 70; Red Pine 2012: 111; Bayer 2019: 35, note 35.

a specific kind of agent acting as a cosmogonic principle. However, apart from the mind, no such agent can be found. This is the point references to 'merely mind' in the Buddha's discourses set out to make.

6:087 The term 'merely mind,' as used in the *sūtra*s, Candrakīrti argues, is in fact short for "merely mind is the generating principle of the world," and should therefore not be understood as saying that merely mind, but no external objects exist.[97] Another example of such abbreviated phrasing, Candrakīrti claims, is the term 'Buddha,' which is short for '*buddha-ṭattva*' ("one who has awakened to reality"); in ordinary usage only *buddha*, not *buddha-tattva*, is used.

6:088 Moreover, if mind was regarded as an ultimately real foundation of all existence, it is unclear why it, in turn, is regarded by the *Daśabhūmikasūtra*, the very *sūtra* the opponent has cited before, as arisen from causes and conditions, such as karma, and primordial ignorance. Since the mind is part of the network of dependent origination like everything else, its existence is thereby regarded as only dependent, but cannot be fundamental.

6:089 What is meant by saying that the mind is the only generating principle of the world is that all living beings and all their inanimate environments are produced by karma. The former are the result of individual karma, while the latter result from collective karma of entire groups of perceivers.[98] Given that karma connects mental entities, constituting a link between intentions and later experiential states, it is therefore the mind that is responsible for the production of the world and all that is in it.

6:090 According to Candrakīrti's interpretation, the aim of the *sūtra*s the Yogācārin refers to is not to deny the existence of matter, but to

[97] For further discussion of this verse see Bayer 2019.

[98] This does not denote a separate kind of karma, but refers to the fact that some karmic potentials of an agent ripen as properties of the agent (like the pattern on the tail of the peacock), while others ripen as properties of the environment the agent finds himself in (such as the biodiversity of different kinds of lotus flowers in the world), and are also experienced by other agents with similar karmic potentials.

deny its role in the creation of reality. Reality, comprising both material and mental aspects, is wholly mind-made, since it is a product of karma, but that does not mean there are no material objects. In his autocommentary Candrakīrti illustrates this with the example of two kings, we might call them King Mind and King Matter, fighting for some territory. King Mind conquers King Matter, but realizes that the subjects of the conquered king are important to him and leaves them unharmed. In the same way, even though mind conquers matter in the fight for the being the single source for the creation of the world, matter still plays a role in the world as something generated by mind, and hence as something that exists. The Yogācāra position would correspond to a situation where all of King Matter's subjects are killed by the victorious King Mind. But this is not what happens; subjects of both kings continue to live peacefully in the newly enlarged territory of King Mind, untroubled by the fact that King Mind has now assumed the role of Chief Generative Principle of the World.

Candrakīrti is particularly worried by Yogācāra's denial of matter 6:091
while it still accepts the mind as existent. He argues that the two should stand and fall together. According to the ordinary perspective on unenlightened beings, mind and matter are both real. From the perspective of a highly realized meditative practitioner, both disappear. There cannot be a position where one exists, but the other does not. Once we are in a state where the first of the five aggregates, matter, does not exist, the remaining four mental aggregates will also be nonexistent. But if there is matter, mind will
exist as well. Similarly, in a state where the four mental aggregates 6:092
have vanished, so has matter, and in a state characterized by the presence of the mental aggregates, matter will be present too. The reasons that the Mādhyamika presents *against* the fundamental reality of matter (such as the argument from the four kinds of causal production discussed above) will equally apply to mental phenomena. And the reason they present *in favor* of the existence of mental phenomena (that they are accepted to exist by everyday

consensus) equally applies to matter. From the perspective of Madhyamaka analysis, neither matter nor mind is real. But when the Mādhyamaka does not analyze and accepts the conventions of the world, both matter and mind are equally taken to be real.

In the Buddha's own teachings, Candrakīrti stresses, mind and matter come as a pair as well. In the Abhidharma's theory of *dharmas*, both physical and mental *dharmas* are considered to be ultimately real. In the Perfection of Wisdom texts, however, the ultimate reality of both is denied.[99] We find no case where the Buddha privileges one member of this interdependent pair[100] over the other, arguing that one is ultimately real, while the other is not.

6:093 Yogācāra undermines the theory of the two truths, since the dependent nature they postulate cannot be conceptualized in this framework. The dependent nature can neither be included under the conventionally real nor can it be included under the ultimately real. It is not conventionally real, since it cannot be understood in terms of the structure of internal mental subjects and external physical objects that characterize our everyday understanding of the world—this structure characterizes the imputed nature, which Yogācāra considers to be nonexistent. Nor can the dependent nature by ultimately real, for all the reasons that the Mādhyamikas have so far adduced against anything being ultimately real. This is also the reason why the Yogācāra could not simply let go of the theory of the two truths, saying that there is only one ultimately real entity, the dependent nature or foundational consciousness, for the Madhyamaka arguments against the ultimate reality of such an entity would still stand. The correct position, which the Yogācārin should accept, is that there are two truths, and that mental and material things should both be included among things causally

[99] The negation of the five aggregates in the Heart-*sūtra* (*Prajñāpāramitā-hṛdaya-sūtra*) is a particularly well-known example. See Lopez 1988: 95–107 for some further background of this passage.

[100] On the interdependence of mind and matter in the Abhidharma ontology see Bhikkhu Anālayo 2018: 9–12, 58.

produced at the level of conventional truth, though neither exists at the level of ultimate truth.

Sūtras *teaching Yogācāra are* sūtras *with interpretable meaning* Other passages from *sūtras* asserting that what appear to be external, material objects is only mind in disguise are interpreted by Candrakīrti not along the lines of his interpretation in 6:090, i.e., as denying a generative principle of the world other than the mind, but are regarded by him as denying the existence of an external, material reality. Nevertheless, Candrakīrti does not believe that the Buddha intended to present in these teachings an ontology of the world at the ultimate level. Instead, the Buddha taught these doctrines to counteract the desire of those who are excessively attached to material things. As such, these teachings have the same status as the teachings on the practice of meditation on the impure (*aśubha-bhāvanā*) discussed in 6:069. Teaching that what appear as attractive bodies are really decomposing skeletons constitutes instructions that need to be understood against a specific context (*neyārtha*), and are supposed to have a specific effect on a specific audience. It is not a teaching on what reality is like at the most fundamental level. The same applies to *sūtra* passages teaching that there is no matter, and that everything is a manifestation of mind. **6:094**

How do we know that these passages are to be understood in such a context-dependent manner? There are both scriptural and philosophical reasons. First, Candrakīrti presents various quotations from central Yogācāra texts in his autocommentary, passages from the *Saṃdhinirmocanasūtra* and the *Laṅkāvatārasūtra* supporting the view that the mind-only teachings are just put forward as provisional teachings for the benefit of specific kinds of disciples, like a medicine prescribed by a physician to cure a specific kind of illness. These teachings are not presented as context-independent. **6:095**

The philosophical reason why the texts in question are to be understood as in need of interpretation, and not to be taken at face value is that the negation of external objects fulfills a specific **6:096** propaedeutic role. The physical world around us being so immediately evident, it presents a natural first target for the Madhyamaka criticism of substantially real entities. Once the insubstantiality of the external world, the object of cognition, has been established by Yogācāra arguments, it is then possible to proceed to establish a more subtle form of insubstantiality, that of the knower, together with that of the mental entities argued to form the basis of our perception of the physical world.[101]

6:097 What is the general criterion for deciding which texts contain teachings with provisional meaning (*neyārtah*) and are therefore in need of interpretation, and which contain teachings expressing the Buddha's definite intent (*nītārtha*) and are to be taken literally? An answer to this question is of major importance to Buddhist hermeneutics, since the difference between philosophical schools is often reflected in which texts are assigned to which category. Candrakīrti presents various passages in support of his view that those texts that do not directly teach dependent origination in terms of nothing ever arising in a substantial manner belong to the group of teachings with provisional meaning. Such texts might teach the existence of a variety of things, whether these are persons or Buddha-nature, yet all these existential claims have to be understood in a specific context, aimed at a particular audience making distinct assumptions and having special explanatory needs. The texts teaching emptiness, on the other hand, convey the Buddha's definite position and can be understood literally.

6a.3 Production from itself and from another

6:098 After this lengthy section on the negation of causal production from another which began in 6:014, Candrakīrti now treats the third possibility, causal production from both, which he associates with the Jains, in a single verse. This is the idea that when some

[101] Compare Śāntarakṣita's *Mudhyamakālaṃkāra* 92–93 (Blumenthal 2004: 170–172, 245).

entity such as a pot is produced, the effect is produced by itself (it is the very lump of clay that is shaped into a pot) and by other things (the various instruments of the potter that are required to turn the lump of clay into a pot).

Given that this conception of causation appears intuitively very plausible, it is strange to see that Candrakīrti dismisses it so quickly. His main point is that if self-production and production from another have each been refuted both conventionally and ultimately, combining both cannot possibly result in a viable theory of causation. If you cannot squeeze oil from one grain of sand, and cannot squeeze oil from another either, squeezing both simultaneously is unlikely to lead to success.

It is certainly the case that the two positions of causal self-production and production from another as described above cannot be consistently combined. If the cause is identical with the effect, then both cannot also be distinct from each other in a such a strong sense that there are no relations between the two.

However, one might think that there is another way of understanding 'production from both' that would escape this criticism. Could one not simply say that the clay is the *potential* cause of the pot, which is then *actualized* by the potter's craft? In this way both play a role in bringing about the pot, though neither could do so on its own. Note, however, that the causal relations the opponent is interested in are those involving intrinsic natures; the first two alternatives are cases in which the cause is either intrinsically the same as the effect, or intrinsically distinct. But once we talk about actualizing potentials, intrinsic natures are no longer in the picture. A potential is not something anything can have 'in a lonely state' (one of the characteristics of having a property by intrinsic nature or *svabhāva*), but can only exist relative to an actualizer. Relative to some actualizer the clay is a potential pot, relative to another a potential pigment, and relative to a third a potential dermatological remedy. Nothing could have all three potentials as intrinsic natures simultaneously since every entity can only have a single intrinsic nature characterizing it in its individuality. It is even more obvious that something cannot be an actualizer unless it is an actualizer of something—nothing can be an actualizer all by itself. As long as the opponent believes that causal relations must involve intrinsic natures, the potential/actualizer distinction is unlikely to be of much use to him.

6a.4 Production from no cause

6:099 The final one of the four kinds of causal production is production from no cause. The proponent of this position argues that there is no specific reason, for example, why mangoes arise from a mango tree but not from other trees, since the world is essentially random.[102] Any fruit could arise from any tree, and any effect from any cause, since cause and effect are not in any way connected.

Unsurprisingly, Candrakīrti points out that this does not seem to be the world we live in. Only mango trees produce mangoes, in specific circumstances and at specific times, and mangoes do not just pop up in our environment at random. If there was no regularity between seeds and sprouts there would be no point in agriculture, since we could never reliably predict which plant may arise by growing a seed.

6:100 Our ability to know the world is normally understood in causal terms: objects affect our sense-organs, consequently producing knowledge of these objects in our minds.[103] But if there are no causal regularities, and hence no instances of causation in the world, our knowledge of the world would be on a par with knowledge of nonexistent objects such as flowers in the sky. Neither could be causally related to us, and as we do not perceive flowers in the sky, we should not be able to perceive ordinary worldly phenomena

[102] This 'accidentalist' position is often attributed to the ancient Indian materialists (Lokāyata or Cārvāka), though the accuracy of this ascription has been debated (see Bhattacharya 2011: 41–42).

[103] Note that Cārvāka epistemology is generally understood to only accept the one epistemic instrument most straightforwardly construed in such causal terms: perception (see Gokhale 2015: 49–85). See also Bhattacharya 2011: 55–63.

either. As such, a denial of causal regularities would undermine any causally based epistemology. However, we do believe that our epistemic contact with the world differs in important ways from our relations to nonexistent objects. As such, we should assume that our cognitions of things in the world, as well as the things congnized, are causally produced at the level of conventional reality, and that these causal regularities account both for the variegated appearance of things, as well as for our knowledge of them.

The materialist opponent might respond by saying that our knowledge of the world does exist, and that is arises like sprouts arise from seeds: things just happen to arise, but without any set of causal regularities operating in the background. Everything in the world just happens to arise from the four elements, earth, water, fire, and wind, which constitute the entire ontology. In particular, everything mental is simply something emerging, without underlying causal regularity, from combinations of these elements (as alcohol emerges from a combination of grain, water, yeast, and so on), but is not itself fundamentally real. As such, there also cannot be any future lives, since the destruction of the material basis of the mind will destroy the mind as well. **6:101**

Candrakīrti is particularly concerned to refute this specific claim, as it stands in direct opposition to the Buddhist conception of the world. He argues that if the materialist claims future lives do not exist because they are not observed, we need to determine whether this non-perception is itself observed. If it is not, our epistemic justification for asserting that future lives are not observed is unclear. For the materialist, observation is the only route to knowledge of the world. Unlike other Indian schools of thought, who accept perception and inference as epistemic instruments, the materialists only accept perception. But if the absence of future lives is observed by perception, this means that nonexistent things can be observed, and that in terms of their epistemic access they are on a par with perceptible existent things. How do we then draw a line between existents and nonexistents? And if everything has to be called existent, as it is perceptible, how can we reasonably call future lives nonexistent? Moreover, as existence and nonexistence are mutually dependent, existence is simultaneously undermined by the denial of nonexistence, and with it the materialist's claim that the elements exist.

In addition, Candrakīrti points out, the materialists have a fundamentally wrong understanding of the four elements, taking them to be substantially real when they are in fact wholly insubstantial. Yet if their understanding of the material world of our everyday acquaintance is already faulty, similar to one suffering from visual illusions like double vision, how could we be convinced by their claims about more complex matters reaching beyond this world, such as whether or not there are future lives? The materialist might say we have knowledge of the world, which just happens to arise as some formations of the elements, like sprouts, happen to arise, but their 'knowledge' is false, since its substantialist presuppositions are refuted by the Madhyamaka arguments Candrakīrti has discussed earlier.

6:102 Not only does the materialist hold incorrect views about fundamental reality, for him these views, as well as others, which he, too, deems to be correct, arise from a single source. As Candrakīrti is addressing a materialist, he points out that their body (which, according to their understanding is also their mind) contains a collection of beliefs, some of which, such as that of the substantial existence of the elements, have already been shown to be false. According to the materialist, beliefs do not arise in an attempt to correctly represent the world, but they just happen to arise from the four elements, as everything else in the world just happens to arise from them. Would it then not be reasonable to expect that other beliefs arising from the same basis (such as the denial of future lives) will also turn out to be false, once we have taken the materialist conception of belief-generation seriously?

6:103 The falsity of the materialist's belief in the substantial existence of the elements has been refuted by the earlier criticism of the four kinds of causal production. As there is no other way in which the elements could have arisen, the elements as conceived by the opponent cannot exist. Moreover, the refutation of the four kinds of causal production not only undermines the postulation of the elements, but equally affects theorists who assume a creator god, time, atoms, intrinsic natures, etc., as the causal origin of the world.

Intrinsic natures are mistaken projections

Existence by intrinsic nature presupposes one of the four kinds 6:104
of causal production, but since none of these actually happens, there is also no existence by intrinsic nature. What is nonetheless apprehended is not any form of intrinsic nature, but merely a superimposition produced by ignorance. Ignorance is not simply an absence of knowledge, but an active force obscuring how things really are. This lets us see substantially real objects where there are in fact only empty entities devoid of intrinsic nature.

How can ignorance cause perception of intrinsic nature that is 6:105
really not there? In the same way as ophthalmological conditions can cause perceptions of hair-like entities where there are none (in the case of vitreous floaters), or perceptions of two objects where there is only one (in the case of double vision). In these cases a perception that is wholly produced by malfunctioning sensory faculties is 'projected outward' and regarded as if it were brought about by some external object interacting with our sense faculties. In the same way our malfunctioning cognitive capacities produce the conception of intrinsically real objects, and we are then led to believe that there is something in the world corresponding to this conception.

In setting out the twelve links of dependent origination, the Buddha 6:106
taught that ignorance (*avidyā*, the first link) brings about the entire cycle of causal development in the following links and that, in reverse, the whole cycle can be made to disappear if ignorance is made to disappear. This teaching of dependent origination, Candrakīrti argues, is

a teaching intended for ordinary beings who have not realized emptiness, at least if ignorance is assumed to be a real cause of karma and the cycle of *saṃsāra*, an assumption the Mādhyamika rejects.[104] As the preceding analysis of the four kinds of causal production has shown, nothing really arises in a manner involving intrinsic natures, and so nothing can really cease in such a manner either. This must apply to dependent origination as described by the Buddha as well, hence the origination of karma from ignorance, and the cessation of karma once ignorance has ceased must be understood as empty too. None of this, of course, undermines dependent origination as a core Buddhist teaching; rather, Candrakīrti contrasts here an Abhidharma understanding of dependent origination involving real causal relations 'out there' with a Madhyamaka view that understands this very teaching as concerned with empty objects related by empty causal relations. There is no substantially real entity called 'ignorance' that has to be eliminated in order to achieve liberation. Instead, liberation comes from the realization that while phenomena manifest, these very phenomena, their cause, and the causal relation connecting them are without intrinsic nature and therefore empty. Realizing that ignorance as a cause of cyclic existence is as empty as everything else, ignorance is brought to an end and *nirvāṇa* is attained.

Emptiness does not mean nonexistence

6:107 The opponent is concerned that if, according to Candrakīrti, everything is empty, and nothing ever really arises on the basis of any substantially real causal relation, even at the level of conventional reality, then all things turn out to be nonexistent even conventionally, like a round square, or a barren woman's son. But since it is absurd to say that everything is nonexistent in this way, we have to conclude that some things are not empty.

[104] For some different perspectives on the nature of dependent origination and its ontological status see Geshe Yeshe Thabke 2020, chapter 3.

However, even if all things are empty, this does not imply that we cannot differentiate between empty existent and empty non-existent things. Consider the case of optical illusions. The visual phenomena that sufferers from optical illusions perceive (floating hairs, duplicate objects, mirages in the desert, etc.) are all equally illusory. But this does not mean that each is associated with every ophthalmological condition. The sufferer from floaters sees falling hairs, but no duplicate moons, and no sons of barren women either. In the same way, even though all things are empty, the roles they play relative to our perceptual faculties are not simply interchangeable: sons and squares do appear to them, but sons of barren women and square circles do not. 6:108

While there is a reason why specific things, but not others appear to those afflicted by optical illusions, and why specific things, but not others appear to ordinary beings afflicted by ignorance, this is not something the Mādhyamika is particularly interested in. Their aim is to get beyond these erroneous misconceptions, and to do so it is not necessary to understand all the specificities involved in the respective causes bringing them about. Moreover, when looking for the reason why specific things appear to the optically deluded, or to beings deluded by ignorance, we need to ask these beings, to which these appearances do indeed appear, and not the clear-sighted, or highly realized practitioners, to which they no longer appear. The source of the structure of conventional reality is to be found at the level of conventional reality, not at the level of ultimate reality.

In fact it is not even necessary to ask one suffering from vitreous floaters why he sees hairs, and no sons of barren women. Ubiquitous illusions familiar to anybody (dreams, mirages, reflections, and so forth) produce quite specific perceptions, but not others, even though the perceptions are all unreal. The hot sand in the desert produces the image of a shimmering lake, but no image of the son of a barren woman, even though lake and son are equally nonexistent. If all nonexistent objects are on a par, as the opponent suggests, then the son of a barren woman should 6:109

actually be perceptible (as some nonexistent objects are), or all nonexistent objects should be equally imperceptible (as the son of a barren woman is).

6:110 There is no conflict between things being on the one hand insubstantial, illusory, and lacking existence 'from their own side' and, on the other hand, appearing vividly to our perceptions. While there are some things of this kind that do not even appear to perception (like sons of barren women, or triangular rectangles), not all are like this, and for this reason the opponent's claim in 6:107, that because everything is empty and causally unproduced by any substantial causal relation, everything must fail to appear, is not true.

6:111 A barren woman's son is obviously ultimately unreal, but he is also unreal at the level of conventional reality, since he does not appear in anyone's perception. He is a mere description, and an inconsistent one at that. The same holds for hairs perceived by sufferers from floaters (they lack ultimate and conventional reality), the latter not because they fail to appear perceptually (they do) but because they only appear to a very restricted number of people afflicted by an ophthalmological condition. Their existence is not generally acknowledged by the world, unlike tables and chairs, for example, which lack ultimate, but possess conventional existence.

It is important to note that Candrakīrti here aligns existence by intrinsic nature with the ontological status of sons of barren women: both fail to exist ultimately *and* conventionally. This is usually regarded as a clear statement of the Prāsaṅgika interpretation of Madhyamaka, according to which Madhyamaka does not support an appearance/reality distinction in relation to entities with intrinsic natures.[105] It is not the case that such entities exist conventionally, and fail to exist ultimately, rather they are wholly nonexistent at both the conventional and at the ultimate level.

[105] See Cozort 1998: 60; Ruegg 2002: 168–202; Tillemans 2003.

Candrakīrti presents scriptural support for the claim that all things are pacified from the outset, intrinsically extinguished, and un-arisen. He interprets this as saying that there was never any *time* when things existed with intrinsic nature or were produced by a substantially real causal relation (e.g., prior to the realization of emptiness), nor is there any *perspective* from which they exist or are produced in this way (e.g., the perspective of the ordinary un-enlightened being, as compared to that of the enlightened being). Intrinsic natures are neither something that first exists, and is then removed as the practitioner advances temporally from a time when he has no direct understanding of emptiness to a time when he does, nor is it removed when the practitioner advances in terms of levels of understanding from seeing the world in terms of conventional truth to seeing the world in terms of ultimate truth. All things are at all times and from all points of view devoid of intrinsic nature and therefore empty. 6:112

The difference between a barren woman's son (which is ultimately and conventionally nonexistent) and a pot (which is ultimately nonexistent, though conventionally existent) is that the latter is accepted to exist by common consensus, and thereby forms part of ordinary interactions and exchanges between people. While there is not anything in the pot that exists with intrinsic nature, and therefore needs to be taken seriously at the level of fundamental ontology, pots are embedded in the network of conventions in a way that mere thought-constructions like sons of barren women are not, and it is this embedding that endows them with conventional reality. 6:113

In his autocommentary Candrakīrti points out that this picture does not change substantially when we consider the pot's constituents, that is, the different bits of matter that constitute it. The Madhyamaka position is not that the pot, being only conventionally real, is a conceptual construction superimposed on these constituents, which are ultimately real (as the Ābhidharmikas argue), but that the same analysis is to be applied at the level of the constituents (and the constituents of the constituents—all the way down):[106] these too exist only nominally, playing a specific role in our network of conventions, but are not grounded in any substantially real entities.

Benefits of realizing dependent origination

6:114 However, given that Candrakīrti denies substantial causal production at both the ultimate and the conventional level, how do we account for ordinary instances of causation, such as seeds producing sprouts? He responds that even though all the four kinds of causal production have been previously refuted, this does not rule out cause and effect arising in dependence. An important feature of this notion of dependent origination is the mutual dependence exhibited by the entities related by it. The scriptural sources Candrakīrti presents in his autocommentary illustrate this by reference to the mutual dependence of long and short, act and agent, and so on. The underlying view of origination is therefore quite different from the conceptions of causation Candrakīrti refutes, where causal powers are always taken to reside in specific objects, forming part of their intrinsic nature. But if any (or indeed all) objects are mutually dependent in this way, their causal powers cannot be intrinsic, because intrinsic properties cannot themselves depend on other properties. The notion of dependent origination thereby charts a middle course between a total absence of causal regularities in the world on the one hand, and the foundation of causal powers in the intrinsic natures of the causal relata on the other. Things arise in a structured manner at the level of conventional reality, but there is no ontologically weighty basis, either conventionally or ultimately, providing the ultimately real foundation of this arising.

[106] The question whether such infinite downward sequences of imputations can be coherently conceptualized is a substantial one. Madhyamaka's Buddhist opponents considered it to be intrinsically problematic (Westerhoff 2016: 346–348) and the question continues to be debated in contemporary metaphysics (see Westerhoff 2020: 152–245 for an overview).

Given dependent origination, all alternative theories Candrakīrti has so far examined turn out to be deficient, since they either assume the existence of some entity outside of the network of dependent origination (causal agents that have their causal nature in and of themselves in the case of the first three kinds of causal production) or clash with the observation that things arise in an ordered manner (in the case of the fourth kind, the absence of causal relations). Only the theory of dependent origination, Candrakīrti argues, is able to provide insight into the fact that no entity is able to 'stand on its own' while at the same time accounting for the fact that the way entities support each other and bring each other into existence is structured, not chaotic. In the same manner, dependent origination undermines a whole set of metaphysical views that either try to ground the world in some ultimate ontology or deny the presence of regularity, structure, or order anywhere in the world. Some examples Candrakīrti mentions include the view that some entities last forever, or that all objects, by their intrinsic nature, are only of a momentary nature, the view that some entities exist substantially, or that the view that everything fails to exist even at the level of conventional reality. **6:115**

Once the idea of intrinsic natures has been refuted, none of these metaphysical views which presuppose such natures can be maintained, as there can be no fire without fuel. Once we realize that no entity exists 'from its own side' but that all things can only exist in a network of dependence relations involving mental entities, our own interests and concerns, those of others, and material entities,[107] the desire to locate the 'core' of individual objects, their intrinsic nature, their haecceity, their *svabhāva* dissipates. As such, theories that 'things as they are in themselves' will continue to exist indefinitely, or will at some point be irretrievably destroyed, are objectively divided into mental and **6:116**

[107] For a quantum-theoretical take on such relationist ideas see Rovelli 2020: 121–131, 2021.

physical things, are intrinsically good or bad, and so on, will lose their explanatory appeal. Like a medicine applied to those suffering from floaters makes the appearance of hairs go away, without affecting in any way the nature of the imaginary hairs, so the view of dependent origination leads to the disappearance of metaphysical views committed to entities that are what they are, independent of their being perceived, or being conceptualized, or indeed independent of other things, without in any way changing the way things exist.

6:117 What keeps beings trapped in cyclic existence are conceptual constructions, and liberation is achieved through the elimination of these constructions. The term 'conceptual construction' does not refer to just any kind of reason-based mental activity, but specifically to the mental construction of substantially real entities with intrinsic natures. Since such entities do not exist, there are only their representational simulacra in the mind, and the attachment to them as if they were more than mind-made fictions causes the continuity of *saṃsāra*.[108] These conceptual constructions are eliminated through the kind of analysis Candrakīrti has described so far, which shows the nonexistence of the types of substantial entities that form the object of metaphysical theories previously discussed.

6:118 It is therefore important to realize that even though Candrakīrti's "Introduction to the Middle Way" and Nāgārjuna's *Mūlamadhyamakārikā* look like philosophical texts, they are not, at least as long as we assume that the principal aim of a philosophical text is to refute rival positions and to establish one's own position. Madhyamaka texts, Candrakīrti argues, are not contributions to philosophical debates, but tools to be applied that help their students overcome conceptual constructions keeping them trapped

[108] As Candrakīrti points out in his autocommentary, if there were entities with intrinsic natures in the world it would be inexplicable why the elimination of their conceptual representations should bring any benefit. It is only because there are none that the removal of the mistaken supposition that there are produces soteriological results.

in cyclic existence. They do so by means of reasoning, and thereby also refute other, contradictory theories. But this is a side effect of achieving a far more important cause than argumentative success, the liberation from existential suffering, as the production of ashes is a side effect of boiling water. Scoring dialectical points is not the primary goal of the Mādhyamika's presentation of his philosophical position. This underlines the claim that Candrakīrti's previous discussion of the Sāṃkhya, Yogācāra, Jain, and Cārvāka positions is not, or at least not in the first instance, meant to be a contribution to ancient Indian philosophical debates, but is taken up in order to demonstrate how to eliminate conceptual constructions that manifest in the form of specific philosophical views.

Not only is the successful defense of one's own position in philo- 6:119
sophical debates not the main purpose of Madhyamaka analysis, it would also be quite counterproductive to conceive of it in this way. Defense of one's own position in a dialectical exchange can provide another source of attachment, attachment to one's own view, and with it the pride of having defeated the opponent, the fear of being defeated in future encounters, and the reinforcement of the belief in a substantial self that holds the view we regard as our own. Yet these are manifestations and sources of the very form of existential suffering the Madhyamaka analysis is setting out to overcome, so turning the reasoned exposition of the Middle Way into further fuel for this suffering precisely undermines the purpose it is supposed to serve. This point constitutes one aspect of the claim that Mādhyamikas propound no views, made in some of the sources Candrakīrti quotes in his autocommentary. Another aspect is the reluctance to treat the Madhyamaka view of universal emptiness as something that is itself ultimately true.[109] The two aspects are, of course, connected: if the Madhyamaka position is not itself ultimately true, attachment to it arising from the desire to align

[109] A brief account of the 'no-thesis view' in Nāgārjuna is given in Westerhoff 2010a: 61–65. For an interesting discussion of its ancestors in early Buddhism see Gómez 1976.

one's own position with the ultimate truth about reality loses its foundation.

6b. Refutation of intrinsically existent persons

6:120 Having dedicated the first major portion of chapter 6, verses 008–119, to the discussion of the selflessness of phenomena, Candrakīrti now turns to the selflessness of the person. The mistaken view that the transitory collection of psycho-physical aggregates constitutes a self (*satkāyadṛṣṭi*)[110] is the principal cause keeping beings trapped in cyclic existence. Refuting this erroneous superimposition is a principal step on the path of Buddhist practice. For Candrakīrti, and for Buddhists in general, a substantial self is of course fully nonexistent, and as such the refutation of a nonexistent entity might appear to be of limited use. However, what does exist is a *conception* of a self that is wholly dependent on the aggregates, which is misapprehended as being substantially real. This misapprehension is the target of the Madhyamika critique.

Considering the logical relation of the two concepts of the selflessness of phenomena and of the selflessness of persons, it is evident that the former implies the latter—if there are no intrinsically existent, substantial phenomena anywhere, there are also no substantial selves. However, in our cognitive and emotional lives our self plays a role unlike all other phenomena. It continuously occupies center stage, it is the fixed point around which our universe resolves. Given this centrality, expecting the realization of its insubstantial status as a mistaken superimposition to follow as a simple corollary from the establishment of universal emptiness is unrealistic. The example of the self needs to be addressed

[110] For more details on this important concept see Huntington 1992: 225, note 3; Lamotte 1944–1980: 4: 1999–2000; Gelongma Karma Migme Chödrön 4: 1640–1641.

specifically in order to equip the practitioner with the conceptual tools to see through its empty nature.

6b.1 Refutation of the self and aggregates as different

The mistaken superimposition of the self can take two forms. One is the result of bad philosophy, where belief in a deficient philosophical system postulating a substantial self makes one adopt the conviction that there is such an entity. The other is an innate psychological mechanism, present even in animals and pre-linguistic children generating the notion of a self which is then considered in terms of attributes it in fact fails to possess. The former is easier to eliminate than the latter; to remove the former, all that is necessary is the adoption of a philosophical system that incorporates the no-self view. Since the innate superimposition of the self is a kind of cognitive default mechanism, removing it requires more than the adoption of a new philosophical system. Instead we need to change the way we more or less automatically conceptualize the world, a result that is much more difficult to achieve. **6:121**

Candrakīrti begins with the view of a self that results from adopting a faulty philosophical system. As in his discussion of the first of the four ways of causal production, production from itself in 6:008–6:013 above, he focuses on Sāṁkhya, indicating the significant place the Sāṁkhya system occupied in the intellectual culture of Candrakīrti's time. Candrakīrti identifies the Sāṁkhya conception of the self with one of its two fundamental categories, the *puruṣa*, a form of non-individuated consciousness characterized by five qualities. The *puruṣa* is permanent, a subject of experiences, but not a creator (this role is mainly filled by the other fundamental category, *prakṛti*, a material source from which the world around us evolves), and it is without qualities and activities which are instead associated with *prakṛti*.

Candrakīrti notes that other non-Buddhist schools, such as Vaiśeṣika and Vedānta, characterize the self with somewhat different features. However, Candrakīrti's refutation of this philosophical notion of the self is not based on features unique to any specific non-Buddhist system of thought, but focuses on properties shared by all of them.

6:122 The key difficulty Candrakīrti sees with non-Buddhist accounts of the self is that they conceive of it as causally unproduced. As for the Buddhists every object is part of the network of dependent origination,[111] describing the self as unproduced groups it together with entities like sons of barren women—things that are fully nonexistent.[112] Yet nonexistent things cannot carry out any function, and so, in particular, the self assumed by the non-Buddhist cannot act as the basis of our ordinary sense of self. Arguing that there are two types of self, one empirical one, that is reborn and suffers, and forms the basis of our ordinary sense of self, and one transcendent one, that is unborn, permanent, and beyond suffering,[113] is unlikely to resolve this problem, for the two selves would have to be either distinct (in which case there is no unitary self), or identical (in which case the self has contradictory properties).

Moreover, the philosophical sense of self which regards it as substantially real, as transcendent, permanent, without qualities or activities and so forth, plays no role in our conventional cognitive, linguistic, or social practices involving selves. As such, besides any worries that the non-Buddhist notion of a self might not exist at the ultimate level, it is hard to see how, given its radical separation from

[111] Note that even if we admit the existence of some causally unproduced entities (abstract objects, say—independent of whether we believe that these are also dependently originated, just not *causally* originated) this would not help much in the present context, as it would be hard to see how such entities could be regarded as a self, for example as an experiencer or as a subject of prudential concern. Similar considerations apply to non-abstract eternal, immutable (and therefore causally unproduced) entities. As such entities cannot change, and change appears to be essential for participating in causal relations, it is hard to see how such an eternal entity could ever participate in causal processes like perceiving, deliberating, or intending we usually assume the self to be involved in.

[112] Buddhist scholastic thinkers were well aware that this raises the intriguing problem of how we can even reason about nonexistent entities—if they are not there at all, how can they be the subject of logical inference? See Tillemans and Lopez 1998; Yao 2020 for some discussion.

[113] See Duerlinger 2013: 96.

any conventional practices, it could even be regarded as conventionally real.

Yet if the self is causally unproduced, and therefore nonexistent like a round square, it also cannot have any properties, since properties are had only by existent objects.[114] In particular, a nonexistent self cannot have properties like the five qualities ascribed to it in the Sāṁkhya system, or those ascribed to it in other, non-Buddhist philosophical theories. 6:123

A self postulated by schools like Sāṁkhya would have to be wholly distinct from the psycho-physical aggregates, since we know these to be impermanent, as all parts of our body and mind are subject to constant and rapid change, while the opponent's self is taken to be permanent. However, since we are not in any perceptual or cognitive contact with such a self that wholly transcends features of the psycho-physical aggregates, such as being connected with a body, perceiving, cogitating, and so on, it is not reasonable to believe that there is this kind of a self. The point is not that entities we cannot perceptually or cognitively apprehend cannot exist, but that entities of this type, even if they existed, would be unfit to play the role of a self. 6:124

Moreover, if our sense of self was in fact based on a transcendent, permanent entity separate from perception, thought, etc., as postulated by philosophical theorizing, this would fail to explain how the philosophically untrained could have a sense of self. Beings without training in Sāṁkhya or related philosophical systems evidently have a sense of self, a sense of self which cannot be based on the results of philosophical analysis concluding that there is some self-like entity radically distinct from any events we usually consider to constitute our cognitive lives.

[114] An ontology that admits nonexistent objects having properties (like the round square being round and square), on the other hand, would have to address the challenge of how these entities could be part of causal relations. Whatever the round square may be, spelling out how it could participate in any causal process is far from straightforward.

6:125 Furthermore, animals and pre-linguistic children, as well as beings born in the other realms included in Buddhist cosmology, arguably have a sense of self, though they have not acquired it through reflection on the existence of a permanent, transcendent entity separate from the psycho-physical aggregates. As such, it is difficult to see how such a philosophical concept of self could provide the basis of the sense of self of beings of this kind.[115]

6b.2 Refutation of the self and aggregates as identical

6:126 After discussing the non-Buddhist position of a self existing beyond the aggregates, Candrakīrti now examines a rival Buddhist view, identified by him as the view of one of the Abhidharma schools, the Saṃmitīya,[116] a view that denies a self distinct from the aggregates.

It is helpful to note at this stage how the dialectical background of the debate about the self shifts depending on which participants are involved. In the case of the debate between non-Buddhists, the argument usually focuses on the *identity of the referent* of the notion of the self (as one might argue which of two actors played a given role in a film). When non-Buddhists and Buddhists debate (as in 6:121–6:125 above), the disagreement concerns the question whether the notion of a self has *any referent at all* (as one might argue whether a specific role involved an actor, or was created using CGI). When Buddhists, who agree that the notion of the self has no referent debate, the argument is generally about the *basis of imputation* of the notion of a self (as one might disagree on whether a man mistakenly identified in the fog was really a tree or really a column).

Candrakīrti distinguishes two forms the Saṃmitīya denial of a self different from the aggregates may take: taking all the aggregates as the self, or taking only the fifth aggregate, the *vijñāna-skandha,* as

115 For further Madhyamaka criticism of the concept of a self postulated by various non-Buddhist schools see Jha 1987: 155–238; Goodman 2022: 98–191.

116 Sometimes called Sammatīya. See Bareau 2013, chapter 20.

the self. Candrakīrti explains the second form as motivated by the central place the mind plays in Buddhist soteriology. If Buddhism is primarily a form of mind-training, if anything is a good candidate for playing the role of a self, it is the mind.

Refutation of the self and aggregates as identical by reasoning

The first difficulty entailed by taking the aggregates as a self is that the self would be multiple, as the aggregates are multiple.[117] Yet we usually regard the self as a unity, rather than as a multiplicity. The second difficulty is that the self would be substantially real, as the aggregates, or at least the *dharma*s they are composed of are substantially real from the Abhidharma perspective. Yet the Buddhist no-self theory denies that selves are substantially real. In this case, abandoning *satkāyadṛṣṭi* would not be abandoning a mistaken superimposition that something unreal was real, but the mistaken denial of a correct view seeing something real as real. This obviously conflicts with the traditional Buddhist conception of *satkāyadṛṣṭi* as a mistaken view. The only way one could then justify the abandoning of *satkāyadṛṣṭi* would be to understand it as abandoning *attachment* to its object (that is, the self), rather than abandoning its object. 6:127

What precisely the views of the Saṃmitīya school about the self were,[118] and how they related to those of the Vātsīputrīya[119] and the Pudgalavāda school,[120] is difficult to determine on the basis of extant sources. All we can do here is try to determine what Candrakīrti must have taken their views to be, based on the assumption that his criticism was successful. In this context it is evident that Candrakīrti did not simply consider the Saṃmitīya

[117] This remains a problem if only the fifth aggregate, and not all five aggregates, is taken to be the self, for the consciousness-aggregate too is a collection of distinct individual mind-moments, and not a single entity.

[118] See Bareau 2013: 156.

[119] See Bareau 2013: 145.

[120] Westerhoff 2018b: 53–60.

school to take the five aggregates, or the fifth aggregate, as the basis of imputation for the mistaken view of the self (the former is the position most commonly associated with the Abhidharma). Taking them merely as the basis of imputation does not commit one to accept that all properties of the basis of imputation are also had by the object imputed on it, as one does not have to accept that a person superimposed on a column misperceived in the fog is an artifact, made of stone, and so on. Yet Candrakīrti's argument relies on the absurd consequence that if the aggregates are multiple and substantial, so is the self. For this to have any traction, the Saṃmitīya view of taking the aggregates as the 'support' of the self Candrakīrti addresses must be based on the assumption that the self and the aggregates share all of their properties. This, at least if we accept the identity of indiscernibles, implies that they are the same thing. The opponent must hence consider the self and the aggregates to be identical, rather than simply taking the self to depend in some way on the aggregates.

6:128 Candrakīrti continues with three further difficulties entailed by the assumption that the aggregates are the self. All of these turn out to be in tension with other claims that Candrakīrti's opponent (*qua* Buddhist) should accept. First, as the aggregates disappear when enlightenment is obtained, this would be identical with the destruction of the self. Yet the Buddhist conception of *nirvāṇa* is not that some substantial entity is destroyed, which is regarded as a nihilistic view, but that we stop holding on to an entity that was never substantially real in the first place.

Second, as the aggregates pass in and out of existence very quickly, in accordance with the momentariness of the underlying *dharmas* the self, too, would come into existence and go out of existence very quickly.[121] The self of the present moment would exist and would be substantially different from the self of a previous

[121] A contemporary version of such a view of momentary selves is Galen Strawson's 'pearl view' of the self. See Strawson 1997: 424, as well as Westerhoff 2020: 129–130.

moment, which no longer exists. As such, any identification with or memory of a self at a previous time (or indeed a previous life) would be problematic.

Third, since the aggregates existing at some previous moment no longer exist at some subsequent moment, the self at the previous moment would be wholly nonexistent at a subsequent moment. Yet that would mean that the karmic consequences of an action would not be experienced by the self that caused it, and that these consequences would obtain for a substantially different self that exists at a later time (namely the aggregates that exist at times after the karmic potentials have been produced). Again, this is not how Buddhists understand karma to work.

It is interesting to see that the last two difficulties connected with personal and karmic continuity are precisely points we would usually see a supporter of a substantial self make against the Buddhist no-self doctrine, and indeed the response Candrakīrti's opponent gives is one the advocate of the no-self doctrine usually gives, arguing that the particular mind-moments we identify as 'me' form part of a causally connected process, and hence can support memory, karma, and other notions in terms of the qualities that each mind-moment (as a cause) passes on to the next mind-moment (the effect). However, as Candrakīrti has already noted previously,[122] this suggestion does not work if the objects connected by the causal relation are supposed to be ultimately real and substantially distinct. For if the nature of one moment involves that of another, they cannot be entities that each exist by their intrinsic nature, as ultimately real entities would, because such existence precisely excludes dependence relations of this kind. On the other hand, if their natures are all completely distinct there is no reason that explains why one set of mind-moments, but not another one, forms part of a causal chain. If there is nothing specific about a group of entities that makes it form a causal chain, any random **6:129**

[122] 6:059–6:061.

selection of entities should do so. Candrakīrti does, of course, accept that personal and karmic continuity should be explained as causal continuity, but argues that this only makes sense if neither the entities connected, nor the relation connecting them, are regarded as substantial, ultimately real entities.

Moreover, there appears to be strong scriptural evidence against the proposed view of the aggregates as the self. In the Buddhist tradition we find a list of 'unanswered questions' or 'indeterminate points' (*avyākṛtavastu*).[123] In relation to these the Buddha argues that various speculative views, such as the view that the world (understood as the perceiver and his experiences) is finite or not, or that the Buddha exists or does not exist after death, are the result of ignorance and cannot be answered. Yet if the self is not distinct from the aggregates, the Buddha should not exist after his death, since aggregates cease when entering *parinirvāṇa*, and as such the world, the perceiver, and his experiences come to an end. In this case the Buddha should not have said that the claim that the Buddha does no longer exist after his death, and the claim that the world is finite, are products of ignorance, and cannot be affirmed, but that these are in fact correct positions.

6:130 If the self was identical with the aggregates in the way the Saṃmitīya position asserts, then the realization of selflessness that constitutes part of enlightenment would simply be the realization that the five aggregates, matter, and the various psychological functions that make up the person, failed to exist. Yet that is not what the Saṃmitīya, who maintains that the aggregates do exist, wants to say. It is evident that this difficulty is not entailed if the self is only taken to be superimposed on the aggregates, rather than considered as identical with them, since the realization that something is imputed on something else does not imply the nonexistence of the latter.

123 See, for example, the *Vacchagottasaṃyutta* (Bhikkhu Bodhi 2000: 1031–1033).

The Saṃmitīya might be tempted to respond that the realization of the nonexistence of the self only applies to the substantial self postulated by the non-Buddhist schools and it is the absence of this *ātman*, not the absence of the aggregates, that is realized by the meditator realizing selflessness. But this move crucially relies on equivocating on the term 'self,' using it to refer to the five aggregates in one part of the argument (e.g., when discussing the workings of karma), and to substantial selves postulated by the non-Buddhist schools in others (when referring to the realization of selflessness). Obviously the term cannot refer to both, since the *ātman* is permanent and unchanging, while the aggregates are not. Yet simply switching the meaning of a term to evade the unwanted consequences of one's thesis is hardly a sustainable argumentative strategy.

If the realization of selflessness was simply the realization of the absence of an *ātman* in the aggregates, matter, for example, would appear very much as it appears to the ordinary perceiver, as even the non-Buddhist who believes in a substantial self does not consider matter to contain an *ātman*. But this means that the realization of selflessness would not actually entail the realization of the empty nature of matter, that is the realization that matter (and by extension, the other aggregates) differ fundamentally in the way they appear to us (as substantial, conceptualization-independent entities) from the way they exist (dependently originated and hence empty). Yet the Buddhists maintain that it is only the realization of emptiness that will lead to the cessation of harmful emotional involvement with entities deemed to be substantially real. The assumption that there is an *ātman* present in these entities is no more than an epiphenomenon of the more fundamental misconception of locating intrinsic natures in entities that really lack them (after all, materialists like the Cārvākas will also realize the absence of an *ātman* in the aggregates but are still trapped in cyclic existence). Therefore, if the realization of selflessness is understood only in the attenuated form of the realization of the absence of an *ātman* in the **6:131** aggregates it is hard to understand how it could be conducive to the attainment of *nirvāṇa*.

Refutation of the self and aggregates as identical by scripture

6:132 As always in the discussion of Buddhist philosophy, the systematic question at hand (in this case, whether or not there is a self separate from the aggregates, and whether it is, as the Saṃmitīya suppose, identical with the aggregates) cannot be discussed without addressing the scriptural question of what position the Buddhist *sūtra*s take on this matter. The opponent claims that because the Buddha asserted that those who see the self only see the aggregates,[124] the aggregates are to be considered as identical with
6:133 the self. However, Candrakīrti notes, as the context of this passage makes clear, the Buddha wants to say that the clinging at the self at the level of conventional truth is not directed at any entity other than the five aggregates (such as a substantial *ātman* postulated by the non-Buddhist schools), and continues to point out immediately afterward in the passage that taking any of the aggregates to be the self is erroneous. As such, the scriptural passage cited by the opponent does not support his position.

Refutation of the self as the collection of aggregates: the analogy of the chariot

6:134 However, even if the Buddha said of *each one* of the aggregates that it is not the self, this still leaves open the possibility that the *collection of all of them together* is identical with the self, in the same way as a forest is not identical with any one of the trees it contains, but is the collection of all of them taken together. This raises the problem that the Buddha also stated that the self is its own master, is what is tamed through spiritual practice, and the witness of one's experiences.[125]

[124] *Khandasaṃyutta*, Saṃyutta Nikāya 22.47 (Bikkhu Bodhi 2000: 885).

[125] The idea of the self as the master (*nātha*) is a major theme in the *Ātmavarga* chapter of the *Udānavarga*; for the notion of the self as tamed (*dama*) see the *Aśvavarga* chapter

But assuming that the opponent, as a fellow-Buddhist, accepts that the self plays these functional roles at the conventional level, it is hard to see how the mere collection of the aggregates, which the opponent identifies with the self, could do so.

Candrakīrti elucidates this point by comparing the relationship between the self and the aggregates to that of a chariot and its parts.[126] Simply collecting together two wheels, an axle, and all the other parts of a chariot will not give us anything we can drive in, so why should we assume that the mere collection of the aggregates can provide us with something that can perform the role of a master, be tamed, or act as a witness? Rather, the functioning chariot is something dependent on its parts, and so a self is something dependent on its aggregates, instead of simply being a collection of the aggregates. **6:135**

We have to distinguish the *mere collection of the chariot-parts* and the *chariot-parts put together in the right way*. Only the latter can fulfill a function, so the situation needs to be described in terms of two entities, the appropriator (*upādātṛ*, the chariot) and the appropriated basis (*upādāna*, the chariot-parts), not just in terms of one, the appropriated basis. Similarly, when referring to the self, we cannot describe it simply in terms of its appropriated basis, the aggregates, as the Saṃmitīya opponent holds, but need to understand it as an appropriator dependent on its appropriated basis. This is why the Buddha describes the self as "dependent on the aggregates."[127]

and 17.10 (Rockhill 1883). For the notion of being a witness (*sākṣitā*) see, for example, Shaw 2006b: 180.

[126] Although any complex material entity could have been used as an example here, that of the chariot is particularly pertinent in the context of discussing the self, given the well-known Indian metaphoric reference to the rider and the chariot representing the *ātman* and the body (see e.g. *Kaṭha Upaniṣad* 3.3, Olivelle 1998: 238–239, and, more generally, Schlieter 2016).

[127] *Saghātāvagga*, Saṃyutta Nikāya 5:10 (Bikkhu Bodhi 2000: 230).

6:136 In the case of the chariot, what distinguishes the mere collection of its parts from a functioning chariot is that the parts are put together to form a certain shape. Similarly, the self might be considered to be the aggregates put together in a certain way. It is unclear, however, how the analogy is supposed to extend from the chariot-parts to the aggregates, since the former are all physical, and so easily arranged into a physical shape. But four of the aggregates are psychological in nature, and while restricting the self to a complex consisting only of the first aggregate, matter, is not a possibility for the Saṃmitīya, the alternative claim that the mental aggregates are put together with matter in a specific 'shape' seems to raise more questions than it answers.[128]

6:137 From a semantic perspective the relationship between the self and the aggregates is that between an agent and what is acted upon, as the self is supposed to be the agent that takes the five aggregates, the body and various psychological states, as its own. If we assume, with the opponent, that the self is simply a collection of the aggregates we would have to conclude that either the agent is identical with what is acted upon, or that there is only what is acted upon, but no agent.

The former option is problematic since Candrakīrti rejects the claim that agent and object of action could be identical.[129] Indeed, such an identity is not assumed in ordinary circumstances. We do not in general accept the identity of agent and object of action: the potter is not identical with the clay he works with, the fire is not identical with the fuel it burns, and so forth. Why, then,

[128] The Saṃmitīya reply here leaves open the option that the 'shape' of the aggregates might be understood not as a physical shape, but as a spatio-temporal causal structure, including material elements (located in time and space) and mental elements (located in time only). If this idea can be made to work (the Saṃmitīya does not provide any details) this would, however, be hard to reconcile with the idea that we are still dealing just with a collection of the aggregates, rather than with an additional, though dependent, entity, namely the structure that the five aggregates jointly form.

[129] See 6:73–6:76, 6:163.

should we accept such an identity in the case of the self and the aggregates?

The latter option seems to be hardly more viable, since agent and object acted upon form a mutually dependent pair: there can only be one when we have the other. In the semantic framework within which we operate, without something to act on, nothing can be described as an agent, and to be conceived of as the object of an action, we must also conceive of something that carries out that action.

Candrakīrti is not trying to argue that semantic or grammatical considerations indicate structures at the level of ultimate reality, as some classical Indian philosophers do, but that when we frame the relation between the self and the aggregates at the conventional level, we need to do so in the structure our linguistic conventions provide. If one entity generates another, like 'left' generates 'right,' and 'up' generates 'down,' we need to accept both if we accept either; we cannot simply declare one to be nonexistent. Of course that does not mean that we have to regard them as ultimately real or substantially existent, and as Candrakīrti points out in his autocommentary, scriptural references to actions without agents should be regarded precisely as rejections of such an ultimately real agent. Instead, entities like 'left,' 'right,' and so on need to be regarded as conventionally and interdependently real within the conceptual framework we use for reflecting about such things in the first place.

The relationship between the self and the aggregates has been 6:138
described by the Buddha, who pointed out that the self is imputed
on the basis of fundamental elements of matter, of the sensory
organs, including the mind, and the pleasant, unpleasant, or neu- 6:139
tral ways in which the mind can be involved with the various sensory objects.

As such, the self is, as an imputed entity, different from the aggregates, yet not the very same thing as them, it does not exist separately from them (as the non-Buddhist's *ātman* would be taken to exist), nor is it identical with them (as the Saṃmitīya conception would have it). Having run out of conceptual locations in which a substantial self could be placed, we are led to the conclusion that such a self fails to exist.

Difficulties with mis-identifying the object of negation

6:140 If the self was identified with the collection of aggregates, or with a single aggregate, as the Saṃmitīya propose, as long as those aggregates are present, some aspect of the self would remain. The opponent might therefore claim that the realization of selflessness can take place while the aggregates still exist because this realization is not the removal of the sense of self that identifies it with the aggregates, but realizes the nonexistence of a self understood in terms of a permanent *ātman* as postulated by the non-Buddhist schools. But as Candrakīrti has argued before, such a transcendent self would be utterly unconnected with any of our physical and psychological properties, and therefore hardly promising as a point of attachment for the cognitive and emotional illusions that keep us bound to cyclic existence. Moreover, the opponent is also committed to the claim that the realization of selflessness leads to liberation, and how the realization of the absence a permanent *ātman* is supposed to bring this about remains unclear.

6:141 If the self and locus of attachment are misindentified, leading to the negation of a sense of self that never led to our entrapment in cyclic existence in the first place, we cannot expect the resulting erroneous 'realization of selflessness' to have any power to liberate us from *saṃsāra*. If we are afraid of a snake hiding in our wall, convincing ourselves of the nonexistence of a wholly different entity (such as an elephant in our room) is not going to remove our fear. On the contrary, being lulled into a false sense of security by the absence of the elephant, we are more likely to be harmed by the snake's bite. In the same way, negating an erroneous sense of self is not only pointless, but also dangerous as it prevents us from apprehending the harm produced by the remaining sense of self not covered by our initial negation.

Self and aggregates are not support and supported

Having negated the existence of a self as a separate entity over and above the aggregates (such as the non-Buddhist's *ātman*) and as the very same thing as the aggregates (the Saṃmitīya position), can we conceive of the two as related by a relationship of dependence or support? As a bowl keeps the yogurt it contains in place, could the self support the aggregates, making them hang together as a unity, or could the aggregates support the self, giving it individuality? Bowl and yogurt are, of course, separate entities that can exist in the absence of one another. Yet, as Candrakīrti has argued before, this is not a helpful way to conceive of the relationship between self and aggregates. If the self existed wholly apart from our physical and psychological states it is unclear that it would be enough of a self to qualify as *our* self, and to function as something we care about in the way in which we care about our self. The bowl, on the other hand, would remain a bowl, whether or not it is filled with yogurt. 6:142

Note that the difference or non-identity between self and aggregates that would be required here is not the intrinsic difference Candrakīrti considers as holding between cause and effect in 6:014, for such a strong notion of difference would preclude the obtaining of any dependence relation. The opponent's idea is rather that of two entities that can stand in a relationship of dependence and support (as the bowl supports the yogurt which depends on it for its spatial coherence), even though each can also exist without the other one. It is this latter consequence which Candrakīrti considers as problematic.

The self does not possess the aggregates

An alternative proposal would be to suggest that the self owns the aggregates, that is, that our body and psychological states each belong to our self which acts as their possessor. We can make sense of ownership in cases where one entity owns another, separate one, for example when a man owns a cow, or where owner and owned are the same, and one entity inheres in another one, for example 6:143

when we speak of me owning my body. But neither the claim that the self and the aggregates are identical because the self is *just the aggregates*, nor the claim that the self is an entity that exists quite separately from them holds up in the light of the preceding criticisms. As such, there appears to be no further conceptual space in which we could develop the ownership model.

The 20 wrong views of the self

6:144 Candrakīrti considers four ways in which each of the five aggregates could be related to the self: being identical with the self, being possessed by the self, having the self contained in it, and containing the self. Formulating this view for each aggregate, matter (*rūpa*), sensation (*vedanā*), discrimination (*saṃjñā*), volition (*saṃskāra*), and consciousness (*vijñāna*), results in a list of twenty possible accounts of the self.[130]

The four ways in which self and aggregate could be related can be spelled out in terms of three relations: identity, possession, and containment. On the basis of these we can formulate six different possibilities:

1. *x* and *y* are identical
2. *x* and *y* are not identical
3. *x* possesses *y*
4. *y* possesses *x*
5. *x* contains *y*
6. *y* contains *x*.

6:145 As Candrakīrti makes clear in his autocommentary, possibility 2 (the two relata being distinct) is not considered here because this has already been discussed as the non-Buddhist view that

[130] This list of twenty views, spelled out as four positions applied to the five aggregates, finds its earliest expression in the Pāli canon and is subsequently taken up in a variety of different Buddhist discussions. Wayman 1984: 215–223 presents a helpful overview. See also Lamotte 1944–1980, 2: 737, note 3, 4:15–17; Thrangu Rinpoche 2012.

the self and aggregates are distinct entities. The possibility of the aggregates possessing the self (possibility 4) is not specifically addressed, perhaps because a possessor is assumed to be unitary (if all the aggregates possess the self, which one is in control in the case of conflict?). This leaves us with the four possibilities listed by Candrakīrti. Their refutations follow from the discussion presented previously. The rejection of the view that the self is nothing but the collection of the aggregates refutes possibility 1, that self and aggregates are identical. Possession (possibility 3) has just been discussed in 6:143. Containment (possibilities 5 and 6) presupposes that the two relata are distinct entities, a possibility that has also been addressed previously.

Candrakīrti compares the mistaken view that the transitory collection of psycho-physical aggregates constitutes a self (*satkāyadṛṣṭi*), which is common to all beings, to a massive mountain-range from which rise, in those beings capable of philosophical analysis, the summits of the twenty wrong views of the self. Once *satkāyadṛṣṭi* is destroyed through the realization of the nonexistence of a substantial self, the twenty wrong views of the self resting on it are abandoned and the first level of enlightenment, the state of a stream-enterer (*śrotāpanna*), is achieved. **6:146**

6b.3 Refutation of the self as neither identical with the aggregates, nor different from them

The opponent now introduces an alternative conception of the self, also associated with the Saṃmitīya, according to which the self exists substantially, insofar as it is the producer of karmic seeds, and the experiencer of their fruit, is the basis for our sense of self, and perceived by the six sense consciousnesses, but cannot be said to be permanent or impermanent, or identical with the aggregates, or different from them.

From the claim that the self cannot be permanent (as it could then not relate to our impermanent physical and psychological states), and that it cannot be impermanent (as this would undermine its continuity, and its ability to experience karmic effects), that it cannot simply be identical with the aggregates (as it would be as impermanent and insubstantial as the aggregates) or distinct from them (for such a transcendent self could not be an object of prudential concern), the opponent does not conclude that there is no self, but that it cannot be described by any of these predicates.[131]

6:147 The Ābhidharmika opponent does not consider the mind, which it takes to be substantially real, as inexpressible in terms of identity and difference relative to the body. He simply regards it as an entity distinct from the body. Candrakīrti argues that there is a logical connection between taking something to be substantially real and taking it to be inexpressible: if an entity is substantially real then it cannot also be inexpressible. Why this implication holds is not explicitly addressed by Candrakīrti.[132] I believe that in the present context the notion of inexpressibility is not to be understood as referring to limits of our representational system. The idea is not that the identity or difference of the self and the aggregates is somehow fixed by the world, yet our conceptual resources could not determine the matter either way. Rather, inexpressibility mirrors ontological indeterminacy: for the Saṃmitīya there *is* no relation of identity or difference that holds between the aggregates and the self as they understand it. However, Candrakīrti argues, substantial things cannot be ontologically related in an indeterminate way to other substantial things. If *a*'s relationship to a substantial *b* is indeterminate in this way, this is an argument against admitting *a* into our ontology, not an argument for admitting an entity that is impoverished in its identity relations with other entities deemed to be substantially real like *b*.

When we say that $\sqrt{2}$ is neither identical with, nor distinct from $\frac{707}{500}$, this means that the set of numbers we presently consider, i.e.,

[131] See Duerlinger 2003: 20–21.

[132] Duerlinger (2013: 141) argues that an entity's substantiality implies, and its inexpressibility excludes having a determinate relation of identity or difference to the "causal basis of its conception."

the set of rational numbers we currently quantify over (or take to be substantially real) does not contain $\sqrt{2}$, not that it does contain it, but that according to the theory of rational numbers the truth-value of any instance of $\sqrt{2} = a$, where a is any rational number, is undecided.

For the Saṃmitīya there is not (and indeed could not be) any ontological indeterminacy about how the mind and the body are related by identity and difference, as they take the self and the aggregates to be both substantially real. Either the self is identical with or distinct from the aggregates (both of these options have been shown to be deficient above), or it fails to be substantial, which is incompatible with the central claim of the Saṃmitīya.

The Saṃmitīya accepts that an insubstantial entity like a clay pot, **6:148**
which depends for its existence on its material parts, is related to these parts neither by the relation of identity, nor by that of difference, and is in this sense inexpressible. It is neither identical with them, since this would imply that the pot, which is one, is also many, nor is it different from them, since that would imply the existence of a separate entity, the pot, over and above all the parts. Candrakīrti agrees, but argues that this is precisely because the pot is empty of intrinsic nature. It is merely a superimposition, a label used in our everyday discourse. In the very same way one should think about the self, which relates to the aggregates precisely as the pot relates to its parts.

Verses 6:147–6:148 look at the implication relation between substantial existents standing in identity-difference relations with other things from two different directions. In the previous verse Candrakīrti has argued that since the Saṃmitīya take the self to be substantial, they would also have to accept that it stands in such identity or difference relations. In the present verse, considering the contrapositive of the implication relation, he argues that since the failure of an entity to stand in identity-difference relations with other things indicates its insubstantial nature, regarding the self as being 'inexpressible' in this way implies that it cannot also be regarded as substantially real.

6:149 Having explained that substantial existence is incompatible with indeterminacy relative to identity relations, but that such indeterminacy *is* compatible with merely nominal existence, Candrakīrti now points out that the Saṃmitīya self lacks the very characteristic of thinghood. Entities that the opponent regards as substantially real, such as the mind, are related by identity and difference to entities deemed substantially real. The mind is identical with itself, but different from matter. Whatever is substantially real is embedded in a network of identity relations, such that any entity is related to any entity (including itself) either by the relation of identity or by the relation of difference. The Saṃmitīya self stands outside of the network of such relations with whatever else is real. Lacking such key features of thinghood, it should not be regarded as a shadowy entity ontologically unrelated to other things, but should be considered as nonexistent.

6b.4 Summarizing the view of the self

6:150 In conclusion, Candrakīrti notes that our sense of self does not have a substantially real basis (since when we analyze it, we only find the individual aggregates). Nor do the self and the aggregates stand in a relation of identity (the self would then be simultaneously one and many) or difference (otherwise we should be able to find a self separate from the aggregates), support and supported, or possessor and possessed (all of these presuppose that the self and aggregates are separate entities). Instead of assuming the existence of a substantially real self that stands in any of these relations, we need to realize that the self is only a conventional designation.

6b.5 The analogy of the chariot

The chariot does not exist in any of the seven ways

6:151 At this stage Candrakīrti comes back to the analogy of the chariot from 6:135, listing seven possible relations the chariot could have to its parts and rejecting them all. He notes that

1. The chariot is not different from its parts.
2. The chariot is not identical with its parts.
3. The chariot does not possess its parts.
4. The chariot does not depend on its parts.
5. The parts do not depend on the chariot.
6. The chariot is not the mere collection of its parts.
7. The chariot is not the arrangement of its parts.

These seven possible relations conceive of the connection of wholes and parts in terms of four concepts, identity, possession, mereological dependence, and collection, each of which, apart from the second,[133] is presented as a pair. We have met the concepts used to construct these seven relations earlier in the text. Candrakīrti's further comments will focus on the final two possible relations. How identity and difference of parts and whole are refuted is evident in the light of the preceding discussion; as Candrakīrti argued above in 6:143, the relationship of possession requires the two relata to be either identical or distinct. The 4th and 5th relation presuppose that the whole is a distinct entity over and above its parts, and is related to them by a dependence relation.

As Candrakīrti has previously discussed in 6:135, if the chariot were the mere collection of the parts, the chariot would still exist if the parts are disassembled. The matter is raised here again in order to introduce a further difficulty for the 7th possible relation. **6:152**

Arguing that the chariot is an arrangement of the parts obviously presupposes the existence of the parts to be arranged. Yet being a chariot-part depends on the existence of the chariot, the whole, something that possesses the parts. The opponent, however, denies the existence of such a part-possessor, since the position he defends is that the chariot is *just* the parts put together. But if there is no

[133] Again, the reason why Candrakīrti does not discuss the inverse of 3, the parts not possessing the chariot is probably related to doubts about the feasibility of a plurality possessing a unitary entity (see the comments on 6:144).

chariot yet, there can also be no parts to arrange into a chariot. If, on the other hand, we simply identify the chariot with the arrangement of the parts, the construction turns out to be impredicative:[134] we need to presuppose the arrangement of the parts in order to construct the very arrangement of the parts we are supposed to bring about.

Some commentators[135] have argued that Candrakīrti's objection here confuses existential and notional dependence. The chariot-parts might well depend notionally on the chariot, meaning that we could not *describe* them as chariot-parts if there was no chariot. But they are not existentially dependent on the existence of the chariot: the chariot's wheels do not stop existing when we take the chariot apart. Hence there is no difficulty with identifying the chariots with the parts put together in a specific way.

Consider, however, a representation of a chariot made from the pieces of a tangram puzzle. While the pieces continue to exist, there seems little justification to regard them as a parts of a chariot-representation, as the same parts could be used to make representations of a cat, a man, or a thousand other things. The same holds for the Ābhidharmika's ultimate constituents, the *dharmas*. These, too, could be reassembled to make various other mascroscopic entities. But this means that it is exceedingly difficult to conceive of the chariot as 'this collection of *dharmas*, assembled in the right way,' as the opponent proposes. First, how do we specify the 'right way' without appealing to the very notion of a chariot we are trying to construct here in the first place? And second, why specify a specific collection of *dharmas*, given that many other collections could also be used to assemble a chariot from them? As such, neither the collection of *dharmas* that make up the chariot, nor the way its members are assembled, can be specified without

134 For further discussion of the problems connected with impredicative definitions see Linnebo 2021; Mittelstraß 1995 s.v. 'imprädikativ/Imprädikativität,' 2: 216–218.

135 Siderits/Katsura 2024.

reference to the chariot. Yet if a non-circular ontological analysis of the chariot as the arrangement of parts is supposed to be successful, precisely such a specification would be required.

The 'arrangement' of the parts of the chariot refers to the parts 6:153
assembled together, producing the specific shape of the chariot. Continuing with the discussion of the 7th possible relation, we can wonder whether the specific shape of the chariot is (a) the shape of the individual chariot-parts, or whether (b) it is the assembled shape of the collection of chariot-parts. If (a), it would either have to be the shape of the individual chariot-parts pre- or post-assembly. In the former case, the chariot-parts did of course have their pre-assembly shape before the chariot was put together, so as there was no chariot then, there should not be one now, if all we mean by 'the chariot is the arrangement of its parts' is that each of the chariot-parts has the pre-assembly shape it has. On the other 6:154
hand, if what we mean by this is that each of the chariot-parts has the post-assembly shape it has, we realize that because the shape of the individual wheels, the axle, and so forth is not observed to change during assembly, the unassembled chariot should again be the same as the assembled chariot. We might worry that the underlying assumption is not actually true. Because no wheel is perfectly rigid, when bearing a load as part of an assembled chariot it will be somewhat more elliptical than when removed from the chariot.[136] In response we should note, first, that this might well be an effect of each of the chariot's parts having further parts in turn. The only position Candrakīrti seems to need to defend here is that at the level of the most fundamental particles (whatever these are taken to be) the properties of each individual particle do not change when you put several of them together. Yet it appears that not even this needs to be presupposed here. Even if the shape of the parts changed post-assembly, this is unlikely to help supporting the position that the whole being the arrangement of its parts is to be spelled out as

[136] Compare the discussion in Siderits/Katsura 2024.

saying that each part has the specific post-assembly shape it has. If we take a large number of rubber bands and form them into a ball, each will have a shape different from the one it had when all the rubber bands were still in the box. Still, if being the ball was just each rubber band having its post-assembly state, this would imply that if we somehow froze each rubber band in its current position, and then laid them all out on our table we would still have a ball, which is obviously false. As such, any way of spelling out the idea that the chariot is the arrangement of its parts as having *only* to do with the specific shape of each particular chariot-part appears unsatisfactory.

6:155 In fact, option (b), that the chariot being the arrangement of the chariot-parts refers to the overall shape or structure exemplified by the *collection* of the parts, rather than by each part individually, is intuitively much more plausible. A difficulty arises, however, since Candrakīrti's interlocutor is supposed to be both a foundationalist in general, and a reductionist about collections. On the one hand, he assumes that each conceptual imputation needs to bottom out in something that is not a conceptual imputation in turn. On the other hand, he believes that collections, sets, classes, and so on are nothing over and above their members, that is, that they are conceptual imputations as well. As such, the collection of chariot-parts could not provide the foundation for the conceptual imputation 'chariot.'

6:156 The best the opponent could offer in response here is that the chariot is a conceptual imputation that is not based on a substantial 'basis of designation,' but that it is a conceptual imputation based on another conceptual imputation. Candrakīrti agrees with this, and argues that this is in fact how all things exist. When we backtrack from an effect to its cause we do not get from something that is not substantially real (since it is designated on the basis of causes and conditions) to something substantially real (whatever the fundamental level of reality is at which the causal powers reside), but we simply discover that at the basis of every unreal entity there is another entity that is equally unreal. In the same way as tracking down an illusory deer will not provide us with real meat, the analysis of conventionally real phenomena will not yield ultimately real phenomena that constitute their foundation.

The opponent might object that Candrakīrti's conception of the 6:157
world as illusory all the way down is hardly satisfactory, since, according to the Abhidharma analysis, the chain of merely imputed entities terminates at the level of fundamentally real *dharmas*. The Ābhidharmika accepts that the chariot is not ultimately real, because it is simply superimposed on the collection of the chariot-parts, and even if he accepts Candrakīrti's point that the collection of chariot-parts, too, is only a conceptually imputed entity he can still assume that it is superimposed on ultimately real entities, namely the most fundamental material entities, the *rūpa-dharmas*. However, in order to regard these as ultimately real we need to provide an account of their origin. Are they self-produced, caused by fundamentally different things, caused by both, or randomly originated? Earlier in the text Candrakīrti has argued against all of these possibilities, and so it seems that even pushing our analysis further to the *rūpa-dharmas* does not provide us with anything substantially real.

The chariot exists as a mere dependent designation

Having shown all seven possible relations between a whole and its 6:158
parts to be problematic, Candrakīrti argues that any analysis that bases itself on them is unsatisfactory from the relative and from the ultimate perspective. Not only will the positions that a partite object is different from its parts, identical with its parts, and so on fail to account for the ultimate ontological nature of part-whole relations, even as an analysis of the mereological intuitions that underlie our conventional thinking about parts and wholes these seven possible relations are unsatisfactory. The opponent might then wonder how we can ever refer to chariots or other partite entities in ordinary discourse. This, however, Candrakīrti responds, is only a problem for the opponent, who believes that the seven conceptual structures

discussed above are the *only* ones that can undergird our ordinary mereological discourse, and that we can only refer to things with parts if our analysis can produce some substantial ground for them either conventionally or ultimately. The Mādhyamika has an alternative to substantial grounds, and therefore he is not committed to the claim that if part and whole are not related to each other by *any* of the seven possible relations, and if our analysis fails to ground partite entities, all talk about parts and wholes becomes nonsensical. This alternative is dependent origination. Wholes are mere imputations on parts, which are in turn only the products of imputational acitivity.[137] As long as we do not try to analyze the final nature of parts and wholes, we can unproblematically refer to partite objects in everyday discourse.

6:159 As such, we cannot only refer to the chariot at the level of conventional reality, but also to the specific implications of that term such as being possessor of parts, a whole, an agent, or an appropriator of its constituents.[138] This point is directed against the Ābhidharmika opponent who would argue that even though there are ultimately real parts, there is no possessor of parts, no whole, no agent, and no appropriator. Candrakīrti has argued above that once we agree that one relatum of such relations is ultimately real, while the other one is not there at all, we end up with a scenario in which neither relatum is there at all, because considerations that speak against the

[137] The question whether this is the case because there is an infinite descent of imputations, or because the imputations form a circular structure can be left open for the time being.

[138] Even though the precise difference between these four terms is not essential for the point Candrakīrti is making here, and even though there appears to be no consensus among Candrakīrti's commentators on how their difference is to be understood, we might try to differentiate them as follows. The 'possessor of parts' conceptualizes the part-whole complex with emphasis on the entity that has the parts, the 'whole' with emphasis on what the parts jointly constitute. Reference to an 'agent' underlines the functional role of a part-whole complex as something that does something (as such, we would not describe it as composed of physical parts, but of functional sub-units that carry out sub-functions of the whole). The 'appropriator' is primarily relevant in the case of the physico-psychological complex that constitutes a person by focusing on the parts that take other parts as their own, as, for example, the non-physical aggregates consider the physical aggregate as their associated body (this is how the role of the appropriator is understood by Tsong kha pa (Jinpa 2021: 462–463)).

ultimate reality of the whole will in due course also question the ultimate reality of the parts. Rather, we should not differentiate between parts and wholes (and other associated pairs of concepts) in terms of ultimate reality, but treat both as having the same ontological status, being conceptually imputed, dependently originated, and hence empty. Both play their roles within the "nominal framework of mere designation."[139] There is no need for ontological analysis to revise the way partite objects are conceptualized in our everyday interaction with them, regarding some of them as part of the ultimate structure of reality, while adopting an error theory toward others.

When analyzing any partite[140] entity in terms of the seven possible relations mentioned in 6:151 in an attempt to detect its intrinsic nature we realize that no such nature is to be found. This then leads the investigator to insight into the empty nature of phenomena, regarding them as existing without any intrinsic nature. Such insight, however, does not undermine the existence of these entities from a conventional point of view, where no analysis of their fundamental nature is attempted. Even though Candrakīrti points out in his autocommentary that analysis renders conventional reality nonexistent, but when left unanalyzed it exists through worldly agreement, this does not mean that Madhyamaka analysis has any ontological consequences that turns existent things into nonexistent things. Rather, things with intrinsic natures were never there in the first place, and analysis removes the mistaken superimposition that they were. Without such analysis, the consensus of everyday conventions continues to produce the belief in intrinsic natures. **6:160**

[139] Jinpa 2021: 463.

[140] Note that Candrakīrti's analysis is not just applicable to the non-atomic, but also to partless entities possessing different properties. For these the question is not how they relate to their parts, but how, as individuals or instantiators, they relate to the properties they instantiate.

6:161 The opponent might object that while the chariot does not vanish in its entirety as the result of Madhyamaka analysis, the mistaken superimposition does. As a consequence, after the investigator has concluded his analysis the chariot-parts still appear to him, but not the whole that the conceptual imputation mistakenly superimposed on it. Candrakīrti responds that once the whole is destroyed, the parts will no longer exist, as once a cloth is burnt, its threads have ceased existing too.

Two things might strike us as curious about this response. First, are there not other scenarios in which the whole is destroyed while the parts are left behind (if we decompose the cloth into its constituent threads, for example)? And second, do we not face the same danger of equivocating between notional and existential dependence raised in relation to 6:152? We might agree that once the chariot is decomposed or burnt we do not want to *describe* the remainders as chariot-parts, nevertheless, whatever individual things constituted the chariot before its destruction (wheels and axle, bits of carbon, *dharma*s, etc.) continue to *exist* after its destruction.

This objection would be justified if the arguments the Mādhyamika brought forward against the substantial existence of wholes did not apply to the parts that compose the wholes. Yet what Candrakīrti has in mind when he points out that the fire of reasoning burns the whole of the chariot, and burns the parts with it, is that the considerations that speak against the intrinsic nature of the one also speak against the intrinsic nature of the other. He is essentially presenting a proof by induction, with the base case being the claim that the chariot does not exist by intrinsic nature because it is mereologically dependent, and the induction step claiming that if something is mereologically dependent, its parts will also be existentially dependent. The Ābhidharmika will obviously accept the base case but not the induction step, with the Mādhyamika pointing out, for example, that since even the simple *dharma*s can only be individuated relative to the compounds in which they occur (since there is otherwise nothing that differentiates two *dharmas* of the same kind), each *dharma* must be existentially dependent on other *dharmas*. If this is accepted, Candrakīrti's inductive proof establishes that nothing, whole or part, can exist by intrinsic nature, i.e., without standing in a web of existential dependence relations involving other things.

As, by following the Madhyamaka arguments, the investigator 6:162
will be led to realize the empty nature of the chariot, without losing hold of the chariot as a conventionally real object that plays a variety of conventional roles,[141] so, when the same arguments are applied to the self, the realization of its empty nature does not undermine properties commonly associated with the self, such as depending on the aggregates, the elements,[142] and the sense spheres,[143] appropriating them as an appropriator, and being an agent acting on the appropriated as an object.

While the empty nature of the chariot does not conflict with the 6:163
fact that it plays a variety of conventional roles, it does, however, rule out that it has properties associated with a fundamentally real entity, such as impermanence, permanence, arising, ceasing, being eternal, or being substantially identical with or different from the aggregates.

If the self were identical with the aggregates, it would be as impermanent and continuously arising and ceasing as they are, but this would not accord with the constancy we associate with the self. We do not consider ourselves to be a substantially different person from the one we were five minutes ago. Moreover, the aggregates the self takes as its own would be the same as the self that is their

[141] Such as those mentioned in 6:159.

[142] *dhātu, khams*, the six sense faculties, their objects, and the sensory cognitions resulting from the contacts of organ and object.

[143] *āyatana, skye mched*, the six sense faculties, and their objects. The twelve *āyatanas* are identical with the first twelve of the eighteen *dhātus*.

appropriator, in tension with the Mādhyamika's reluctance to accept entities that reflexively act on themselves.[144]

If, on the other hand, the self was different from the inconstant aggregates and as such permanent and eternal, we would, implausibly, have to assume that we are the same self now that we were on the day we were born, that we would be if we suffered from total amnesia, or that we were several lifetimes ago. If the self was frozen in time in this way, it is unclear how it could be related to the changing physical and psychological states that we consider to make us 'us.' In addition, since a permanent self seems introspectively inaccessible, we would face the problem how an entity that we cannot in any way have direct epistemic access to could be the focus of our prudential concern in quite the same way as the self is.[145]

Any substantially real entity would have to be located somewhere in the conceptual space laid out by such ontologically fundamental concepts as permanence or identity. It would have to be either impermanent, and arising and ceasing, or permanent and eternal; it would either have to be the same as its constituents, or different from them. Since the self can be shown to be neither, Candrakīrti infers that the self is not substantially real.

6:164 It might still be unclear what the 'self-grasping mind,' that is, the part of the mind that classifies phenomena into those that constitute me, or are associated with me, and all other 'other' ones the mind takes as its object. As we have seen above, it cannot be an entity over and above the aggregates, such as a substantial soul that some non-Buddhist opponents postulate, nor can it just be the collection of the aggregates, as the Ābhidharmikas believe. Candrakīrti identifies it as the substantial self mistakenly superimposed on the aggregates (rather than just the aggregates themselves). In the case of the rope mistaken for a snake, our fear is not directed at the rope

[144] See above, 6:73–6:76 and Śāntideva's *Bodhicaryāvatāra* 9:17–19.

[145] Candrakīrti cites various passages from Nāgārjuna's *Mūlamadhyamakakārikā* in support of the claim that the self has none of the properties of permanence, impermanence, and so on. For a detailed analysis of these see Duerlinger 2013: 155–186.

(who would be afraid of a rope?), nor is it directed at a snake quite separate from the coiled-up shape in front of us (we are afraid of the entity that we believe to be present on the path right in front of us), but at the snake superimposed on the rope, which is of course fully nonexistent. In the same way the self-grasping mind neither engages with an *ātman* nor with the aggregates but with an imputed self that is projected by ignorance as a substantially real entity on the aggregates. This imputed self continues to exist until analysis begins to investigate whether the imputation of the self *as substantially real* in fact has any basis which could be regarded as substantially real.

Once the self has been realized as being mere imputation, all the entanglements that keep beings trapped in cyclic existence, which group around the view of 'mine' relating to the self, together with the superimposition of the substantially real self, drop away. Once there is no agent, action, which stands in a mutual dependence relation with it, ceases. Grasping and the accumulation of karma having ceased, the practitioner obtains liberation. He may then either enter the *nirvāṇa* of the *arhat* or continue on the bodhisattva path. **6:165**

Other entities are similarly dependently designated

The sevenfold analysis of the chariot is applicable to all other things. **6:166** These, too, are not different from or identical with their parts or constituents, do not possess them, do not depend on them, are not depended on, and are not the mere collection or the arrangement of their parts or constituents. Instead they are mistaken imputations erroneously regarded as substantially real by general worldly consensus. When operating within such worldly consensus their existence in this way should not be questioned,[146] just as the Buddha,

[146] It is only when we employ the Madhyamaka technique to analyze such entities in order to find their intrinsic nature in the context of philosophical and meditative inquiry that the disagreement between conventional acceptance of intrinsic natures and their ultimate rejection becomes important.

who saw the empty nature of all things, did not take issue with the ontological status everyday agreement ascribed to the entities in its focus.

6:167 Conceptual pairs like part and whole, quality and qualified, desire and the one who desires, characteristic and characterized all exist through mutual imputation, and as such we cannot have one member of the pair without the other. Given that Candrakīrti regards the dependence relation involved here as existential, this implies that we cannot account for them in terms of an ontological analysis which regards one part of a pair as substantially real, and the other one as only derivative, as the former could not exist without the latter also existing. This failure of not being able to provide a specific analysis of these pairs in terms of ultimately real entities does not, however, imply that such concepts cannot be used in an ordinary, transactional context that do not involve attempted analyses seeking to ascertain what is fundamentally real.

6:168 In addition to conceptual pairs like part and whole, quality and qualified, and so on, cause and effect, too, are imputed by mutual dependence. Even though the idea of temporal sequence appears to be essential to the notions of cause and effect, we cannot say that one is prior to the other. If the cause is prior to the effect, there is not yet any effect relative to which it could be a cause, and if the effect is prior to the cause, the effect would have come into existence without the cause. One might object that this is once again mixing up different senses of dependence and priority: surely the effect cannot exist before its cause, but the cause can very well exist before the effect, it just cannot be *described* as a cause. If the seed does not produce a sprout, it can no longer be described as a cause, but this does not mean that it does not exist.

This concern might be justified if Candrakīrti tried to argue from mutual imputational dependence to the nonexistence of causation. This, however, is not the case. Rather, Candrakīrti's aim is to show that the frameworks of ultimately real existence and of causation cannot be combined. The opponent's position is that the causal structure is anchored all the way down at the fundamental level of reality, not that the causal network is simply a conceptual shadow projected on a fundamentally non-causal world.[147] What he means by this is a level of entities existing by their intrinsic natures, that is, entities having natures they have in a lonely state, independent of other things, and entities having natures that characterize only them, but not other entities. Yet the idea of a causal network contradicts both of these assumptions. First, 'being a cause' is a relational property, so it is hard to conceive of anything having this property just on its own. Second, without any specific effect it could be related to, the cause-ness of any entity becomes wholly indistinct. As any liquid could be a glue, for it is always conceivable that we can cook up some substances that can be made to stick together by it, anything could be a cause, as long as we are free to choose what counts as the effect. As such, 'being a cause' would no longer count as picking out a nature that only characterizes a single entity, but it will characterize many of them indiscriminately. If, therefore, the framework of ultimately real things with intrinsic natures and the framework of causal structures are incompatible, we have to let go of one, and the Mādhyamika recommends we let go of intrinsic natures. As a result, there is no scope anymore for analyzing the causal relation in terms of one or two ultimately real relata.[148] Instead, they have to be understood as being mutually dependent on another, and without assuming that their causal description is in any way grounded in the fundamental level of reality.

If 'being a cause' and 'being an effect' were properties located at **6:169**
the fundamental level of reality, there should be an answer to the question what the spatial and temporal relations between entities

[147] Note that this is not the Mādhyamika's position either, for his arguments question the coherence of the idea of a world 'as it is in itself' wholly free from all conceptual structures.

[148] The former would be the position that takes both cause and effect as ultimately real, the latter might take only one (the present entity) as ultimately real, considering the other to be either a memory or an anticipation.

characterized by these properties look like. Focusing for the time being on their temporal relation, we should then be able to ask whether cause and effect are temporally contiguous, so that there is no moment of time between the last moment of the cause and the first moment of the effect, or whether they separated by one or more moments. If they are contiguous, cause and effect are just one event and merge into one another like a river flowing into the ocean. As there is no fact to the matter where the river ends and the ocean begins, other than agreements to label things in specific ways, there would also not be any imputation-independent division of events into the part that constitutes the cause, and the part that constitutes the effect. But if the cause *c* is separated from the effect *e* by at least one moment, how is its relation to *e* different from that to some other event *f* that also begins one moment after *c*? Neither pair 'meets' in any way, so why does *c* not fail to produce *e*, as it fails to produce *f*, or why does it not produce *f* as it produces *e*? We might well have good reasons (based on expectations, habit, subjective probabilities, etc.) to regard *c*-*e* but not *c*-*f* as a causal sequence, yet it is hard to find the justification for this in the events themselves, rather than in our way of thinking about the events. As a consequence, as it seems impossible to answer the question of the contiguity between causes and events in a satisfactory manner, given that there is no third possibility apart from the two answers just discussed, we should drop the assumption that causes and effects have the kind of existence where this question could be settled in a wholly objective, rather than in a mind-dependent manner. In other words, causes and effects cannot be intrinsic properties of ultimately real things, but are conceptual imputations that prove to be of great utility in everyday transactions, but crumble under the pressure of analysis setting out to determine their ultimate features.

6:170 If cause and effect cannot be understood as either contiguous or as non-contiguous, we cannot account for the causal relation at all in any ultimate sense. In this case the supposed cause does not ultimately produce any effect, and because nothing can be taken to be a cause without producing an effect, it cannot be understood as a cause. How, then, are we are going to account for causality?

Candrakīrti replies that the whole problem of contiguity only arises if we presuppose that cause and effect connect entities that exist with intrinsic natures in an ultimate way, so that there is an objective, mind-independent, ultimate fact to the matter of how cause and effect are temporally related. But the Mādhyamika does not make this assumption, instead he regards the causal relation as illusion-like, as a mistaken mental imputation without any grounding in ultimate reality. As such, the problem of the presence or absence of contiguity disappears. If an illusionist creates the impression of an elephant flying through the air, we are not going to try to find the ultimate laws of motion that explain the specific trajectory of the elephant in space. The reason for this is that the elephant is not a real object in the first place, so that the assumption that it had some kind of nature in and of itself that made it exhibit some behavior is not one we could usefully entertain. This does not mean that the flying elephant no longer appears, just as causation (rice producing rice-sprouts, barley producing barley-sprouts, and so forth) still appears, but once we understand their empty nature we will no longer endeavor to find out truths about these entities grounded in the ultimate way things are.

Is the Madhyamaka position self-refuting?

In an intriguing move, the opponent now turns the problem of the contiguity or non-contiguity of cause and effect against the Mādhyamika's own argument. Is Candrakīrti's refutation 'in contact' or contiguous with what it refutes or not? And if neither possibility is plausible, does this not undermine the Mādhyamika's own argument, making it impossible for him to refute his opponent's position? 6:171

Those used to thinking about philosophical arguments or proofs as abstract entities, existing over and above any specific written or spoken manifestation, might find this argument curious. What could even be meant by the temporal or spatial contiguity of an entity that is not in space or time with 'what is to be refuted'? However, in the present context we have to think of philosophical arguments as specific moves in a debate. As such, they obviously take spatiotemporal form (as a sequence of sounds) and are deemed to have causal power (to change the opponent's beliefs). Yet if there is a general problem with causes discharging their effects either in a contiguous or non-contiguous manner,[149] the Madhyamaka arguments will not have any causal power to convince their opponents. The argument they have just presented is self-refuting:[150] by undermining the causal relation it simultaneously undermines the causal power of any argument to convince somebody of an argument undermining the causal relation.

6:172 Another consequence, in addition to Candrakīrti's argument being self-undermining, is that the Madhyamaka argument would refute any claim whatsoever. The Mādhyamika argues that some events *c* and *e* deemed to be cause and effect are not in contact, yet if causation can take place without contact, anything could cause anything else. Thinking of arguments and positions refuted in causal terms, as implied by the previous verse, then also entails that the Madhyamaka argument would refute any position. As a cause not in contact with its effect would equally produce everything else that it is also not in contact with, a similarly contactless refutation would fail to be in contact with what it refutes, as it fails to be in contact with any other statement, and would equally refute all of them as well. In any case, the opponent objects, the Madhyamaka refutation of causal relations with or without contact, which crucially depends on the idea that causation without contact entails that anything could cause anything else does not work, as can be demonstrated by specific examples. A magnet can attract iron even

[149] As mentioned in 6:169.

[150] The supposedly self-refuting nature of Madhyamaka arguments is also discussed in Nāgārjuna's *Vigrahāvyartanī*. See Westerhoff 2010: 43–65, 66–67, 85–86.

though it is spatially separated from it, and the eye can see a distant object. Still, the magnet does not attract *all* pieces of iron, and the eye does not see *all* objects. (Note that the opponent here focuses on the spatial, not on the temporal non-contiguity of cause and effect.) In fact, all the Mādhyamika is doing is engaging in debate for the sake of arguing, he has no position of his own to defend. As such, he cannot be regarded as a serious participant in a debate, since such participants would try to establish a position they regard as true.

Candrakīrti responds to the self-refutation charge by pointing 6:173
out that the question whether, in the final analysis, two things are contiguous or non-contiguous is only sensible for entities deemed to be ultimately real, for entities that have specific intrinsic natures allowing us to settle questions about their ultimate way of being. This is the way the opponent understands causes and effects, and as such he should be able to provide us with an answer concerning the question of contiguity. The Mādhyamika, however, does not regard his own arguments (or, for that matter, anybody else's) as ultimately real,[151] and so the difficulty does not apply to him. Faced with the incompatibility of intrinsic natures and causal relations, the Mādhyamika does not drop the causal relations, but the intrinsic natures. Given that a similar incompatibility arises between intrinsic natures and logical relations, and the Madhyamaka perspective is not invested in intrinsic natures, it can abandon them in favor of retaining logical relations, and thereby the ability to dialectically engage the opponent's argument, at the level of conventional reality.

Moreover, there is no tension between the problem of contiguity 6:174
being unresolved for an entity, and the entity fulfilling a function in a straightforward way. Candrakīrti mentions two examples, a projection of the sun for studying a solar eclipse, and the reflection of a 6:175

[151] When Candrakīrti argues that he has no position (*pakṣa*), this is to be understood as having no position that entails the existence of anything with intrinsic natures. See also Westerhoff 2010: 61–65.

face in a mirror. It is evident that both reliably fulfill functions in a familiar manner, providing precise information about the shape of the eclipse, or the location of some blemish on our face. Why is the question of whether their cause is contiguous or non-contiguous with them unresolved? In the case of the projection, Candrakīrti argues that it is wholly impossible to decide the question in either way because the projection does not exist to the slightest extent while he characterizes the reflection in the mirror as 'untrue.' This is not taken to mean that projections and reflections do not appear, but that they arise "dependent on no more than conventional practice." Instances of reflected sunlight abound, yet we pick some specific one and treat it as indicative of the sun's perceived shade during an eclipse. Such a choice cannot be made outside of a convention-based framework incorporating beliefs about optics, the motions of the heavenly bodies, the position of the observer, and so on. Similarly, objects in a mirror are not anywhere 'out there,' but are make-believe projections we interact with in a convention-based way (by regarding the person in the mirror as identical with us, despite their being an enantiomorph, by considering the mirror to reverse left and right, rather than up and down,[152] by applying the razor to our own face, rather than to the mirror, and so on). If reflections and projections can only exist within the transactional reality of a set of conventions, subjecting them to an ontological analysis trying to uncover their ultimate relations to some other fundamentally real entities would presuppose that we strip them first of all their conventionally constructed aspects. Yet stripping them in this way dissolves the entity we were trying to analyze. We do not end up with an entity 'as it is in itself,' but with no entity. Trying to take such conventionally constructed entities out of the framework of conventions they are located in is like trying to take a bubble out of water. As such, the problem of contiguity must remain unresolved for the Mādhyamika, though that does not

[152] See Westerhoff 2010b: 161–173; Eco 2018, section 4.

detract in any way from the utility of projections and reflections in astronomy and cosmetics. For Çandrakīrti, this point generalizes: because all entities derive their identity from the framework of transactional reality in which they (and we) are located, the project of ultimate ontological analysis the opponent has in mind is equally futile for them.

In Candrakīrti's autocommentary an interlocutor suggests to dissolve the difficulty of the self-refuting nature of the Mādhyamika's argument against causation by distinguishing between productive and explanatory causes.[153] Smoke, for example, is not the productive cause of fire, since smoke does not bring about fire, but it can in some circumstances be its explanatory cause, by causing us to know that fire is present where the smoke is observed.[154] He then points out that the Mādhyamika critique referred to was only formulated as a criticism of productive causes, and now the Mādhyamika's opponent uses it to apply to explanatory causality too. As such, the Madhyamaka argument is not self-undermining, since the form of causation criticized is not the same as the one operating in the argument criticizing causation. Candrakīrti, however, considers this to be an insufficient reply, since the Mādhyamika criticism of causation will affect all forms of causation, whether they are productive or explanatory. As such, he argues that we should prefer responding with the claim that the problem of contiguity remains unresolved for all kinds of causation, but that this undermines neither production nor explanation at the conventional level.

The question whether the Mādhyamika's argument (as a cause) was contiguous or non-contiguous with the refutation of the opponent (the effect) would only have any traction if either the argument, or what the argument was trying to establish, existed in a substantial manner. Only in this case could we conceive of the kind of ultimate analysis in terms of fundamental facts about temporal **6:176**

153 On the distinction between these two types of causes see also Wangchuk 2019: 278.
154 See Tauscher 1981: 117, note 61.

relations between causes and effects leading to an interesting conclusion. However, Candrakīrti takes neither his own arguments, nor their targets, to exist with intrinsic nature.

In his autocommentary Candrakīrti discusses the example of someone suffering from floaters, who uses references to the different types of hair he erroneously perceives in an argument. No part of this argument will affect or refute someone who is free from the perception of floaters. In the same way, none of the opponent's arguments, built around the notion of intrinsic nature, will affect the Mādhyamika, who rejects the existence of any entities with intrinsic natures.

In his autocommentary Candrakīrti also briefly addresses the two counterexamples the opponent introduced in 6:172, that of the magnet, and that of the object seen in a distance. We should note first that it is not clear whether these cases are really examples of causation without contact. This is certainly questionable from a contemporary understanding: the magnet is connected with the iron via a magnetic field, the eye with the object seen by the light traveling between them. But even if these are cases of contactless causation, the opponent still owes an explanation of why causation without contact then does not entail the ubiquity of causal relations. Why does not every iron object feel the pull from a given magnet, and why is not every object seen, independent of where it is located? Moreover, even if we somehow resolve these problems for cases of apparent causation without spatial contact, establishing the opponent's case in favor of contactless causation presumably also requires providing examples of causation without *temporal* contact, which so far have not been supplied. As a consequence, the opponent has not explained how the supposed counterexamples of the magnetic field, the eye, and so forth can be understood in such a way that they establish the possibility of causation without contact. Candrakīrti, on the other hand, does not have to explain this, since the problem only arises if the entities involved in the examples are understood as existing with intrinsic nature, a supposition that the Mādhyamika denies.

The Mādhyamika explains the empty nature of things in terms of examples like dreams and illusions, examples which are also accepted by his opponent. As such, the Mādhyamika can say: "When I describe things as empty, I mean that they are like these" and expect to be understood by the opponent. However, there is no example of a substantially real entity existing with intrinsic nature that the Mādhyamika would accept; for this reason the opponent cannot say: "When I describe things as existing with *svabhāva*, I mean that they are like this." Given that in Indian logical theory the provision of an example both parties agree on is an essential part of a valid argument, this indicates an imbalance in the dialectical situation. The Mādhyamika can present an argument like "all things are empty because they are dependently originated, as in a dream," where the existence of dreams is accepted by both parties in the debate, yet the opponent cannot produce a valid counterpart along the lines of "all things exist with intrinsic nature, because of *x*, like a *y*," since there is no *y* with intrinsic nature the Mādhyamika accepts. 6:177

Not only is it difficult for the proponent of intrinsic natures to produce acceptable arguments for his view, his whole project, Candrakīrti argues, is flawed. Ordinary beings are already trapped in a conceptual prison due to their innate belief in a real self.[155] Why bind them any tighter in a network of arguments purporting to provide support for a philosophical view in substantially real entities?

Candrakīrti explains that the discussion relating to contiguity or non-contiguity between cause and effect introduced in 6:169–6:170 provides a further consideration in support of the Madhyamaka view of emptiness, in addition to the "remaining arguments" for the selflessness of phenomena and the selflessness of persons presented earlier in the chapter, even though it does not add any independent support to the Madhyamaka position. The response to criticism of the contiguity argument is to be based on the previously presented arguments for emptiness focused on the notions of dependent origination 6:178

[155] See 6:121.

(refuting the intrinsic nature of phenomena) and dependent designation (refuting the intrinsic nature of persons). With respect to the alleged self-refutation of the Mādhyamika position, the defender should point out that the lack of 'real causal power' to refute the opponent would only be a problem if there were such a thing as real causal power. However, previous arguments for emptiness (such as the rejection of the four kinds of causal production) have shown this not to be the case.

Candrakīrti also addresses the criticism that Madhyamika constitutes a pathological form of philosophical debate known as *vitaṇḍā*, where one debater only aims at refuting the other's position, without attempting to establish a position of his own. However, this characterization is not applicable to Madhyamaka since, first, there is no such thing as the opponent's position to be refuted in any substantially real sense, and, second, the Mādhyamika presents a position at the level of conventional truth by rejecting the existence of entities with intrinsic natures.

The 16 types of emptiness

6:179 The final major portion of the 6th chapter is dedicated to the classification of different types of emptiness. They differ only to the extent different empty entities are considered under each type—the emptiness they exhibit is identical for all of them. The first classification differentiates two types of emptiness familiar to anyone who has followed Candrakīrti's exposition so far, the emptiness of phenomena (discussed in 6:008–6:119) and the emptiness of persons (6:120–6:178). From the perspective of the Mahāyāna these play a role in differentiating the realizations attained in the different vehicles.[156] The emptiness of persons is realized by the *arhat*s; this, too, is realized by the practitioners of the Mahāyāna, who additionally also realize the emptiness of phenomena.

[156] How far exactly the *arhat*'s realization of emptiness goes is a complex question. See Mi pham (Padmakara 2004: 310–314) for some discussion.

Candrakīrti next considers classifications of emptiness into 16 types and into four types. Both are based on the *Perfection of Wisdom in 100,000 Lines* (*Śatasāhasrikā-prajñāpāramitā*). The 16-fold classification includes the following types of emptiness: 6:180

1. Emptiness of the internal,
2. Emptiness of the external,
3. Emptiness of the external-internal,
4. Emptiness of emptiness,
5. Emptiness of the great,
6. Emptiness of the ultimate,
7. Emptiness of the compounded,
8. Emptiness of the uncompounded,
9. Emptiness of that which has transcended boundaries,
10. Emptiness of what is without end and beginning,
11. Emptiness of non-elimination,
12. Emptiness of nature,
13. Emptiness of all phenomena,
14. Emptiness of intrinsic characteristics,
15. Emptiness of non-apprehension,
16. Emptiness of the nature of nonexistence.

The four-fold classification consists of:

1. Emptiness of existence,
2. Emptiness of nonexistence,
3. Emptiness of intrinsic nature,
4. Emptiness of extrinsic nature.

Candrakīrti equates these types of emptiness with the Mahāyāna and points out that none of them exists in the slightest in any ultimate sense; they are all, without exception, merely conventions at the level of relative truth.

The presentation of the 16 types of emptiness does not imply that emptiness is in some way internally differentiated; all of the 16 types involve the same kind of emptiness. Nor are the various types presented in order to display different argumentative strategies employed for establishing emptiness in particular instances. Finally, the discussion of the different types is not aimed at a single addressee. Whoever has realized one type of emptiness will more easily realize the others. Nevertheless, some may find some of the 16 instances of emptiness discussed more straightforward than others; moreover, attachment to the different entities found to be empty may manifest in different forms, relative to the entity this attachment is directed at. For this reason 16 different types of emptiness are discussed.

6:181 The *emptiness of the internal* (1) refers to the emptiness of the five physical sense-faculties (vision, hearing, smelling, tasting, touching) together with the mind's cognitive faculties. These six are
6:182 dependently originated, changeable, and hence not constant. But they are also not perishing, that is, they do not simply, by their own nature, pass out of existence. An entity that existed with intrinsic nature would either have to be unchangeable and frozen in time, since it could never lose or modify this nature, or it would have to be extremely short-lived, bringing about its own destruction through itself immediately after arising. The Buddhist conceptualization of reality, influenced as it is by the principle of momentariness, cannot readily incorporate entities of the first type, though the Abhidharma's ontology of *dharmas* is based on entities of the second type. The five sense-faculties and the cognitive faculties, however, cannot be straightforwardly seen as belonging to either type, and hence do not qualify as things with intrinsic natures.

Verse 6:181 refers to the nature of vision, etc., and in his autocommentary Candrakīrti points out that this nature is something non-fabricated and independent of other things,[157] known by

[157] The epithets by which *svabhāva* is characterized in Nāgārjuna's *Mūlamadhyamakakārikā* 15:2.

cognition free from ignorance. The opponent immediately raises the charge of contradiction: how could Candrakīrti incessantly deny that *anything* has an intrinsic nature and then accept that some things do? The puzzle is resolved by realizing that 'nature' in this sense[158] is not the intrinsic nature that ordinary beings see in things (as when the Ābhidharmikas identify the fire's intrinsic nature as heat, and so on), but their emptiness, conventionally characterized as non-fabricated and independent of other things, which is neither existent nor nonexistent and by nature pacified.

The *emptiness of the external* (2) and of the *external-internal* (3) **6:184**
are discussed next. The former refers to the objects of the sense-
faculties, material objects, sounds, scents, and so on, while the **6:183**
latter subsumes the physical bases of the sense-faculties, the eye, the ear, the nose, etc., since they are both external, physical objects and give rise to internal phenomena, that is, to the sense faculties. External and external-internal entities are to be regarded as empty for the very same reason as the internal.

The Madhyamaka theory of emptiness is not simply a philosoph- **6:185**
ical theory, but also a metaphilosophical theory applicable to itself.
This idea is captured by the *emptiness of emptiness* (4). Not only **6:186**
are all phenomena and all persons empty of an ultimately real intrinsic nature, but the theory of emptiness is empty in this way as well. What this means is that not only all *entities* in the world lack a substantial ground in terms of atomic material parts, first causes, or conceptualization-independent aspects, but that there is also no ground of ultimately real *truths* a theory might hope to capture. An ultimately true theory of some set of entities would contain only truths that do not hold in virtue of anything else, truths that do not need any other truths to ground them.[159] But the Mādhyamika argues that there are no ultimately true theories, and so the theory of emptiness cannot be such a theory either. In particular, the

[158] See Jinpa 2002: 97–104; Westerhoff 2009: 40–46.

[159] For further discussion of the nonexistence of ultimately true theories see Westerhoff 2020, chapter 4.

notion of intrinsic nature is nothing more than a mistaken superimposition projected onto the world by perceivers in the grip of ignorance. As such, the world's emptiness of such intrinsic nature cannot be a feature the world has in and of itself, independent of perceivers' superimpositions. The theory of emptiness is a projection aimed at removing another projection, not a set of truths about the world that hold no matter what. As such, emptiness is empty of the nature of emptiness, that is, of the absence of *svabhāva* as a fundamental, mind-independent feature of the world. Emptiness is explained as not only stopping the mind from grasping at entities and persons deemed substantially real, but also as stopping it from grasping at theories deemed ultimately true.

6:187 The *emptiness of the great* (5) focuses on the nature of space.
Candrakīrti gives two reasons for space being without limits. First,
space pervades the whole of existence; there is no animate or in-
6:188 animate world separate from space. Second, when meditators cultivate immeasurable love, immeasurable compassion, and so on, they do so by generating the relevant emotions relative to all beings throughout space. By doing so they aim at generating these qualities to an immeasurable degree, by focusing on an immeasurable number of objects toward which they could be directed. Since each of these beings occupies a finite portion of space, the space containing them all must be immeasurable as well. Understanding the 'greatness' of space in this way, both in terms of its all-pervading nature and in terms of its limitless extent, might tempt one to infer its ontological fundamentality. Space being an indispensable basis of the animate and inanimate world, one might want to conclude that it plays an important role in the grounding of reality as a substantially real entity. Such a fundamental status in indeed ascribed to space in Vaiśeṣika, a non-Buddhist school of Classical Indian philosophy,[160] which Candrakīrti explicitly mentions in

[160] *Vaiśeṣikasūtra* 1.1.5 (Sinha 1986: 17–19); see also Aṇṇambhaṭṭa's *Tarkasaṃgraha* (Swami Virupakshananda 1994: 29–30, 48). Umāsvāti's *Tattvārthādhigamasūtra* 5:1–3

the autocommentary. Unsurprisingly, Candrakīrti regards this as a mistake and argues that the emptiness of space was specifically taught to refute this mistaken view of space. From the Madhyamaka perspective, space is as empty as everything else.[161] Even if we accept it as all-pervading and limitless this would not contradict the view that it is also empty, since the possession of certain properties or the ability to fulfill certain functions at the level of conventional reality is not considered to be in conflict with an entity's ultimate emptiness.

An entity of supreme importance in the Buddhist world-picture is liberation or *nirvāṇa*, which Candrakīrti characterizes by the term 'ultimate.' Given its exalted nature, this is an obvious candidate for something that should be accorded the status of an ultimately real entity in Buddhist ontology, if anything is, and indeed it is considered in this way by the Sarvāstivāda Abhidharma. Candrakīrti notes that the *emptiness of the ultimate* (6) is taught in order to refute this mistaken view of *nirvāṇa*. Characterizing *nirvāṇa* as ultimate (*paramārtha*) does not indicate a particular fundamental status, but signifies that it is the highest (*parama*) aim (*artha*) to be realized by the Buddhist path. Like all other phenomena, it is empty because it is neither unchangeable nor impermanent, as an ultimately real entity existing with intrinsic nature would be assumed to be. Liberation is not unchangeable, since any individual being that becomes liberated changes from a previous unliberated to a later liberated state. The liberated state can only be conceived of in contrast with the previous unliberated state it changed from. As such, the presence of change is an essential

6:189

6:190

(Tatia 1994: 123–124) also lists space (*ākāśa*) as a substance (*dravya*). For further discussion see Jhaveri 1956; Bumistrov 2018.

161 For Madhyamaka discussion of the nature of space (*ākāśa*) see Nāgārjuna's *Mūlamadhyamakakārikā* 5:1 (Siderits/Katsura 2013: 60) and Candrakīrti's *Prasannapadā* on 24:19 (May 1959: 239, note 849), where he cites Āryadeva's *Catuḥśataka* 9:5 (Lang 1986: 88–89; Geshe Sonam Rinchen 1994: 205–206), La Vallée Poussin 1988–1990: 1: 134, note 23; Qvarnström 1989; Mason 2012; Aitken 2021: 10.

precondition of the existence of a liberated state. Nor is the liberated state impermanent, since once *nirvāṇa* is obtained one can never revert to the previous state of being bound in cyclic existence.

6:191 Candrakīrti next addresses the dichotomy of compounded and uncompounded objects in order to explain the *emptiness of the*
6:192 *compounded* (7) and the *emptiness of the uncompounded* (8). The example of compounded entities considered are the three realms of cyclic existence in which sentient beings are reborn: the desire realm, the material realm, and the immaterial realm. The first includes the familiar six realms of rebirth discussed in Buddhism, including the realms of animals and humans, while the second and third are realms that retain only some features of matter found in our world (in case of the material realm) or are wholly mental (in case of the immaterial realm); beings are reborn in these realms as a result of having mastered specific forms of meditation. All of these realms have arisen from causes and conditions and are therefore empty, as dependent entities cannot be ultimately real.

Uncompounded entities, on the other hand, do not arise or endure, are devoid of impermanence, and so do not cease. *Nirvāṇa* is recognized by all Buddhist schools as an uncompounded entity; some schools also recognize other entities, such as space (*ākāśa*) or suchness (*tathatā*, synonymous with emptiness), as uncompounded. Candrakīrti does not mention any specific examples of uncompounded entities, nor does he refer to specific arguments demonstrating their emptiness. His rejection of uncompounded entities is supposed to cover whatever different Buddhist schools might subsume under this notion, and the reasons for their emptiness are evident in the light of the preceding discussion. To the extent that all of these entities are still dependent by relying on the conceptualizing mind for their existence they cannot be substantially real objects existing by their intrinsic natures. Uncompounded things are therefore empty of the intrinsic nature of being uncompounded things.

Buddhism traditionally positions itself as a middle way between the extreme views of permanence and annihilationism. How exactly these extremes are understood differs somewhat from context to context. They may, for example, be taken to be two different positions on the nature of the person—the belief in a permanent soul, or the belief that all mental functions cease at the death of the physical body, or two different views of objects—that all objects exist substantially, or that nothing exists at all.[162] The exact content of the two extreme views is of secondary importance in the context of Candrakīrti's argument. His main point is that the middle position, that is, the position Buddhism identifies as the correct view equally far removed from the two mistaken extremes, is empty too, and this is what is indicated by the *emptiness of that which has transcended boundaries* (9). In other words, the final position Buddhist philosophical inquiry arrives at cannot be considered as an ultimate truth expressing the nature of things as they are in themselves. Tsong kha pa[163] criticizes the Yogācāra position which considers its own view that everything is mental as a position located between two extremes, namely the view that our mental representations have external objects as a foundation, or that they have no foundation whatsoever. The difficulty, he argues, is that they take the resulting position of everything being mental to be ultimately true, and the mind to be ultimately real. For the Mādhyamika, on the other hand, all philosophical positions are conceptualization-dependent. This is especially clear in the case of the 'middle way.' It is formulated as an antidote to two extreme positions leading to the perpetuation of suffering. As such, it is of exclusively instrumental value, aimed at the refutation of these positions; its objective is not to provide an alternative position characterizing the most fundamental level of reality. **6:193**

[162] For the understanding of the extreme view of annihilationism in the Madhyamika discussion see Westerhoff 2016.

[163] Jinpa 2021: 498.

6:194 The *emptiness of what is without end and beginning* (10) designates the emptiness of *saṃsāra*. Buddhist cosmology conceives of cyclic existence as without a beginning in time;[164] it also lacks a temporal end insofar as it continues to perpetuate itself endlessly through the actions of beings in it, unless they find an escape from it through the Buddhist path to liberation.

Entities without boundaries have no middle.[165] An infinite space can have no middle point, since such a point, being defined as one equidistant from opposite points on its perimeter, is either undefinable, or every point satisfies this condition. Insofar as the location of other points is to be determined in relation to the boundary, these cannot be fixed either. Of course it is possible to simply *postulate* a middle point, an origin of the coordinate system, and define all other locations in relation to this. But first this is obviously a mere imputation (there is nothing special about the point picked as the origin in itself), and secondly all other locations are only relationally defined relative to the origin, without assuming that these location-descriptions reveal anything about the intrinsic nature of the respective points in space.

Candrakīrti applies these considerations to a temporal process without boundaries. There can be no midway point of *saṃsāra* equidistant from its beginning and end. The impossibility of relating this point to the boundaries of cyclic existence generalizes to relating any other sub-sections of this cycle, such as individual births and deaths, to the ends of *saṃsāra*. We can relate these to an arbitrary point in time we picked, and we can relate temporal locations to one another, but we cannot speak of specific temporal points in which a life begins or ends in a non-arbitrary, non-relational way, linking these points with temporal locations in a mind-independent, fundamentally real temporal sequence.

164 See Tola/Dragonetti 1980.
165 *Mūlamadhyamakakārikā* 11: 1–2, see Siderits/Katsura 2013: 123–124.

Candrakīrti describes cyclic existence as dream-like; as the 6:195
dream creates its own temporal (and spatial) structure that cannot be related in any robust way to the spatio-temporal structure of the waking world, so the arising and ceasing of life in *saṃsāra*, and the beginning, duration, and end of temporal processes, are not related to ultimate, substantial temporal process, but can only be understood as existing in a mind-dependently imputed and relational way. As events in a dream still appear, so the sequence of birth and death still appears in cyclic existence, but this cyclic existence, being neither unchangeable nor passing out of existence on its own accord, is as empty of intrinsic nature as all other phenomena.

The discussion of the *emptiness of non-elimination* (11) refers to 6:196
the emptiness of an entity that is not eliminated. Candrakīrti does not explicitly state what it is that "is not eliminated." According to
some commentators this refers to the Mahāyāna, others equate 6:197
it with the six perfections, or with *nirvāṇa* without remainder. As *nirvāṇa* is already covered by the *emptiness of the ultimate* (6) and the *emptiness of the uncompounded* (8) the first two appear more plausible, and given the centrality of the six perfections to the Mahāyāna path there is less of a difference between these two concepts than one might think. Both remain a constant element of a Buddhist's practice, independent of the specific stage the practitioner has achieved. Unlike the 'three poisons' of anger, greed, and ignorance, and the mistaken views of the substantial existence of phenomena and persons, which have to be eliminated on the way to enlightenment, the Buddhist path (which Candrakīrti identifies with the Mahāyāna path) and the set of the virtues cultivated while progressing on it is never to be given up, until Buddhahood is obtained.

Even though the Buddhist path is aimed to lead beyond the conventional reality that constitutes cyclic existence, this does not entail that the path itself has any ontological status at the level of ultimate reality. It is simply an expedient tool to bring about a specific effect—liberation from *saṃsāra*—but this does not exclude it from the set of entities that are empty. Even the Great Vehicle is, in the end, a means of transportation that is going to be left behind once one has reached the destination.

6:198 The *emptiness of nature* (12) is related by several commentators[166]
to the *emptiness of emptiness* (4), and indeed it takes up the ontolo-
6:199 gical status of emptiness again from a different angle. In the discus-
sion of the emptiness of emptiness, the mistaken presupposition to be dislodged was that, given that we had established by reasoning that all things are empty, we should then be justified in treating the theory of emptiness as a final account of how things are in themselves. In the present context the emphasis is on the fact that advanced Buddhist practitioners up to the Buddhas do not bring about the emptiness of things in some way by their cognition or perception. This emptiness obtains whether or not there are Buddhas in the first place; it constitutes the uncreated, unconstructed *nature* of things. Once we talk about natures, however, we might then consider these to be substantially real entities described by an ultimately true theory. The emptiness of things, conceived as their nature, is of course not to be understood in this way. Emptiness is a nature that is itself empty; it only exists in a conventional, mind-dependent way, rather than as a characteristic possessed by things 'from their own side.'

6:200 A comprehensive Abhidharma classification of all phenomena subsumes them under the eighteen sense spheres: the six sense faculties, their objects, and the sensory cognitions resulting from the contacts of organ and object. Candrakīrti also mentions the contact of the six sense faculties with their objects, and the feelings that result as a consequence (the 6th and 7th member of the twelve links of dependent origination) separately, as well as material and immaterial and compounded and uncompounded phenomena. Even though these are, strictly speaking, all included in the eighteen

[166] Tsong kha pa (Jinpa 2021: 499), Go rams pa 358.

sense spheres, contact and the resulting feelings are mentioned in particular since these are the immediate cause of sensory attachment, while the latter two pairs constitute alternative classificatory schemes that cover the same range of phenomena as the eighteen sense spheres in a more concise manner.[167]

The collection of everything that exists is an obvious further candidate for something that exists ultimately by its intrinsic nature. The *emptiness of all phenomena* (13) is taught in order to refute the idea that 'all there is' could be regarded as a substantial entity that constitutes the foundation of existence.[168]

Candrakīrti now turns to the discussion of the *emptiness of intrinsic characteristics* (14), which will continue up to 6:215. In his exposition he discusses a list of key concepts from the Buddhist worldview, beginning with the constituents of the physical world, and ending with the Buddha's omniscience. For each he briefly presents the concept's intrinsic characteristic, the quality we use in order to define it and distinguish it from other things, concluding in 6:215 that despite the fact that these concepts possess intrinsic characteristics, this does not contradict the position that they are, like all things, empty of intrinsic nature. Intrinsic characteristics play an epistemological role, they allow us to pick out specific entities, while intrinsic natures claim to play an ontological role, indicating ultimately real, self-sufficient foundational entities. **6:201**

Candrakīrti's descriptions of the relevant intrinsic characteristics are very brief and obviously not meant to be self-contained. They are intended as reminders for an audience who has studied these materials in considerable detail and is familiar with the explanation of these concepts in the commentarial literature.

[167] Dewar 2008: 473–474.

[168] For a discussion of the question whether 'all there is' should be regarded as an entity at all see Westerhoff 2020: 277–295.

The precise constitution of the list of concepts Candrakīrti discusses is of secondary importance in relation to the key philosophical point he wants to make (that despite having intrinsic characteristics, these things are all empty). It is clearly meant to cover the entire spectrum of existence, from the most mundane (the everyday material world) to the most sublime (the omniscient knowledge of the Buddha), following the bodhisattva path, while also covering key Buddhist concepts that play an important role in the Mahāyāna *sūtras* and commentaries.

6:203 Candrakīrti first presents the intrinsic characteristics of the five physico-psychological aggregates as described in the Abhidharma.[169] The intrinsic characteristic of matter is destruct-
6:202 ibility; that of feeling, experience; that of perception, the grasping of characteristic features; that of dispositions, intentional action; and that of consciousness, awareness with respect to its objects. Collectively, the aggregates have suffering as their intrinsic nature, and the eighteen sense spheres have the intrinsic nature of a poisonous snake.

In the context of a perceptual process in which the five aggregates take part, these characterizations are relatively straightforward. Material objects, which constitute a significant subset of objects perceived are, in the light of the Buddhist understanding of impermanence, all constituted by a sequence of rapidly arising and disintegrating momentary entities (*rūpa-dharma*). As these entities self-destruct without external causes, destructibility is identified as the intrinsic characteristic of matter. Epistemic contact with objects produces specific experiential hedonic states (pleasant, unpleasant, or neutral), while their perception requires that specific discriminating features are distinguished (telling blue objects from yellow objects, and so forth). Dispositions arise in the context of trying to acquire certain perceived objects, and of avoiding others;

[169] See, for example, the Abhidharmakośa's *Dhātunirdeśa*, in particular La Vallée Poussin 1988–1990: 1: 63–89.

this process is based on intentional actions and produces specific karmic potentials. Consciousness involves particular objects (material things, sounds, etc.) appearing in awareness. Collectively all of these aggregates have a nature of suffering since they fuel craving, which is one of the chief drivers of cyclic existence, which is characterized by suffering. Candrakīrti introduces the example of the poisonous snake again[170] in order to characterize the sense spheres. As with concealed snakes, beings might be deceived about these, yet they eventually bite and harm them.

The sense spheres are further described as entrance-gates for suf- **6:204**
fering, since suffering arrives through the sensory faculties, as they produce sensory cognitions when connected with their objects. Dependent origination, understood in terms of its twelve links, is specified as having the intrinsic characteristic of being a collection of mutually connected causes and effects.

Candrakīrti continues his discussion of the emptiness of intrinsic **6:205**
characteristics by briefly describing the intrinsic characteristics of the six perfections that form the core of Mahāyāna ethics.[171] The perfection of generosity is characterized by giving, virtue by not being **6:206**
inflamed, patience by the absence of anger, effort by faultlessness, meditation by concentration, and wisdom by the absence of attachment. Generosity includes all forms of giving, including giving material goods, one's own body, or even the meritorious potential accumulated through Buddhist practice. Virtue means not being set alight by afflictive emotions, while patience is expressed in particular by freedom from anger. Effort continuously upholds virtuous conduct without any defilements, meditation focuses the mind, collects together and joins the various virtuous factors, leading to the perfection of wisdom, which is characterized by abandoning attachment to any entity erroneously conceived of as fundamentally real.

[170] See 6:141.

[171] For an in-depth discussion of the six perfections from a Madhyamaka perspective the reader may want to consult Śāntideva's *Bodhicaryāvatāra* (Crosby/Skilton 1995).

6:207 Next Candrakīrti turns to three important sets of meditative states within Buddhist practice.[172] These are the four absorptions of the form realm, meditation on the four immeasurables, and the four formless absorptions. They are characterized as having the absence of anger as intrinsic natures, since they can be brought about only when anger is abandoned.

6:208 The 37 factors of enlightenment, a conglomeration of individual lists of practices considered to encompass the entire Buddhist path already referred to in 4:002, is taken up next. Their intrinsic characteristic is that they lead to liberation.

6:209 Candrakīrti then considers another set of central concepts, the 'three doors to liberation':[173] emptiness, signlessness, and desirelessness. The first, emptiness, has the intrinsic characteristic of lacking the perception of substantially real entities. Signlessness is characterized as the pacification resulting from not objectifying the properties of things, while desirelessness is the presence of suffering in the absence of confusion, as one sees the suffering of cyclic existence and is not confused about its true nature when it appears otherwise.

A further set of meditative practices, the eight liberations,[174] is described as having the intrinsic characteristic of being conducive to liberation.

6:210 The ten powers of the Buddha,[175] specific epistemic capacities of enlightened beings that Candrakīrti will come back to in 11:28–30 have the intrinsic characteristic of being "decisive in form" since they produce complete certainty about the objects known.

The four fearlessnesses,[176] four pronouncements of the Buddha about his enlightenment, that he is fully awakened, has removed all

[172] See above, 3:011, for more information on these states.

[173] *vimokṣamukha*. For further discussion see Conze 1962: 59–69. See also Lamotte 1944–1980: 3: 1221–1222; Gelongma Karma Migme Chödrön 3:1001.

[174] *aṣṭavimokṣa*. See Engle 2016: 345–346, note 906; Rahula/Boin-Webb 2001: 205, note 18. See also Red mda' ba 324–325, Padmakara 2010: 431–432. See below, p. 211, note 17.

[175] *daśabala*. On these see Engle 2016: 345, note 905, 622–639. See 8:003.

[176] *vaiśāradya*. See Lamotte 1944–1980: 3: 1596–1571; Gelongma Karma Migme Chödrön 3:1284–1286. See also Lamotte 1973: 2: 298–299.

defilements from his mind-stream, taught what the impediments to liberation are, and that following the Buddhist path will lead to the cessation of suffering, have the intrinsic characteristic of being "well established in form." This means that they cannot be refuted by any opponent, as they are grounded in the Buddha's direct knowledge of his enlightenment experience.

The four superlative individuating knowledges[177] of the Buddhas and bodhisattvas, knowledge of things, words, etymologies, and the resulting elocutionary confidence, which Candrakīrti will mention again in his autocommentary to 9:001, have the intrinsic characteristic of being uninterrupted because they are not obstructed by any obstacles. The Buddha also possesses the highest degree of the four 'divine abodes,' mental states that play a special role as objects of meditative focus,[178] but also as ethical qualities: love, compassion, sympathetic joy, and equanimity. The Buddha's great love has the intrinsic characteristic of bringing benefit to other beings, both in terms of ordinary temporal benefit and in terms of guiding them to liberation. The intrinsic characteristic of great compassion is to liberate beings from suffering, that of great sympathetic joy is delight in the happiness of others and in the wish that others may never be without happiness, and that of great equanimity being unalloyed by attraction to what is pleasant or aversion to what is unpleasant. **6:211** **6:212**

The Sanskrit and Pāli traditions ascribe eighteen unique qualities to a Buddha,[179] relating to the perfections of his body, speech, and mind. Candrakīrti's autocommentary presents a very detailed picture of each with quotations from Mahāyāna *sūtras*. These unique qualities result from the Buddha's enlightened state and, as a being who has become enlightened cannot subsequently go back to an **6:213**

[177] *pratisaṃvid:* See Lamotte 1944–1980: 3: 1614–1624; Gelongma Karma Migme Chödrön 1322–1330; Dayal 1932: 259–267 for further discussion of these.

[178] See 6:207.

[179] *āveṇikabuddhadharma*. On these see Lamotte 1944–1980: 3: 1625–1627; Gelongma Karma Migme Chödrön 3: 1331–1333; Dalai Lama/Thubten Chodron 2019: 47–51.

unenlightened state, these qualities are described as having the intrinsic characteristic of being irremovable.

6:214 The final topic Candrakīrti considers in his examination of intrinsic characteristics is the omniscient cognition of a Buddha. This has the intrinsic characteristic of being perception, indicating that Buddhas do not have to resort to other epistemic instruments, such as inference, which is only necessary in cases where one's perceptual capacities are insufficient. Since the Buddhas know everything there is to know directly, they do not have to resort to reasoning as an alternative route to knowledge. Moreover, the Buddha's omniscient knowledge is really the only kind of perception there is in a strict sense. Other forms of cognition we might ordinarily label as perception, such as the perceptions of ordinary beings, or even those of realized beings below the state of full Buddhahood do not qualify.[180] This is because they are limited in scope, accessing only some, but not all aspects of the apprehended object.

6:215 Candrakīrti concludes this exposition of the 14th type of emptiness, the *emptiness of intrinsic characteristics*, by pointing out that even though compounded entities (such as the aggregates, elements, and sense spheres) and uncompounded entities (such as space or *nirvāṇa*) have specific intrinsic characteristics, they are all empty of any substantial, mind-independent intrinsic nature.

6:216 The *emptiness of non-apprehension* (15) is explained by Candrakīrti in relation to time. Assuming the Abhidharma theory of momentariness and presentism,[181] neither the past nor future events can be observed, since the former do not exist anymore, and the latter do not exist yet. Present events, being momentary phenomena without any temporal thickness, cannot be observed when they exist either—since perceptual processes take time, once a momentary phenomenon is perceptually registered it has already passed out of existence.

[180] We meet this phenomenon in other contexts. For Dharmakīrti, for example, much of what we ordinarily classify as perceptions (such as everyday cognitions of medium-sized dry goods) does not qualify as perception (see Westerhoff 2018b: 223–224).

[181] For further discussion of these see Siderits 2007: 119–123, 2022: chapter 7.

The unobservability or non-apprehension of events taking place 6:217
in the past, present, and future is not fundamentally real but is itself empty, as it exists purely in dependence on these events. It does not permanently persist by its own nature, nor does it cease existing by this same nature. As a dependent phenomenon it has no intrinsic nature in the first place.

Things do not have the nature of being conjunctions, that is, the na- 6:218
ture of being arisen from a conjunction of causal factors, because they are conditionally originated. Causally originated things do not have the intrinsic nature of being causally originated, since causation itself is not a fundamentally real property of the world, but, according to Madhyamaka analysis, something that is originated in dependence on conditions, and specifically arisen in dependence on conceptualizing minds.[182] Assuming that being part of the causal nexus is a mark of the real,[183] things lacking the intrinsic nature of participating in the network of causes might be considered as unreal or nonexistent. Yet this lack does not constitute their intrinsic nature either, it is not fundamentally real but is as empty as everything else. This emptiness is described as *the emptiness of the nature of nonexistence* (16).

Condensed classification into four kinds of emptiness

After this discussion of the 16 types of emptiness, Candrakīrti takes 6:219
up a shorter classification of emptiness into four types, beginning
with the *emptiness of existence* (1) and the *emptiness of nonexist-* 6:220
ence (2). The first refers to the emptiness of conditioned things like the five aggregates, the second to the emptiness of unconditioned things[184] like space or *nirvāṇa* (nonexistent objects like sons of

[182] See Siderits 2004: 411–413; Westerhoff 2018b: 110–112.

[183] An idea we find frequently in Buddhist thought; see e.g. Westerhoff 2018b: 66–67, 207, 231–232, 250, note 103, 256.

[184] *asaṃskṛta*. Sautrāntika Abhidharma, unlike Sarvāstivāda, regards space (*ākāśa*) and liberation (*nrivāṇa*) as nonexistents, rather than as real things. See Frauwallner 1956: 117–121; Tauscher 1981: 185, note 484; La Vallée Poussin 1988–1990: 1: 280–286.

barren women are not what is meant here). The former are empty because their conditioned nature prevents them from 'standing on their own,' ontologically speaking, the latter lack intrinsic natures because they are absences (the absence of obstruction in the case of space, the absence of suffering in the case of liberation), and absences, being essentially dependent on conceptualization (we characterize something as an absence of *x* on the basis of a mistaken expectation to find an *x* in this place) cannot exist as independent, substantial entities.

6:221 The *emptiness of intrinsic nature* (3), *svabhāvaśūnyatā*, is in this context not to be understood as the lack of a substantially real foundation of all things, but refers to the nature of all things (the fact that they lack *svabhāva*, their emptiness) being empty too[185] because it is not fabricated. The intrinsic nature of things (understood as their emptiness) is not brought about by realized beings from *arhat*s up and, as the Perfection of Wisdom texts point out, is not produced by knowledge or perception. It does not originate from any causes and conditions. The intrinsic nature of things is to be empty of intrinsic nature. This nature being empty too is what is referred to here by the emptiness of intrinsic nature.

6:222 The final member of the shorter, fourfold classification of types of emptiness is the *emptiness of extrinsic nature* (4). Extrinsic na-
6:223 ture[186] remains what it is whether or not Buddhas appear in the world, and Candrakīrti characterizes it as the limit of reality, since it transcends cyclic existence and is the true nature of reality. It is permanent and unchangeable, and is what is understood through highest knowledge, which is without conceptualizations. Its emptiness is the emptiness of the highest nature.

[185] Trisoglio 2003: 323.

[186] *parabhāva*. In Candrakīrti's exposition in 6:221–223, *svabhāva* and *parabhāva* refer to the same thing: the emptiness of all phenomena. In other contexts (e.g. *Mūlamadhyamakakārikā* 1:2, 15:6, 22:4, 22:9) the pair *svabhāva* and *parabhāva* refers to opposite notions that are both rejected by the Mādhyamika. See Tauscher 1981: 186–187, note 492, for some discussion of the different conceptual dimensions of the term *parabhāva*.

Despite the fact that emptiness is characterized as reality's true nature, as permanent, as what is perceived by perfected knowledge of the enlightened mind, and as transcending *saṃsāra*, it is not presented as a mind-independently real, independently existent, ultimate foundation of reality. Madhyamaka argues that there is no such foundation, and hence emptiness cannot exist in this way either. Even emptiness described as the highest nature, as the final one of the classifications of emptiness into 2, 16, and 4 types, as they are set out in the Perfection of Wisdom *sūtra*s and as Candrakīrti has just discussed, is as empty as everything else.

Conclusion

6:224

By means of the analysis presented from 6:008 onward, the bodhisattva develops the understanding that the three realms of cyclic existence[187] are originally unborn, that is, not causally produced by any substantially real causal relation, and for this reason also do not really abide or cease. This is not merely an intellectual assent to the theory of universal emptiness resulting from being persuaded by Madhyamaka arguments, but a realization at the experiential level, as vivid and evident as the perception of an Indian gooseberry, which, due to its transparent nature, can be seen clearly inside and outside when held in the palm of one's hand. Nevertheless, this realization, leading to a meditative state called 'cessation,'[188] is achieved by relying on the obscurational, transactional conventional truth through which all of the Buddhist path is expressed, even though at the level of ultimate truth there is no such meditative state to enter, and no one to enter it.

[187] See 6:191.

[188] *nirodhasamāpatti, gog pa'i snyoms 'jug*. See Tauscher 1981: 190, note 503. The state of *nirodhasamāpatti* is commonly associated with the cessation of all mental activity, but there is a considerable discussion in the commentarial literature of the question whether this kind of cessation is meant here, or whether it refers to the cessation of all conceptual superimpositions that obscure the direct perception of emptiness.

6:225 Despite remaining in this state of deep meditative absorption, the bodhisattvas still generate compassion for suffering beings. While their mind belongs to *nirvāṇa*, their actions still take place in *saṃsāra*. As Candrakīrti pointed out in 1:008, already on the 1st bodhisattva stage the bodhisattva surpasses the realized beings on the non-Mahyāyāna Buddhist path in terms of merit, due to the awakening mind he has generated. Having passed beyond this 6th bodhisattva stage to the 7th, he also outshines them in term of intelligence. While the Mahāyāna considers the bodhisattva's motivation as superior from the start, it is only after realizing the teachings set out in this chapter that the bodhisattva's insight into emptiness also goes beyond the understanding of emptiness achieved by his highly realized non-Mahāyāna fellow Buddhists, the *arhat*s and *pratyekabuddha*s.

6:226 Candrakīrti concludes the 6th chapter with a poetic image combining various philosophical concepts in memorable way. The leader of a group of wild geese flies ahead of his companions, the ordinary geese, propelled by the wind, crossing a great ocean. The wild goose, a prominent figure in Indian literature, stands for a being striving for enlightenment, and the foremost of them, their king, is the bodhisattva. The wings which carry him ahead of the others through the space of emptiness are the conventional and ultimate truth, or compassion and wisdom; he is propelled by the karmic force of the virtue he has accumulated since beginningless time. The ocean crossed by the geese represents the immeasurable qualities of the Buddha which the practitioners fully traverse, ultimately becoming fully enlightened Buddhas themselves.

Chapter 7

Section 7. Obtaining the 7th bodhisattva stage

Advancing to the 7th bodhisattva stage, called Far Progressed, the bodhisattva achieves the power to enter the meditative state called 'cessation' he achieved on the previous level instantaneously at any moment. Ordinarily, the entry into and exit from any meditative state takes place in a gradual, temporally extended way, but the 7th stage bodhisattva is able to enter into the direct realization of emptiness in an instantaneous manner. This leads to the dissolution of the boundary between the meditative state, in which emptiness is directly perceived, and the post-meditative state, in which appearances persist in their non-empty manifestation. The two states blend into one another, since the bodhisattva can alternate between them very quickly. The bodhisattva does not abide in the meditative state for long periods because of his intention to help all sentient beings. The 7th bodhisattva stage is accordingly characterized by perfecting the second key component of the Buddhist path, method or compassion, which the bodhisattva uses to help other sentient beings (the other key component, wisdom, was perfected on the previous stage). 7:001

Chapter 8

Section 8. Obtaining the 8th bodhisattva stage

8:001 Subsequently the bodhisattvas advance to the 8th stage, called Immovable. On this stage the bodhisattva's progress becomes irreversible. The difference between the 7th and the 8th stage is compared to dragging a ship across land into the water. While its progress is first laborious and slow, once the ship floats on the water it moves forward effortlessly, without needing to be pulled, and at much greater speed than previously. The aspirations the bodhisattvas have made previously become completely purified of all defilements at this stage. When the bodhisattvas have entered the meditative state of "cessation" they are roused from this again by the Buddhas, who impress on them that they have not yet obtained full enlightenment. The key distinction between bodhisattvas and the realized practitioners of the lower vehicles is that even though there might be no difference in their realization of ultimate reality, the bodhisattva needs to acquire a vast amount of merit to generate the karmic potential to benefit all sentient beings. As such he cannot abide permanently in meditative states, but needs to arise from them in order to engage in meritorious activities.

8:002 On the 8th stage the bodhisattvas have removed all afflictive stains which lead to the continuation of birth in the three realms of cyclic existence from their minds. They have also eliminated the roots of these afflictive stains. Nevertheless, despite being free from attachment or any form of defilement, and having no superior in the realm of *saṃsāra* they have transcended, the bodhisattvas have not yet achieved the full enlightenment of the Buddhas.

8:003 Once attachment to the three realms of cyclic existence has been completely removed, however, and once rebirth in *saṃsāra* no longer takes place, the question arises how the bodhisattvas can still remain active in the world, generating the amount of merit required for obtaining full enlightenment. They do so by acquiring ten different kinds of magical powers (such as being able to materialize anything, appear to take birth in any world, work miracles, etc.)[1] which equip them with a mental body. This mental body can move anywhere and is not obstructed by anything, making it possible to act in cyclic existence without actually being reborn.

[1] See 6:210.

Chapter 9

Section 9. Obtaining the 9th bodhisattva stage

9:001 The 9th bodhisattva stage is called Perfect Intellect; on this stage the ninth of the bodhisattva's ten perfections, the perfection of power, is fully purified and he attains the four superlative individuating knowledges of the Buddhas and bodhisattvas: knowledge of things, words, etymologies, and the resulting elocutionary confidence. Candrakīrti explains these as knowing the characteristics of all things, the ability to differentiate all things, being able to express all things clearly, and having continuous knowledge of the specific causes of things.[1]

[1] Note that the relevant Sanskrit term *pratibhāna* or *pratibhāṇa* can refer both to readiness and confidence in speech, as well as to a form of insight or understanding. Candrakīrti focuses on the latter sense here; obviously the two are connected, as it is the insight into things spoken about that gives rise to elocutionary confidence. See Dayal 1932: 265–266.

Chapter 10

Section 10. Obtaining the 10th bodhisattva stage

Finally, the bodhisattva obtains the 10th stage, called Cloud of Dharma. At this stage the bodhisattva is empowered by all the Buddhas who send out rays of light from a curl of hair located between their eyebrows. These rays enter through the crown of the bodhisattva's head. The final three bodhisattva stages are characterized in terms of regal succession; Candrakīrti notes in his autocommentary on 8:001 that the bodhisattvas obtain a status comparable to princes on the 8th stage, become regents on the 9th, and are anointed as kings on the 10th stage. The rays of light emanating from the Buddhas thus confirm the bodhisattva's succession in the royal line of enlightened beings. **10:001**

At this stage the bodhisattva masters the final of the ten perfections, the Perfection of Knowledge, which differs from the Perfection of Wisdom to the extent that the former fully penetrates conventional truth, while the latter is directed at ultimate truth, free from the duality of perceiving subject and perceived object.[1] As rain falls from a cloud, at the stage called 'Cloud of Dharma' a continuous, effortless stream of compassion, blessings, and teaching issues forth from the bodhisattva, nourishing the virtues present in all living beings.

[1] Jinpa 2021: 526; Padmakara 2004: 329.

Chapter 11

Explanation of the qualities of each bodhisattva stage in terms of its special enumerated features

11:001 Having described the succession through the ten bodhisattva stages,
Candrakīrti now discusses the qualities the bodhisattvas acquire at
11:002 each stage in numerical form, beginning with the first. At this stage
the bodhisattvas acquire twelve abilities. They can, in a single instant,
(1) see a hundred Buddhas and (2) receive the blessings of a hun-
11:003 dred Buddhas and understand that they have been blessed by them,
can (3) accomplish a hundred eons of the path to enlightenment,
can (4) see a hundred eons into the past and future, (5) enter and exit
a hundred meditative concentrations, (6) make a hundred worlds
tremble and (7) fill them with light,[1] (8) generate a direct realization
of emptiness in a hundred beings, thereby bringing them to the 1st
bodhisattva stage as well, (9) travel to a hundred pure realms, (10)
teach a hundred different aspects of the Buddha's teachings, and (11)
manifest in a hundred forms, each of which is (12) accompanied in
turn by a retinue of a hundred bodhisattvas.

11:004 At the succeeding bodhisattva stages the numbers associated
with these twelve qualities increase. While a bodhisattva at the 1st
stage can see a hundred Buddhas in an instant, a bodhisattva at the
11:005 2nd stage can see a thousand, and so on. The associated numbers
increase as follows:

2nd stage: 1,000 (10^3)
3rd stage: 100,000 (10^5)
4th stage: 10^9
5th stage: 10^{10}

[1] Dzogchen Pönlop Rinpoche (1999: 51) interprets this as the ability to "display or manifest 100 different worlds."

6th stage: 10^{12}
7th stage:[2] 10^{23}.

From the 8th stage the associated quantities are no longer represented by numerical terms, but by reference to the number of atoms contained in sets of worlds. The basic unit is the trichiliocosm, consisting of a billion worlds.[3] On the 8th stage a bodhisattva has gone beyond conceptual thought; the number associated with his twelve qualities at this stage corresponds to the number of atoms in one hundred thousand trichiliocosms (i.e., 10^{14} worlds). On the 9th stage this number increases to the number of atoms in one hundred thousand "countless" trichiliocosms (i.e., 10^{64} worlds). 11:006 11:007 11:008

At the 10th stage the number associated with the twelve qualities is inexpressibly large. It exceeds the number of all atoms added together, not just in the trichiliocosms just mentioned, but also in an inexpressible number of buddha-fields[4] beyond these.

At the 10th stage the bodhisattvas are also able to display manifold manifestations at any instant, as many as the pores on their skin, of Buddhas and bodhisattvas, and of beings belonging to the six realms, from the hells upward to the god-realms, gods like Indra and Brahma, and so forth. The aim of all of these manifestations is to provide the right kind of medium through which to help other beings to obtain enlightenment. 11:009

Having concluded the description of the qualities of the 10th bodhisattva stage, Candrakīrti now turns to what lies beyond this stage, that is, the qualities of a fully enlightened Buddha. As the way of the wanderer at night is illuminated by the full moon, having 11:010

[2] Translators disagree on the numerical value associated with the 7th stage. What is clear, however, is that in the progression from the 1st to the 7th stage the numerical values associated with the twelve qualities increase, and that the rate of their increase increases as well.

[3] Sakadata 1997: 93–94; Huntington 2018: 44.

[4] *buddhakṣetra*. Candrakīrti here refers to pure buddha-fields (*viśuddhabuddhakṣetra, dag pa'i zhing khams*), specific environments with marvelous qualities created by Buddhas at the time of their awakening, through their accumulated merits, in which they lead beings to liberation.

obtained the 10th stage the bodhisattva sees the path to full enlightenment clearly laid out in front of him, and moves onward to the attainment of full Buddhahood.

Candrakīrti also refers here to the Mahāyāna idea that Buddhas obtain enlightenment in Akaniṣṭha,[5] the highest heavenly realm of the form realm. Accordingly, the enlightenment of the historical Buddha Śākyamuni under the bodhi tree was a mere manifestation, since the Buddha had already obtained enlightenment earlier in a heavenly realm.

Section 11. Explanation of the level of Buddhahood

The Buddha's knowledge

11:011 The Buddha has understood that all things have the same characteristic of being unborn, that is, not causally produced by any substantially real causal relation, and hence empty. Even though all phenomena are distinct and differentiated, they are identical and undifferentiated to the extent they are all empty, as a variety of pots may have different shapes, though the space enclosed by them always has the same nature. Having realized the essential identity of all things in terms of their emptiness, the Buddha knows the nature of all phenomena and is thereby omniscient.

11:012 However, one may object that if reality is completely pacified by nature, then there is no possibility for the mind to know it by representing its structure. The differentiation of reality into its different aspects requires a causal relation. However, if all things are unborn, which, looking back at the preceding verse, is what Candrakīrti has in mind when he notes that the "reality of things

[5] *Laṅkāvatārasūtra* 2:11, *Sagathakam* 774 (Suzuki 1932, 46, 284–285). See Red Pine 2012: 59, 81; Suzuki 1930: 375–376. See also Sakadata 1997: 66–67, 126; Huntington 2018: 80–84.

is pacification," differentiation seems to be impossible because the causal relation is wholly absent at this stage. If, in the absence of such differentiation, we cannot ascertain distinct *objects* making up reality, it is difficult to see how we could conceive of a knowing *subject*. (In addition, any epistemic relation between perceiver and perceived presumably also requires the presence of a causal relation.) Yet if there is no act of knowing, there cannot be any knowledge of reality, and as such, no Buddha who could correctly claim to know and teach the nature of this reality.

Note that this is specifically a problem for a Buddha, not for ordinary beings, who see the world in terms of superimpositions of intrinsic nature, the duality of perceiver and perceived, and so on. On the basis of their mistaken understanding of reality they can negotiate conventional truths in successful manner. For a Buddha, on the other hand, for whom all mistaken superimpositions have disappeared, such projected structures are no longer relevant. The question then remains how, once everything that we usually take to constitute the structure of the known world and the structure of the knower's cognitive representations has disappeared, we can still speak of knowledge in any reasonable sense.

Candrakīrti responds by referring to the Sautrāntika theory of **11:013**
perception. The Sautrāntikas endorse a form of representationalism according to which mental representations (*ākāra*) accurately mirror the external object perceived. The picture is slightly complicated by the fact that the Sautrāntikas combine this with the Buddhist theory of momentariness and with presentism. As a result, their theory of perception has to account for the fact that by the time our mind perceives any object (a patch of blue color, say), the object that caused the mental representation has already gone out of existence. Strictly speaking, our representation is therefore directed at something that does not exist (anymore), yet the Sautrāntika explains that we can still speak of epistemic contact with reality in this context, since the mental representation of the color blue we perceive now is an exact mental representation of the

earlier momentary instance of the blue patch that caused the representation.[6] The key point is that according to this epistemological theory, which Candrakīrti accepts at the level of conventional truth, mental representations are veridical because they precisely reflect the object represented.[7] Candrakīrti then points out that if we accept this account of what it means to represent truthfully, the Buddha's mind, seen through the perspective of epistemic standards we accept, represents reality truthfully, since after enlightenment, the Buddha's mind is as unborn and free from superimposition as reality itself.[8] As such, it can represent it with maximal accuracy.

We do, of course, have to accept that this conception of "faithful representation" only makes sense when trying to conceive of the relation of the Buddha's mind to the world from *our* vantage point, and hence in a metaphorical manner. In the case of the Buddha's cognition we cannot assume, that from the Buddha's perspective there is an unborn mind *as a subject* knowing an unborn reality *as an object*, since the division between subject and object has vanished for him.

The Buddha's activity

11:014 Having accounted for how there could be *knowledge* of reality in terms of knower and known having identical structures, Candrakīrti now turns to the second challenge voiced in 11:012, that of accounting for the Buddha as the *knower* of reality. A specific problem is connected with explaining the understanding of the Buddha as someone who teaches the ultimate truth. If the

[6] For more on the Sautrāntika theory of perception see Dhammajoti 2007: 158–162.

[7] Scherrer-Schaub 1991: 258–259, note 492, section 3.3; 153–154, note 154. For more on Candrakīrti's epistemology see Thakchoe 2010, 2013.

[8] The commentarial literature (e.g., Jinpa 2021: 534) uses the image of water being poured into water to underline this point, as the perceiver and perceived are inextricably mixed at this stage.

transformation of the Buddha's mind through enlightenment has eliminated all mental defilements, including desire and craving, what would actually motivate the Buddha to teach? Even if we can understand that, from the vantage point of conventional truth, the Buddha's mind accurately represents ultimate truth, how can we make sense of the Buddha's endeavor to teach, in the absence of any facilitating psychological factors?

The answer lies in the vast store of merit the Buddha has accumulated during his training as a bodhisattva on the way to enlightenment. This allows him to project different emanations,[9] including bodily manifestations displaying psychological states, which appear to ordinary beings in the form of a Buddha. There is no need for the Buddha to really be subject to psychological states, like the desire to teach, as long as he can generate an emanation that convincingly portrays such states to beings to be liberated. In fact not even the display of a living being like a Buddha is necessary to make it possible for the Buddha to teach. Through the force of his accumulated karmic potential he can also bring about teaching by purely inanimate means, through the sound of wind rustling in the trees, the sounds of flowing water, the shapes of rocks, and so forth.

In the same way as the potter sets his wheel in motion once, but 11:015
subsequently does not need to sustain its motion when forming the
pot, as it keeps on spinning by the force imparted to it at the begin- 11:016
ning of the process, so, after enlightenment, the Buddha does not need to expend any effort when acting, teaching, and so forth, since all his activities unfold as products of previously accumulated merit. This merit includes karmic potential accumulated by the Buddha-to-be on the bodhisattva path, and merit generated by other beings wishing to hear the Buddha's teachings. While the Buddha seems

[9] Candrakīrti refers here to two different manifestations of the Buddha, the two 'bodily' manifestations (*rūpakāya*) distinguished in Mahāyāna doctrine of the 'three bodies' (*trikāya*) of the Buddha. These are the *nirmāṇakāya*, the form the Buddha manifests to ordinary sentient beings, and the *saṃbhogakāya*, the perfected form the Buddha adopts to teach bodhisattvas in the buddha-fields.

to resemble sentient beings in cyclic existence in many ways (he has a human body, speaks a human language, eats and drinks, get sick, and so forth) such resemblance is only apparent. The normal psychological and motivational processes that generate behavior in ordinary sentient beings are wholly absent in the case of a Buddha, though the Buddha generates an emanation that produces the impression that they are present.

The three bodies of the Buddha

11:017 Candrakīrti already referred to the first two of the "three bodies" of a Buddha distinguished in Mahāyāna Buddhology in 11:014 and now turns to the third, the *dharmakāya*. At this stage all objects of knowledge have been completely burned away by the fire of the Buddha's wisdom;[10] the eradication of all objects of knowledge also entails the eradication of knowledge and the knower. The resulting peaceful state, free from knowledge, knower, or known, is a form of the Buddha without the temporal dimension of arising and passing away; moreover, no kind of mental activity operates at this level. This, however, does not contradict the fact that (from the perspective of conventional truth) the Buddha has perfect knowledge of ultimate reality, given that, as discussed in 11:013, the nature of reality and the nature of the Buddha's mind coincide. In addition, the Buddha can display, again at the level of conventional truth, a spatio-temporal physical body that appears to teach this knowledge of reality to ordinary beings.

11:018 Through his emanations, generated by the power of intentions the bodhisattva has accumulated on the way to Buddhahood, the Buddha can benefit countless sentient beings, like a wish-fulfilling

[10] Candrakīrti here refer to a famous Buddhist metaphor where the analysis of conventional phenomena is compared to the rubbing of two sticks, producing the fire of wisdom which subsequently completely consumes the sticks.

tree, a boon-giving miraculous tree already mentioned in early Indian sources, or like the similar effective wish-fulfilling gem. These miraculous entities have no minds, and do not fulfill their beneficial activity by means of mental states. In the same way, the fully enlightened Buddhas are without concepts or mental activity, but carry out their beneficial activity simply by the continued force of previously accumulated intentions.

The perfected form of the manifestation of the Buddha, the *saṃboghakāya*, which Candrakīrti refers to in this verse by the term "body of peace," is distinct from the Buddha's manifestations in human form (the *nirmāṇakāya*), such as the historical Buddha Śākyamuni. It appears only to bodhisattvas on the higher bodhisattva stages, but not to other bodhisattvas or ordinary beings. The *saṃboghakāya* is endowed with five specific properties: abiding in the heavenly realm of Akaniṣṭha, lasting until the end of cyclic existence, displaying the minor and major marks of physical perfection had by a Buddha as the result of his accumulated merit, being surrounded exclusively by bodhisattvas, and always teaching the Mahāyāna.

Candrakīrti uses the phrase "physical body in accordance with **11:019**
the cause" in order to refer to the Buddha's *nirmāṇakāya* manifestation which is physical, and hence perceptible to ordinary beings, but conforms to the other two bodies of the Buddha, the *dharmakāya* and the *saṃbhogakāya*, in arising from the same source. In this body the Buddha can know and demonstrate all the past rebirths he took on the path to buddhahood, instantly and in their correct order, like a reflection in a clear mirror. This idea is already found in the Pāli canon, where the Buddha's enlightenment experience is associated with the attainment of three knowledges, the first of which is the ability to remember all his past lives.[11] Many of these lives are related by the Buddha in the *jātaka* tales.[12]

[11] *pūrvanivāsānusmṛti*. See e.g. the *Mahāsacakkasutta*, Majjhima Nikāya 36, I 249, Bhikkhu Ñāṇamoli / Bhikkhu Bodhi 2001: 341.

[12] See Shaw 2006a.

11:020 Within this body, and in fact within a single pore of this body, the
Buddha is able to display different miraculous projections of scenes
11:021 from his path to buddhahood, such as the buddha-fields and how he
took birth there, the monastic community that attended him in the
11:022 past, the teaching he taught, and the different situations in the past
in which he practiced the six perfections.

11:023 He can similarly show the Buddhas of the past, and future, and
those of the present, wherever they are located, together with their
11:024 teachings, as well as the entire sequence of their spiritual development, from first making the resolve to become Buddhas up to their obtaining of enlightenment. Having known that all of the events that constitute the Buddha's path to enlightenment are of the same nature as a magical display, he can demonstrate them all by means of his miraculous powers.

11:025 He can similarly demonstrate the actions of beings below the realization of a fully enlightened Buddha, from bodhisattvas, to *arhats*, to ordinary mortals.

11:027 The miraculous powers of the Buddhas include the ability to
manipulate the display of space. They are able to display entire
11:026 universes in a single particle, without the particle increasing in size, or the universe shrinking.[13] The Buddhas are also able to manipulate the display of time. Though free from any conceptualizing activity, they can display an immeasurable amount of actions in any instant, as many as there are particles in the entire earth, until the end of cyclic existence.

The ten powers of the Buddha

11:028 Next, Candrakīrti considers the ten powers of a Buddha, which take the form of ten specific epistemic abilities:

[13] This notion of the interpenetration of the microscopic and the macroscopic is developed at length in the *Avataṃsakasūtra* (see Cleary 1993: 189–190).

1. The power of knowing what is the case and what is not, 11:029
2. The power of knowing the consequences of actions,
3. The power of knowing the dispositions of different beings, 11:030
4. The power of knowing the different elements,
5. The power of knowing which faculties are superior and which are not,
6. The power of knowing the ways leading to all destinations,
7. The power of knowing the defilement and purification of all meditative absorptions (*dhyāna*), grades of liberation (*vimokṣa*), meditative concentrations (*samādhi*), and attainments (*samāpatti*),
8. The power of knowing how to remember previous lives,
9. The power of knowing death and birth,
10. The power of knowledge of the eradication of the taints.

These ten powers are described by Candrakīrti in greater detail in the following verses, and illustrated by quotations from the *Tathāgata-mahākaruṇā-nirdeśa-sūtra*.

The power of knowing what is the case and what is not (1) is 11:031
to understand which *kinds* of karmic consequences follow which actions; in particular it is to know that virtuous, but not non-virtuous intentions will give rise to hedonically positive states and to know how particular kinds of meditative achievements lead to progress on the path to enlightenment.

The power of knowing the consequences of actions (2) involves 11:032
detailed knowledge of the connection between *specific* actions and the results they bring about; how virtuous, non-virtuous, and neutral actions, or some mixture of these, carried out by each being in the past, present, or future give rise to their specific experiences that are hedonically positive, negative, or neutral or a mixture of these, and how the practice of the Buddhist path leads to gradually becoming free from cyclic existence.

The power of knowing the dispositions of different beings (3) 11:033
is the knowledge of their different psychological states, including

afflictive emotions like desirous attachment and aversion, but also virtuous states of mind like faith. These act like seeds, bringing about specific dispositions, and the Buddha knows all of these, in their full variety, for all beings, at any moment.

11:034 The power of knowing the different elements (4) extends to the knowledge of the nature of the eighteen sense spheres: the six sense faculties, their objects, and the sensory cognitions resulting from the contacts of sense faculty and object. (In the *sūtra* quotation Candrakīrti adds in the autocommentary, this knowledge is described as a comprehensive insight into the elements of Buddhist ontology, including the constituents of matter, space, the three realms, the compounded and uncompounded, and *saṃsāra* and *nirvāṇa*.) The nature of all of these is to be empty, and the Buddha understands their emptiness in terms of all of the divisions of that concept (such as the 16-fold division discussed above in 6:180).

11:035 The power of knowing which faculties are superior and which are not (5) relates to the knowledge of the nature and mutual interaction of epistemic processes ordinary beings employ in order to interact in the world. The Buddhas know how sentient beings form conceptualizations, which give rise to defiled mental states such as desire, and to pure states, such as faith, how these states can take on forms of superior, intermediate, or inferior strength, and how these in turn operate in relation to the different epistemic faculties enumerated in the Abhidharma texts.[14]

11:036 The power of knowing the ways leading to all destinations (6) amounts to knowing where the practices of each individual lead, whether they will bring it to the state of a fully enlightened Buddha, to states of realization like those of an *arhat*, or to rebirth in one of the six realms of cyclic existence.

[14] Candrakīrti refers in particular to the 22 faculties (*dvāviṃśatiḥ indriyāṇi*, *dbang po nyi shu rtsa gnyis*), a set of faculties dominant in the epistemic constitution of beings. See Chapter 2 of Vasubandhu's *Abhidharmakośa* (Lamotte 1988–1990: 1: 158–159), Lamotte 1944–1980: 3: 1494–1495, Gelongma Karma Migme Chödrön 3: 1224–1225.

The power of knowing the defilement and purification of all meditative absorptions, grades of liberation, meditative concentrations, and attainments (7) is the knowledge of the causes and nature of the various meditative states constituting an integral part of the Buddhist path. 11:037

Candrakīrti specifically refers to different, partly overlapping[15] kinds of meditative training, the four absorptions of the form realm,[16] the eight liberations,[17] calm abiding,[18] and the nine attainments.[19]

The enumeration of the ten powers of the Buddha concludes with the three specific epistemic powers characterizing the Buddhas' enlightenment experience. The first of these, the power of knowing how to remember previous lives (8), enables the Buddhas to recall all of their own previous lives, as well as all the previous lives of all other sentient beings as well as their causes in the greatest detail. Not only do they know their external circumstances, such as the place and circumstances they were born in, but their knowledge even extends to the internal features of each life of each sentient being, knowing the succession of mental states that constitute each one. In this way they know the karmic potential of each being, knowledge they can they use to teach each one in the most effective manner. 11:038

The power of knowing death and birth (9) involves knowledge of the birth and death of every single being anywhere in the cosmos, 11:039

[15] The four formless absorptions (*catasra ārūpyasamāpattayaḥ*) and the absorption of cessation of concept and feeling (*saṃjñāveditanirodhasamāpatti*) are included in the eight grades of liberation; the nine attainments subsume the four absorptions of the form realm, the four formless absorptions, and the absorption of cessation of concept and feeling.

[16] See 6:207.

[17] *aṣṭau vimokṣāḥ*. Lamotte 1944–1980: 3: 1289–1299, Gelongma Karma Migme Chödrön 3: 1056–1064. See Padmakara 2010: 431–432. See below, p. 188, note 174.

[18] *śamatha*. Lamotte 1944–1980: 5: 2428–2429, note 4, Gelongma Karma Migme Chödrön: 5: 2016, note 383.

[19] *samāpatti*. Lamotte 1944–1980: 2: 1023, note 3, Gelongma Karma Migme Chödrön: 2: 793, note 446; Dalai Lama/Thubten Chodron 2019: 211–260. See Padmakara 2010: 432.

and all the causes and conditions that lead from there to its specific next rebirth. As opposed to the previous power, this is directed at the future, not at the past. This is not to be understood in the sense of an omniscient knowledge of a predetermined future, but in the sense of the Buddha's knowing how, given the potentials a being has accumulated until now, it would be reborn in its next life. As this power involves knowing whenever a being is born anywhere, the Buddha is able to teach all beings without limit. Moreover, using his divine eye, the second of the three specific epistemic powers, he not only knows the arising and cessation of each individual being's life, but also arising and cessation on a cosmic scale, knowing the origination and destruction of each universe.

11:040 The power of knowledge of the eradication of the taints (10) is the final of the three specific epistemic powers a Buddha acquires when achieving enlightenment. It is the knowledge that all the mental contaminants have been eliminated, leading to complete liberation from *saṃsāra*. Candrakīrti points out that only the fully enlightened Buddhas have completely removed these contaminants, as well as the karmic tendencies that underlie them; in the case of other highly realized practitioners such as the *arhat*s, while the contaminants have been removed, some remnants of the underlying karmic tendencies stay behind, as a residue remains when oil has been emptied out of a pot.

Describing the Buddha's qualities

11:041 The description of the Buddha's qualities by bodhisattvas, *arhat*s, and so on are limited not because the qualities expressed are lim-
11:042 ited, but because the expressive resources of the non-Buddhas are not able to represent their full range, as a bird cannot traverse the full expanse of limitless space. For this reason, Candrakīrti, who sees himself as outside of the group of highly realized Buddhist practitioners, considers it to be even less feasible for him to provide

an account of even a fraction of the qualities of the Buddhas, basing himself instead on the description of them provided by Nāgārjuna.

Candrakīrti's description in the "Introduction to the Middle Way" has characterized the Buddha's qualities by the concepts 'profound' and 'vast.' The former includes emptiness, which is profound because it is difficult to understand and realize, and the latter the ten bodhisattva stages, since the qualities developed along them are limitless. The realization of these two, of the emptiness of all things, and of the perfections that characterize the path of the bodhisattva, leads to the attainment of Buddhahood. 11:043

The physical embodiment of the Buddha and its activity

Despite having completely passed beyond cyclic existence, the Buddha nevertheless manifests in *saṃsāra* in physical form. In this he displays the various biographical events of a Buddha's life, teaches the Buddhist teaching, and thereby leads sentient beings to liberation. 11:044

The nature of all phenomena, their emptiness, is the same for each one; there is no ultimate differentiation into different types of emptiness relative to the objects that are empty, such as the emptiness of material objects, emptiness of mental objects, and so forth—all these are only distinguished in terms of the descriptions provided for them. As such, the Buddha's wisdom realizing emptiness is also the undifferentiated realization of this emptiness; it does not present him with different aspects of emptiness, in the way in which the representation of a patterned cloth would consist of different representations of distinct parts of the pattern. As the realization of emptiness is undifferentiated in this sense, realizing the emptiness of any one phenomenon is equivalent to realizing the emptiness of all, as understanding the properties of space contained in a single pot is equivalent to understanding the properties of any portion of 11:045

space. And since it is the realization of this undifferentiated emptiness of all things that leads to Buddhahood, the differentiation into different vehicles such as the Mahāyāna and the vehicles of the *arhats* and *pratyekabuddhas* is only taught for conventional and propaedeutic reasons. The distinction of the different vehicles was taught in relation to the particular inclinations and capacities of different beings, not because there were in any ultimate sense different background ontologies (of the Abhidharma and the Mahāyāna), or different paths and different goals these paths would lead to.

11:046 Despite the fact that there is only a single liberated state, vehicles such as those of the *arhats* and *pratyekabuddhas* have been taught to lead to final *nirvāṇa*. This is because the minds of many beings are covered by obscurations to such an extent that they can only access the Buddha's wisdom in a somewhat attenuated form. Having trained them along these paths, the Buddha will then teach the undifferentiated, highest truth of emptiness to them.

11:047 Candrakīrti illustrates this point by drawing on an example from the 7th chapter of the *Saddharmapuṇḍarīkasūtra*,[20] describing a guide who leads a group of merchants on a journey bound for an island of jewels far away. The group gets stuck in a seemingly endless forest and wants to turn back. To enable them to reach the island the guide conjures up an illusory city in the middle of the forest where the merchants can rest. After they have regained their strength, the guide declares the city to be a mere magical apparition, subsequently guiding them to the real island of jewels.

In the same way, the Buddha teaches the spiritual goals of the paths of the *arhats* and *pratyekabuddhas* as if they were the final destinations of the Buddhist path. This is only done, however, for the sake of those whose reach cannot extend to full Mahāyāna enlightenment. Once they have achieved the intermediate goals of *arhat*ship and *pratyekabuddha*hood, the Buddha will teach them

[20] Kern 1963: 181–183.

that these are not the final goal yet, and will show them how to realize the fully enlightened state that crowns the Mahāyāna path.

The continuity of the Buddha's teaching

The Buddha's manifestation of a physical embodiment in the form of a *nirmāṇakāya* (such as the historical Buddha Śākyamuni) after obtaining enlightenment in a pure realm is not a one-off event. Rather, the Buddha generates such manifestations in as many eons as there are atoms in all of the buddha-fields. According to the view presented by Candrakīrti, the Buddha's enlightenment did not take place in Bodhgaya in ancient India; rather, the Buddha became enlightened before this time in a heavenly realm, and continues to send out manifestations of historical beings which *appear* to obtain enlightenment on earth. Candrakīrti points out that this is a secret not commonly taught, indicating that only those with sufficiently large accumulations of merit would find such power to produce *nirmāṇakāya* emanations plausible. For this reason this idea is only taught to students distinguished in this respect. 11:048

Buddhahood arises from the two forces of wisdom and compassion, compared by Candrakīrti to the mother and the wet-nurse, respectively. Understanding the interconnectedness of all things and feeling great love for all sentient beings, the Buddha will continue to manifest his enlightened activity, and not enter into any form of *nirvāṇa* in which his enlightened activities cease as long as the world itself exists, and until all beings in the entire world have been liberated. 11:049

The pleasures resulting from the five sense faculties are like poisoned food that sentient beings, ignorant of its real nature, consume, leading to much suffering. The Buddha knows this, and hence feels pain greater than a mother seeing her own children eat poison. As such he would never pass into a state where he does not display his enlightened actions, until all beings have been liberated. 11:050

11:051 The suffering of cyclic existence, birth and death, being separated from what is pleasant, meeting the unpleasant, is the result of considering things to be substantially real or substantially unreal. Belief in the substantial reality of karma supports actions resulting in rebirth in the human or divine realm, with their associated suffering, suffering that takes place within the realms, and suffering associated with falling out of these realms once the karmic potential has been exhausted. The belief that karma is substantially unreal tends to facilitate actions leading to rebirth in the lower realms which are characterized by a multiplicity of suffering that take place within these realms. Seeing this, the Buddha will continue his enlightened activity until all beings are liberated.

Section 12. Origin and uniqueness of Candrakīrti's exposition of Madhyamaka

11:052 Candrakīrti points out that his exposition of Madhyamaka in the "Introduction to the Middle Way" takes as its basis Nāgārjuna's *Mūlamadhyamakakārikā*, the *sūtra*s, and oral instructions.
11:053 Nevertheless, it is not simply a paraphrase of other teachings; in fact, Candrakīrti claims, no tradition other than Madhyamaka presents the teaching of emptiness correctly. His exposition of Madhyamaka presented here is unique and not found elsewhere.

In particular, it would be mistaken to understand Madhyamaka as accepting the ontologies of the Sarvāstivāda or Sautrāntika Abhidharma as correct on the level of relative truth, while postulating universal emptiness as the ultimate truth, since the supramundane teaching of Madhyamaka cannot be understood as a simple extension of the mundane teachings of the Abhidharma. The Madhyamaka criticism of intrinsic natures, which the Abhidharma endorses, is directed against any form of *svabhāva*, not simply against *svabhāva* conceived of as ultimately real.

Candrakīrti is here emphasizing a point that is commonly regarded as a unique feature of the Prāsaṅgika interpretation of Madhyamaka,[21] that is, the view that objects with intrinsic natures (such as the *dharmas* postulated by the Abhidharma) do not even exist at the level of conventional truth.

In a poetic image Candrakīrti compares Nāgārjuna's teachings to a vast ocean whose brilliant color has frightened away some thinkers, having the appearance of an infinite extension, with no visible boundaries or ground which the mistaken superimposition of an intrinsic nature could latch onto. Instead of this awe-inspiring aquatic expanse, Candrakīrti here presents his audience with a more confined body of water, a pond filled with buds of lotus flowers, said to open only at night. These correspond to the minds of the audience, which fully unfold to a comprehensive understanding of Madhyamaka when moistened by the nightly dew and illuminated by the rays of the moon, the exposition by Candrakīrti, who bears the moon (*candra*) in his name. 11:054

Other Buddhist teachers of the past (Candrakīrti explicitly refers to the Yogācārins Vasubandu, Diṅnāga, and Dharmapāla) lacked the relevant karmic potential to comprehend the full range of Nāgārjuna's teaching of emptiness, which appears frightening to those not predisposed to it from previous mental acquaintance. Other traditions, whether they are rival schools of Buddhist thought, or non-Buddhist systems promoting a substantial self, should be regarded as the product of philosophical ingenuity, but not as a reflection of the Buddha's enlightened mind. As such, one should fail to be impressed by any tradition other than Madhyamaka. 11:055

Candrakīrti concludes his work by a poetically framed dedication of the merit acquired from composing it. He expresses the aspiration that this merit should fill the entire extent of space, 11:056

[21] For later Tibetan discussions of this point see Thurman 1984: 306–344; Ruegg 2002: 168–202; Cozort 1998: 60.

illuminating the blue-black sky darkened by mental afflictions and defilements like the constellations of shining autumn stars.[22] He also refers to this merit as a mind-made serpent stone that will enable the entire world to quickly obtain Buddhahood. The serpent stone is a stone or jewel said to be found in the head of snakes and is considered to be effective against poison, or, more generally, able to fulfill its bearer's wishes. This simile works on a variety of levels; like the serpent stone, the merit acquired through the study of emptiness is able to neutralize the poisons of mental afflictions and conceptual constructions, and will bring about the greatest of all goods, liberation; the reference to snakes and the miraculous gems they possess also concludes the text by pointing back to the origin of Madhyamaka: to the *nāga*s as guardians of the Perfection of Wisdom texts, and to Nāgārjuna, whose Middle Way expounds their teachings.

[22] The fourth of the six seasons (*ṛtu*) distinguished in the ancient Indian calendar, autumn (*śaradā*) follows the rainy season (*varṣā*) and is characterized by clear skies.

Bibliography

Edwin A. Abbott: *Flatland. A Romance of Many Dimensions*, Penguin, London, 1998.

Alison Aitken: "No unity, no problem: Madhyamaka metaphysical indefinitism," *Philosopher's Imprint* 21:3, 2021, 1–24.

William L. Ames: "The notion of *svabhāva* in the thought of Candrakīrti," *Journal of Indian Philosophy* 10, 1982, 161–177.

William L. Ames: "Bhāvaviveka's own view of his differences with Buddhapālita," in Georges B. J. Dreyfus and Sara L. McClintock (eds.): *The Svātantrika-Prāsaṅgika Distinction. What Difference Does a Difference Make*? Wisdom Publications, Boston, 2003, 41–66.

William L. Ames: *The Lamp of Discernment: A Translation of Chapters 1–12 of Bhāvaviveka's Prajñāpradīpa*, University of Hawai'i Press, Honolulu, 2019.

Bhikkhu Anālayo: *Rebirth in Early Buddhism & Current Research*, Wisdom Publications, Boston, 2018.

James B. Apple: *Atīśa Dīpaṃkara*. The Illuminator of the Awakended Mind, Wisdom Publications, Boston, 2019a.

James B. Apple: *Jewels of the Middle Way. The Madhyamaka Legacy of Atiśa and His Early Tibetan Followers*, Wisdom Publications, Boston, 2019b.

Dan Arnold: *Buddhists, Brahmins, and Belief*, Columbia University Press, New York, 2005.

André Bareau: *The Buddhist Schools of the Small Vehicle*, University of Hawai'i Press, Honolulu, 2013.

Achim Bayer: "The world arises from mind only. Candrakīrti's affirmation of *cittamātra* at *Madhyamakāvatāra* 6.87," in Volker Caumanns, Marta Sernesi, Nikolai Solmsdorf (eds.): *Unearthing Himalayan Treasures*. Festschrift for Franz-Karl Erhard, Indica et Tibetica Verlag, Marburg, 2019, 27–48.

Robert Beer: *The Encyclopedia of Tibetan Symbols and Motifs*, Shambala, Boston, 1999.

Ramkrishna Bhattacharya: *Studies on the Cārvāka/Lokāyata*, Anthem Press, London, New York, Delhi, 2011.

Michel Bitbol: "Two aspects of *śūnyatā* in quantum physics: relativity of properties and quantum non-separability," in Siddheshwar Rameshwar Bhatt (ed.): *Quantum Reality and Theory of Śūnya*, Springer, Singapore, 2019, 93–117.

James Blumenthal: *The Ornament of the Middle Way. A Study of the Madhyamaka Thought of Śāntarakṣita*, Snow Lion, Ithaca, NY, Boulder, CO, 2004.

Bhikkhu Bodhi: *The Connected Discourses of the Buddha*, Wisdom Publications, Boston, 2000.

Bhikkhu Bodhi: *The Numerical Discourses of the Buddha*, Wisdom Publications, Boston, 2012.

Leigh Brasington: *Right Concentration: A Practical Guide to the Jhānas*, Shambala, Boston, London, 2015.

Johannes Bronkhorst: "Sāṃkhya in the Abhidharmakośa Bhāṣya," *Journal of Indian Philosophy* 25:4, 1997, 393–400.

Johannes Bronkhorst: "*Satkāryavāda* and *asatkāryavāda*," in Folke Josephson (ed.): *Categorisation and Interpretation: Indological and Comparative Studies from an International Indological Meeting at the Department of Comparative Philology, Göteborg University. A Volume Dedicated to the Memory of Gösta Liebert*. Meijerbergs institut för svensk etymologisk forskning, Göteborgs universitet, Göteborg, 1999, 43–55.

Karl Brunnhölzl: *A Lullaby to Awaken the Heart: The Aspiration Prayer of Samantabhadra and Its Commentaries*, Wisdom Publications, Boston, 2018.

Brett Buchanan: *Onto-Ethologies. The Animal Environments of Uexküll, Heidegger, Merleau-Ponty, and Deleuze*, State University of New York Press, Albany, 2008.

Mikel Burley: *Classical Sāṃkhya. An Indian Metaphysics of Experience*, Routledge, London, New York, 2007.

Sergei Burmistrov: "The concept of *dravya* in Yogācāra and Vaiśeṣika: a comparative philosophical analysis," *Written Monuments of the Orient* 4:1, 2018, 55–77.

Tim Button: *The Limits of Realism*, Oxford University Press, Oxford, 2013.

José Ignacio Cabezón: *A Dose of Emptiness. An Annotated Translation of the sTong thun chen mo of mKhas-grub dGe-legs-dpal-bzang*, State University of New York Press, Albany, 1992.

Patrick Carré: *Soûtra des Dix Terres, Dashabhûmika*, Fayard, Paris, 2004.

Shaila Catherine: *Wisdom Wide and Deep. A Practical Handbook for Mastering Jhāna and Vipassanā*, Wisdom Publications, Boston, 2011.

Arindam Chakrabarti: *Realisms Interlinked. Objects, Subjects, and Other Subjects*, Bloomsbury, New Delhi, London, Oxford, New York, Sidney, 2020.

David Chalmers: *Reality+. Virtual Worlds and the Problems of Philosophy*, W.W. Norton, New York, 2022.

Lama Chimpa, Alaka Chattopadhyaya: *Tāranātha's History of Buddhism in India*, Indian Institute of Advanced Study, Simla, 1970.

Thomas Cleary: *The Flower Ornament Scripture. A Translation of the Avatamsaka Sutra*, Shambala, Boston, London, 1993.

Ian Coghlan: *Buddhapālita's Commentary on Nāgārjuna's Middle Way (Buddhapālita-Mūlamadhyamakakārikā-Vṛtti)*, American Institute of Buddhist Studies, Wisdom Publications, New York, Boston, 2022.

Edward Conze: "The ontology of the Prajñāpāramitā," *Philosophy East and West* 3:2, 1953, 117–129.

Edward Conze: *Buddhist Thought in India. Three Phases of Buddhist Philosophy*, George Allen & Unwin, London, 1962.

The Cowherds: *Moonshadows: Conventional Truth in Buddhist Philosophy*, Oxford University Press, Oxford, 2013.

The Cowherds: *Moonpaths: Ethics and Madhyamaka Philosophy*, Oxford University Press, Oxford, 2015.

Daniel Cozort: *Unique Tenets of the Middle Way Consequence School*, Snow Lion, Ithaca, NY, 1998.

Kate Crosby and Andrew Skilton: *Śāntideva. The Bodhicaryāvatāra*, Oxford University Press, Oxford, 1995.

The Dalai Lama, Thubten Chodron: *Following in the Buddha's Footsteps*, Wisdom Publications, Boston, 2019.

The Dalai Lama, Thubten Chodron: *In Praise of Great Compassion*, Wisdom Publications, Boston, 2020.

Mario D'Amato: "Mapping the Mahāyāna: some historical and doctrinal issues," *Religion Compass* 2:4, 2008, 536–555.

Har Dayal: *The Bodhisattva Doctrine in Buddhist Literature*, Kegan Paul, Trench, Trübner, London, 1932.

Tyler Dewar: *The Karmapa's Middle Way: Feast for the Fortunate, The Ninth Karmapa, Wangchuk Dorje*, Snow Lion, Ithaca, NY, 2008.

Bhikkhu KL Dhammajoti: "The Sarvāstivāda doctrine of simultaneous causality," *Journal of Buddhist Studies* 1, 2003, 17–54.

Bhikkhu KL Dhammajoti: *Abhidharma Doctrines and Controversies on Perception*, Centre of Buddhist Studies, University of Hong Kong, Hong Kong, 2007.

Bhikkhu KL Dhammajoti: *Sarvāstivāda Abhidharma*, 4th edition, Centre of Buddhist Studies, University of Hong Kong, 2009.

Bhikshu Dharmamitra: *The Ten Grounds Sutra. The Daśabhūmikasūtra. The Ten Highest Levels of Practice on the Bodhisatta's Path to Buddhahood, As Translated from Sanskrit by Kumārajīva (c 410 CE). A Trilingual Edition (Chinese/English/Sanskrit)*, Kalavinka Press, Seattle, 2019.

Jan Willem de Jong: *Cing chapitres de la Prasannapadā*, Librairie orientaliste P. Geuthner, Paris, 1949.

Jan Willem de Jong: "Review of Mervyn Sprung, T. R. V. Murti and U. S. Vyas: *Lucid Exposition of the Middle Way. The Essential Chapters from the Prasannapadā of Candrakīrti*," *Indo-Iranian Journal* 23:3, 1981, 227–230.

James Duerlinger: *Indian Buddhist Theories of Persons. Vasubandhu's "Refutation of the Theory of a Self,"* Routledge, London, New York, 2003.

James Duerlinger: *The Refutation of the Self in Indian Buddhism. Candrakīrti on the Selflessness of Persons*, Routledge, London, New York, 2013.

John Dunne: "Thoughtless Buddha, passionate Buddha," *Journal of the American Academy of Religion* 64:3, 1996, 525–556.

Dzogchen Pönlop Rinpoche: *Commentary on the Madhyamakavatara. Chandrakirti's Entrance to the Middle Way by Mikyö Dorje, Karmapa VIII*, Nithartha Institute, Seattle, 1999.

Umberto Eco: "Sugli specchi," in *Sugli specchi e altri saggi. Il segno, la rappresentazione, l'illusione, l'immagine*, La nave di Teseo, Milan, 2018.

Helmut Eimer: *Skizzen des Erlösungsweges in buddhistischen Begriffsreihen*, Religionswissenschaftliches Seminar der Universität Bonn, Bonn, 1976.

Vincent Eltschinger: "Candrakīrti," in Jonathan Silk (ed.): *Brill's Encyclopedia of Buddhism*, vol. 2, Brill, Leiden, Boston, 2019, 125–131.

Artemus B. Engle: *The Bodhisattva Path to Unsurpassed Enlightenment: A Complete Translation of the Bodhisattvabhūmi*, Snow Lion, Boulder, CO, 2016.

Peter Fenner: *The Ontology of the Middle Way*, Kluwer, Dordrecht, 1990.

Erich Frauwallner: *Philosophie des Buddhismus*, Akademie-Verlag, Berlin, 1956.

Jonardon Ganeri: *Philosophy in Classical India. The Proper Work of Reason*, Routledge, London, New York, 2001.

Richard Garbe: *Die Sāṃkhya-Philosophie. Eine Darstellung des Indischen Rationalismus*, H. Haessel, Leipzig, 1894.

Jay Garfield: "Vasubandhu's Treatise on the Three Natures: a translation and commentary," in Jay Garfield: *Empty Words: Buddhist Philosophy and Cross-Cultural Interpretation*, Oxford University Press, Oxford, 2002, 128–151.

Jay Garfield: *Engaging Buddhism. Why It Matters to Philosophy*, Oxford University Press, New York, 2015.

Rupert Gethin: *The Buddhist Path to Awakening*, Oneworld, Oxford, 2001.

Pradeep P. Gokhale: *Lokāyata/Cārvāka. A Philosophical Inquiry*, Oxford University Press, Oxford, 2015.

Ari Goldfield, Jules Levinson, Jim Scott, and Birgit Scott: *The Moon of Wisdom. Chapter Six of Chandrakirti's Entering the Middle Way with Commentary from the Eighth Karmapa, Mikyö Dorje's Chariot of the Dakpo Kagyü Siddhas*, Snow Lion, Ithaca, NY, Boulder, CO, 2005.

Luis O. Gómez: "Proto-Mādhyamika in the Pāli Canon," *Philosophy East and West* 26:2, 1976, 137–165.

Charles Goodman, *The Tattvasaṃgraha of Śāntarakṣita: Selected Metaphysical Chapters*, Oxford University Press, New York, 2022.

Masaaki Hattori: *Dignāga, On Perception, being the Pratyakṣapariccheda of Dignāga's Pramāṇasamuccaya*, Harvard University Press, Cambridge, MA, 1968.

Megumu Honda: "Sāṃkhya philosophy described by his opponent Bhavya," *Journal of Indian Buddhist Studies* 31, 1967, 436–442.

Megumu Honda: "Annotated Translation of the Daśabhūmikasūtra," in Denis Sinor (ed.): *Studies in South, East, and Central Asia: Presented as a Memorial Volume to the Late Professor Raghu Vira*, International Academy of Indian Culture, Delhi, 1968, 115–276.

C. W. Huntington, Jr., Geshe Namgyal Wangchen: *The Emptiness of Emptiness. An Introduction to Early Indian Mādhyamika*, Motilal Banarsidass, Delhi, 1992.

Eric Huntington: *Creating the Universe. Depictions of the Cosmos in Himalayan Buddhism*, University of Washington Press, Seattle, 2018.

Marzenna Jakubczak: "Why didn't Siddhārtha Gautama become a Sāṃkhya philosopher, after all?" in Irina Kuznetsova, Jonardon Ganeri, Chakravarthi Ram-Prasad (eds.): *Hindu and Buddhist Ideas in Dialogue: Self and No-Self*, Ashgate, Farnham, 2012, 32–46.

Ganganatha Jha: *The Tattvasaṅgraha of Śāntarakṣita with the Commentary of Kamalaśīla*, Oriental Institute, Baroda, 1987.

Indukala H. Jhaveri: "The concept of *ākāśa* in Indian philosophy," *Annals of the Bhandarkar Oriental Research Institute* 37:1/4, 1956, 300–307.

Thupten Jinpa: "Tsongkhapa's qualms about early Tibetan interpretations of Madhyamaka Philosophy," *Tibet Journal* 24:2, 1999, 3–28.

Thupten Jinpa: *Self, Reality, and Reason in Tibetan Philosophy. Tsongkhapa's Quest for the Middle Way*, RoutlegeCurzon, London, New York, 2002.

Thupten Jinpa: *Tsongkhapa. A Buddha in the Land of Snows*, Shambala, Boulder, CO, 2019.

Thupten Jinpa: *Illuminating the Intent. An Exposition of Candrakīrti's "Entering the Middle Way,"* Wisdom Publications, Boston, 2021.

Geshe Kelsang Gyatso: *Ocean of Nectar: Wisdom and Compassion in Mahayana Buddhism*, Tharpa Publications, London, 1995.

Stephen A. Kent: "Early Sāṃkhya in the 'Buddhacarita'," *Philosophy East and West* 32:3, 1982, 259–278.

Johan Hendrik Kern: *Saddharma-Puṇḍarīka or The Lotus of the True Law*, Dover Publications, New York, 1963.

Khenchen Kunzang Pelden, Minyak Kunzang Sönam: *Wisdom. Two Buddhist Commentaries*, Editions Padmakara, Saint-Léon-sur-Vézère, 1999.

Khensur Jampa Tegchok: *Practical Ethics and Profound Emptiness. A Commentary on Nagarjuna's Precious Garland*, Wisdom Publications, Boston, 2016.

Leonard W. J. van der Kuijp, "Phya-pa Chos-kyi seng-ge's Impact on Tibetan Epistemological Theory," *Journal of Indian Philosophy* 5:4, 1978, 355–369.

Leonard W. J. van der Kuijp: "Jayānanda. A twelfth century *guoshi* from Kashmir among the Tangut," *Central Asiatic Journal* 37:3/4, 1993, 188–197.

Louis de La Vallée Poussin: "Madhyamakāvatāra. Introduction au Traité du Milieu de l'Ācārya Candrakīrti, avec le commentaire de l'auteur, traduit d'après la version tibétaine," *Le Muséon* 8, 1907, 249–317; 11, 1910, 271–358; 12, 1911, 236–328.

Louis de La Vallée Poussin: *Abhidharmakośabhāṣyam of Vasubandhu*. English translation by Leo M. Pruden, Asian Humanities Press, Berkeley, 1988–1990.

Étienne Lamotte: *Le traité de la grande vertu de sagesse de Nāgārjuna (Mahāprajñāparāmitāśāstra)*, Institut orientaliste, Université de Louvain, Institut Orientaliste, Louvain-la-neuve, Louvain, 1944–1980.

Étienne Lamotte: *La Somme du Grand Vehicule d'Asaṅga (Mahāyānasaṃgraha)*, Université de Louvain, Institut Orientaliste, Louvain-la-neuve, Louvain, 1973.

Karen Lang: *Āryadeva's Catuḥśataka. On the Bodhisattva's Cultivation of Merit and Knowledge*, Akademisk Forlag, Copenhagen, 1986.

Karen Lang: "Spha-tshab nyi-ma-grags and the introduction of Prāsaṅgika Madhyamaka into Tibet," in Lawrence Epstein, Richard F. Sherburne (eds.): *Reflections on Tibetan Culture. Essays in Memory of Turrell V. Wylie*, Edwin Mellen Press, Lewiston, Queenston, Lampeter, 1989, 127–141.

Richard Lannoy: "The Terror of Time," in Hari Shankar Prasad (ed.): *Time in Indian Philosophy: A Collection of Essays*, Sri Satguru Publications, Dehli, 1992, 415–422.

Gerald J. Larson: *Classical Sāṃkhya. An Interpretation of Its History and Meaning*, Motilal Banarsidass, Delhi, 1979.

Horst Lasic, Xuezhu Li, Anne MacDonald: Candrakīrti's *Madhyamakāvatāra bhāṣya* Chapters 1 to 5, Austrian Academy of Sciences Press, Vienna, 2022.

David Lewis: *Philosophical Papers II*, Oxford University Press, New York, 1986.

Xuezhu Li: "*Madhyamakāvatāra-kārikā* Chapter 6," *Journal of Indian Philosophy* 43, 2015, 1–30.

Christian Lindtner: "Candrakīrti's *Pañcaskandhaprakaraṇa*," *Acta Orientalia* 41, 1979, 87–145.

Christian Lindtner: "Atiśa's introduction to the two truths, and its sources," *Journal of Indian Philosophy* 9:2, 1981, 161–214.

Christian Lindtner: "The Laṅkāvatārasūtra in early Indian Madhyamaka literature," *Asiatische Studien* 45:1, 1992, 244–279.

Christian Lindtner: "Candrakīrti's Pañcaskandhaprakaraṇa," in Karl H. Potter: *Encyclopedia of Indian Philosophies*, vol. 21: *Buddhist Philosophy from 600 to 750 A.D.*, Motilal Banarsidass, Delhi, 2017, 229–240.

Oystein Linnebo: "Predicative and Impredicative Definitions," *The Internet Encyclopedia of Philosophy*, 2021, https://iep.utm.edu/predicat/.

Joseph Loizzo: *Candrakīrti and the Moon-Flower of Nālandā: Objectivity and Self-Correction in India's Central Therapeutic Philosophy of Language*, PhD dissertation, Columbia University, 2001.

Joseph Loizzo: *Nāgārjuna's Reason Sixty with Chandrakīrti's Reason Sixty Commentary*, American Institute of Buddhist Studies, New York, 2007.

Donald S. Lopez, Jr.: *The Heart Sūtra Explained. Indian and Tibetan Commentaries*, State University of New York Press, Albany, 1988.

Dan Lusthaus: *Buddhist Phenomenology. A Philosophical Investigation of Yogācāra Buddhism and the Ch'eng Wei-shih lun*, RoutledgeCurzon, London, New York, 2002.

Anne MacDonald: "Knowing nothing: Candrakīrti and yogic perception," in Eli Franco, Dagmar Eigner (eds.): *Yogic Perception, Meditation and Altered States of Consciousness*, Austrian Academy of Sciences Press, Vienna, 2009, 133–169.

Anne MacDonald: *In Clear Words. The Prasannapadā, Chapter One*, Verlag der Österreichischen Akademie der Wissenschaften, Vienna, 2015.

William Magee: "Dzong-ka-ba on Candrakīrti's assertion of 'non-dependence on another' as the object to be negated in the view of emptiness," *Canadian Journal of Buddhist Studies* 4, 2008, 29–53.

Garth Mason: The Relation of *ākāśa* to *pratītyasamutpāda* in Nāgārjuna's Writings, PhD University of South Africa, 2012.

Jacques M. May: *Prasannapadā Madhyamakavṛtti. Douze chapitres traduits du sanscrit et du tibétain, accompagnés d'une introduction, de notes et d'une édition crititque de la version tibétaine*, Adrien-Maisonneuve, Paris, 1959.

Robert McGuire: *The Madhyamaka Speaks to the West: A Philosophical Analysis of śūnyatā as a Universal Truth*, PhD dissertation, University of Kent, 2015.

Esho Mikogami: "A Refutation of the Sāṃkhya Theory in the *Yogācārabhūmi*," *Philosophy East and West* 19:4, 1969, 443–447.

Jürgen Mittelstraß: *Enzyklopädie Philosophie und Wissenschaftstheorie*, J. B. Metzler, Stuttgart, Weimar, 1995.

Tirupattur Ramaseshayyar Venkatachala Murti: *The Central Philosophy of Buddhism. A Study of the Mādhyamika System*, Allen & Unwin, London, 1955.

Jundo Nagashima: "The distinction between Svātantrika and Prāsaṅgika in late Madhyamaka: Atiśa and Bhavya as Prāsaṅgikas," *Nagoya Studies in Indian Culture and Buddhism: Saṃbhāṣa* 24, 2004, 65–98.

Bhikkhu Ñāṇamoli, Bhikkhu Bodhi: *The Middle Length Discourses of the Buddha*, Wisdom Publications, Boston, 2001.

John von Neumann: *Theory of Self-Reproducing Automata*, University of Illinois Press, Urbana, London, 1966.

Guy Newland: *Compassion: A Tibetan Analysis. A Buddhist Monastic Textbook*, Wisdom Publications, London, 1984.

Geshe Ngawang Samten, Jay Garfield: *Ocean of Reasoning. A Great Commentary on Nāgārjuna's Mūlamadhyamakakārikā*, Oxford University Press, Oxford, New York, 2006.

Michael Nichols: *Malleable Mara: Buddhism's "Evil One" in Conversation and Contestation with Vedic Religion, Brahmanism, and Hinduism*, PhD dissertation, Northwestern University, 2010a.

Michael Nichols: "Scholarly approaches to the concept of 'evil' and the figure of Māra in South Asia," *Religion Compass* 4:9, 2010b, 530–537.

Andrew J. Nicholson: "Hindu disproofs of God. Refuting Vedāntic theism in the Sāṃkhya-sūtra," in Jonardon Ganeri (ed.): *The Oxford Handbook of Indian Philosophy*, Oxford University Press, Oxford, 2017, 598–619.

Bhikkhu Ñyāṇamoli: *The Path of Purification (Visuddhimagga)*, Shambala, Berkeley, London, 1976.

Eugéne Obermiller: *Prajñāpāramitā in Tibetan Buddhism*, Paljor Publications, Delhi, 1998.

Reiko Ohnuma: "The gift of the body and the gift of dharma," History of Religions 37:4, 1998, 323–359.

Peter Oldmeadow: *Study of the Wisdom Chapter (Prajñāpāramitā Pariccheda) of the Bodhicaryāvatārapañjikā of Prajñākaramati*, PhD dissertation, Australian National University, 1994.

Patrick Olivelle: *The Early Upaniṣads. Annotated Text and Translation*, Oxford University Press, New York, Oxford, 1998.

Douglas Osto: "No-Self in Sāṃkhya: A Comparative Look at Classical Sāṃkhya and Theravāda Buddhism," *Philosophy East and West* 68:1, 2018, 201–222.

Padmakara Translation Group: *Introduction to the Middle Way: Chandrakirti's Madhyamakavatara with Commentary by Jamgön Mipham*, Shambala, Boston, London, 2004.

Padmakara Translation Group: *Treasury of Precious Qualities. Book One: Sutra Teachings, by Jigme Lingpa. Commentary by Longchen Yeshe Dorje, Kangyur Rinpoche*, Shambala, Boston, London, 2010.

Roy W. Perrett: "Computationality, mind and value: the case of Sāṃkhya-Yoga," *Asian Philosophy*, 11:1, 2001, 5–14.

Karl H. Potter: *Encyclopedia of Indian Philosophies*, vol. 21: *Buddhist Philosophy from 600 to 750 A.D.*, Motilal Banarsidass, Delhi, 2017.

Red Pine: *The Lankavatara Sutra. Translation and Commentary*, Counterpoint, Berkeley, 2012.

John Powers: *A Bull of a Man. Images of Masculinity, Sex, and the Body in Indian Buddhism*, Harvard University Press, Cambridge, MA, 2008.

Olle Qvarnström: "Space and substance. A theme in Madhyamaka-Vedānta polemics," *Studies in Central and East Asian Religions* 1, 1989, 3–34.

Olle Qvarnström: "Sāṃkhya as Portrayed by Bhāviveka and Haribhadrasūri. Early Buddhist and Jain Criticisms of Sāṃkhya Epistemology and the Theory of Reflection," *Journal of Indian Philosophy* 40:4, 2012, 395–409.

Geshe Rabten: *Echoes of Voidness*, Wisdom Publications, London, 1983.

Walpola Rahula, Sara Boin-Webb: *Abhidharmasamuccaya. The Compendium of the Higher Teaching (Philosophy) by Asaṅga*, Asian Humanities Press, Freemont, CA, 2001.

N. Ross Reat: *The Śālistambasūtra*, Motilal Banarsidass, Delhi, 1993.

Susan Rochard: *Meditation on Selflessness. An Inquiry into Candrakīrti's Analysis of the Self with Reference to Theravāda, Tibetan, and Western Sources*, PhD dissertation, University of Cambridge, 2012.

William Woodville Rockhill: *Udānavarga. A Collection of Texts from the Buddhist Canon*, Trübber, London, 1883.

Carlo Rovelli: *Helgoland*, Penguin, London, 2021.

David Seyfort Ruegg: *The Literature of the Madhyamaka School in India*, Harrassowitz, Wiesbaden, 1981.

David Seyfort Ruegg: "Does the Mādhyamika have a thesis and philosophical position?," in Bimal Krishna Matilal (ed.): *Buddhist Logic and Epistemology*, D. Reidel, Dordrecht, 1986, 229–237.

David Seyfort Ruegg: *Three Studies in the History of Indian and Tibetan Madhyamaka Philosophy*. Studies in Indian and Tibetan Madhyamaka Thought, Part 1, Arbeitskreis für Tibetische und Buddhistische Studien, Universität Wien, Vienna, 2000.

David Seyfort Ruegg: *Two Prolegomena to Madhyamaka Philosophy*. Studies in Indian and Tibetan Madhyamaka Thought, Part 2, Arbeitskreis für Tibetische und Buddhistische Studien, Universität Wien, Vienna, 2002.

Akira Sakadata: *Buddhist Cosmology. Philosophy and Origins*, Kōsei, Tokyo, 1997.

Mattia Salvini: *Convention and agency in the philosophies of the Mahāyāna*, PhD dissertation, School of Oriental and African Studies, University of London, 2008.

Stanisław Schayer: *Ausgewählte Kapitel aus der Prasannapadā (V, XII, XIII, XIV)*, Nakładem Polskiej Akademji Umiejętności, Cracow, 1931.

Cristina Anna Scherrer-Schaub: *Yuktiṣaṣṭikāvṛtti. Commentaire à la soixantaine sur le raisonnement ou Du vrai enseignement de la causalité par le Maître indien Candrakīrti*, Institut Belge des Hautes Études Chinoises, Bruxelles, 1991.

Jens Schlieter: "'Master the chariot, master your Self': comparing chariot metaphors as hermeneutics for mind, self and liberation in ancient Greek and Indian sources," in Richard Seaford (ed.): *Universe and Inner Self in Early Indian and Early Greek Thought*, Edinburgh University Press, Edinburgh, 2016, 168–185.

Al Seckel: *Incredible Visual Illusions*, Eagle Editions, Royston, 2004.

Sarah Shaw: *The Jatakas*. Birth stories of the Bodhisattva, Penguin, London, 2006a.

Sarah Shaw: *Buddhist Meditation. An Anthology of Texts from the Pāli Canon*, Routledge, London, New York, 2006b.

Mark Siderits: "Causation and emptiness in early Madhyamaka," *Journal of Indian Philosophy* 32, 2004, 393–419.

Mark Siderits: *Buddhism as Philosophy. An Introduction*, Ashgate, Aldershot, 2007.

Mark Siderits: "Is reductionism expressible?," in Mario D'Amato, Jay L. Garfield, Tom F. Tillemans (eds): *Pointing at the Moon: Buddhism, Logic, Analytic Philosophy*, Oxford University Press, Oxford, New York, 2009, 57–69.

Mark Siderits: *Personal Identity and Buddhist Philosophy: Empty Persons*, 2nd edition, Ashgate, Aldershot, 2015.

Mark Siderits: "Buddhist reductionist action theory," in Jake H. Davis (ed.): *A Mirror Is for Reflection. Understanding Buddhist Ethics*, Oxford University Press, Oxford, New York, 2017, 276–294.

Mark Siderits: *How Things Are. An Introduction to Buddhist Metaphysics*, Oxford University Press, Oxford, 2022.

Mark Siderits, Shōryu Katsura: *Nāgārjuna's Middle Way. The Mūlamadhyamakakārikā*, Wisdom Publications, Boston, 2013.

Mark Siderits, Shōryu Katsura: *Introduction to Madhyamaka Philosophy: The Sixth Chapter of Candrakīrti's* Madhyamakāvatāra, Wisdom Publications, Boston, 2024.

Nandalal Sinha: *The Vaiśeṣika Sūtras of Kaṇāda, with the Commentary of Saṅkara Miśra and Extracts from the Gloss of Jayanārāyaṇa Together with Notes from the Commentary of Chandrakānta and an Introduction by the Translator*, S. N. Publications, Delhi, 1986.

Geshe Sonam Rinchen, Ruth Sonam: *Yogic Deeds of Bodhisattvas. Gyel-tsap on Āryadeva's Four Hundred*, Snow Lion, Ithaca, NY, 1994.

Geshe Sopa: "The Tibetan 'Wheel of Life': iconography and doxography," *Journal of the International Association of Buddhist Studies* 1984, 7:1, 125–145.

Geshe Sopa: "The special theory of *pratītyasamutpāda*: The cycle of dependent origination," *Journal of the International Association of Buddhist Studies*, 1986, 9:1, 105–119.

Per K. Sorensen: *Candrakīrti Triśaraṇasaptati. The Septuagint on the Three Refuges*, Arbeitskreis für Tibetische und Buddhistische Studien, Universität Wien, Vienna, 1986.

Mervyn Sprung, T. R. V. Murti, and U. S. Vyas: *Lucid Exposition of the Middle Way. The Essential Chapters from the Prasannapadā of Candrakīrti*, Routledge & Kegan Paul, London, 1979.

Theodore Stcherbatsky: *The Conception of Buddhist Nirvāṇa*, Publishing Office of the Academy of Sciences of the USSR, Leningrad, 1927.

Ernst Steinkellner: *A Tale of Leaves. On Sanskrit Manuscripts in Tibet, Their Past and Their Future*, Royal Netherlands Academy of Arts and Sciences, Amsterdam, 2004.

Jürgen Stöter-Tillmann, Tashi Tsering: *Rendawa Shönnu Lodrö's Commentary on the "Entry into the Middle", Lamp which Elucidates Reality*, Central Institute of Higher Tibetan Studies, Varanasi, 1997.

Jürgen Stöter-Tillmann, Tashi Tsering: *Removal of Wrong Views. A General Synopsis of the "Introduction to the Middle" and Analysis of Difficult Points of Each of Its Subjects by Go-rams-pa Bsod-nams-seng-ge*, International Buddhist Academy, Kathmandu, Nepal, 2005.

Jürgen Stöter-Tillmann, Tashi Tsering: *Autocommentary on the "Introduction to the Centre,"* Dr. Tashi Tsering, Varanasi, 2012.

Galen Strawson: "The self," *Journal of Consciousness Studies*, 4:5–6, 1997, 405–428.

Daisetz Teitaro Suzuki: *Studies in the Lankavatara Sutra*, Routledge & Kegan Paul, London and Boston, 1930.

Daisetz Teitaro Suzuki: *The Laṅkāvatāra Sūtra. A Mahāyāna Text*, Routledge, London, 1932.

J. Takakusu: "K'uei-chi's version of a controversy between the Buddhist and the Sāmkhya Philosophers. An appendix to the translation of Paramārtha's 'Life of Vasu-bandhu,'" *T'oung Pao* 5:4, 1904, 461–466.

Nathmal Tatia: *Tattvārtha Sūtra. That Which Is. Umāsvāti/Umāsvāmī with the Combined Commentaries of Umāsvāti/Umāsvāmī, Pūjyapāda and Siddhasenagaṇi*, HarperCollins, San Francisco, London, Pymble, 1994.

Helmut Tauscher: *Candrakīrti—Madhyamakāvatāraḥ und Madhyamakāvatārabhāṣyam (Kapitel VI, Vers 166–226)*, Wiener Studien zur Tibetologie und Buddhismuskunde, Vienna, 1981.

Helmut Tauscher, "Some problems of textual history in connection with the Tibetan translations of the *Madhyamakāvatarāḥ* and its commentary," in Ernst Steinkellner, Helmut Tauscher (eds.): *Contributions on Tibetan and Buddhist Religion and Philosophy. Proceedings of the Csoma de Körös Symposium held at Velm-Vienna, Austria, 13–19 September 1981*, vol. 2, Motilal Banarsidass, Delhi, 1995, 293–304.

Helmut Tauscher: *Phya pa chos kyi seṅ ge: dBu ma śar gsum gyi stoṅ thun*, Arbeitskreis für Tibetische und Buddhistische Studien Universität Wien, Vienna 1999.

Helmut Tauscher: "Phya pa chos kyi seng ge as a Svātantrika," Georges B. J. Dreyfus and Sara L. McClintock (eds.): *The Svātantrika-Prāsaṅgika Distinction. What Difference Does a Difference Make*? Wisdom Publications, Boston, 2003, 207–255.

Helmut Tauscher: "Candrakīrti, *Madhyamakāvatāraḥ* and *Bhāṣya* thereon," in Karl H. Potter (ed.): *Encyclopedia of Indian Philosophies*, vol. 21: *Buddhist Philosophy from 600 to 750 A.D.*, Motilal Banarsidass, Delhi, 2017, 150–172.

Sonam Thakchoe: "How many truths? Are there two truths or one in the Tibetan Prāsaṅgika Madhyamaka?," *Contemporary Buddhism* 5:2, 2004, 31–51.

Sonam Thakchoe: "Candrakīrti's theory of perception: A case for non-foundationalist epistemology in Madhyamaka," *Acta Orientalia Vilnensia* 11:1, 2010, 93–124.

Thrangu Rinpoche: *The Open Door to Emptiness: An Introduction to Madhyamaka Logic*, Namo Buddha Publications, Glastonbury, CT, 2012.

Robert Thurman: *The Central Philosophy of Tibet. A Study and Translation of Jey Tsong Khapa's Essence of True Eloquence*, Princeton University Press, Princeton, NJ, 1984.

Tom J. F. Tillemans, Donald S. Lopez, Jr.: "What can one reasonably say about nonexistence? A Tibetan work on the problem of *āśrayāsiddha*," *Journal of Indian Philosophy* 26, 1998, 99–129.

Tom Tillemans: "Metaphysics for Mādhyamikas," in Georges B. J. Dreyfus and Sara L. McClintock (eds.): *The Svātantrika-Prāsaṅgika Distinction. What Difference Does a Difference Make?* Wisdom Publications, Boston, 2003, 93–123.

Tom J. F. Tillemans: "How far can a Mādhyamika Buddhist reform conventional truth? Dismal relativism, fictionalism, easy-easy truth, and the alternatives," in The Cowherds: *Moonshadows: Conventional Truth in Buddhist Philosophy*, Oxford University Press, Oxford, 2013, 151–165, and Tom J. F. Tillemans: *How Do Mādhyamikas Think? And Other Essays on the Buddhist Philosophy of the Middle*, Wisdom Publications, Boston, 2016, 47–63.

Fernando Tola, Carmen Dragonetti: "*Anāditva* or beginninglessness in Indian philosophy," *Annals of the Bhandarkar Oriental Research Institute* 61, 1–4, 1980, 1–20.

David Tomlinson: *Buddhahood and Philosophy of Mind: Ratnākaraśānti, Jñānaśrīmitra, and the Debate over Mental Content (ākāra)*, PhD dissertation, University of Chicago, 2019.

Raffaele Torella: *The Philosophical Traditions of India. An Appraisal*, Indica, Varanasi, 2011.

Alex Trisoglio (ed.): *Introduction to the Middle Way. Chandrakirti's Madhyamakavatara, with commentary by Dzongsar Jamyang Khyentse Rinpoche Given at the Centre d'Etudes de Chanteloube, Dordogne, France, 1996, 1998, 1999, 2000, Arranged According to Gorampa's Commentary*, Khyentse Foundation, 2003.

Jakob von Uexküll: *Theoretische Biologie*, 2nd edition, Julius Springer, Berlin, 1928.

Paraśurāma Lakshmaṇa Vaidya: *Saddharmalaṅkāvatārasūtram*, Mithila Institute, Darbhanga, 1963.

Swami Virupakshananda: *Tarka Saṁgraha with the Dīpika of Aṇṇambhaṭṭa and Notes*, Shri Ramakrishna Math, Chennai, 1994.

Kevin A. Vose: *Resurrecting Candrakīrti. Disputes in the Tibetan Creation of Prāsaṅgika*, Wisdom Publications, Boston, 2009.

Maurice Walshe: *The Long Discourse of the Buddha*, Wisdom Publications, Boston, 1995.

Dorji Wangchuk: "Where Buddhas and Siddhas meet. Mipam's Yuganaddhavāda philosophy," in Michael Sheehy, Klaus-Dieter Mathes (eds.): *The Other Emptiness: Rethinking the Zhentong Buddhist Discourse in Tibet*, State University of New York Press, Albany, 2019, 273–322.

Alex Wayman: *Buddhist Insight*, Motilal Banarsidass, Delhi, 1984.

Brian Weatherson: "Humean supervenience," in Barry Loewer, Jonathan Schaffer (eds.): *A Companion to David Lewis*, John Wiley & Sons, Chichester, 2015, 101–115.

Jan Westerhoff: *Nāgārjuna's Madhyamaka. A Philosophical Introduction*, Oxford University Press, Oxford, 2009.

Jan Westerhoff: *The Dispeller of Disputes: Nāgārjuna's Vigrahavyāvartanī*, Oxford University Press, New York, 2010a.

Jan Westerhoff: *Twelve Examples of Illusion*, Oxford University Press, New York, 2010b.

Jan Westerhoff: "On the nihilist interpretation of Madhyamaka," *Journal of Indian Philosophy*, 2016, 44:2, 337–376.

Jan Westerhoff: *Crushing the Categories. Nāgārjuna's Vaidalyaprakaraṇa*, American Institute of Buddhist Studies, Wisdom Publications, 2018a.

Jan Westerhoff: *The Golden Age of Indian Buddhist Philosophy*, Oxford University Press, Oxford, 2018b.

Jan Westerhoff: *The Non-Existence of the Real World*, Oxford University Press, Oxford, 2020.

Lynn White: *Medieval Technology and Social Change*, Oxford University Press, 1962.

Paul Williams: "Some aspects of language and construction in the Madhyamaka," *Journal of Indian Philosophy* 8, 1980, 1–45.

Paul Williams: *The Reflexive Nature of Awareness. A Tibetan Madhyamaka Defence*, Curzon, Richmond, 1998.

Joe Wilson: *Candrakīrti's Sevenfold Reasoning. Meditation on the Selflessness of Persons*, Library of Tibetan Works & Archives, Dharamsala, 1980.

The Yakherds: *Knowing Illusion: Bringing a Tibetan Debate into Contemporary Discourse*. Vol. 1: *A Philosophical History of the Debate*, Oxford University Press, Oxford, 2021a.

The Yakherds: *Knowing Illusion: Bringing a Tibetan Debate into Contemporary Discourse*. Vol. II: *Translations*, Oxford University Press, Oxford, 2021b.

Geshe Yeshe Thabke: *The Rice Seedling Sutra. Buddha's Teaching on Dependent Arising*, Wisdom Publications, Boston, 2020.

Yoshiasu Yonezawa: "**Lakṣaṇaṭīkā*, Sanskrit notes on the *Madhyamakāvatārabhāṣya* chapter VI, *Journal of Naritasan Institute for Buddhist Studies*, 36, 2013: 107–175.

Yoshiasu Yonezawa: "A Survey of the **Lakṣaṇaṭīkā*," *Journal of Indian and Buddhist Studies* 62:3, 2014, 1236–1242.

Monika Zin, Dieter Schlingloff: *Saṃsāracakra. The Wheel of Rebirth in the Indian Tradition*, Dev Publishers & Distributors, New Delhi, 2022.

Synopsis

Chapter 1

Section 1. The importance of compassion

1:001 *Arhats* and *pratyekabuddhas* arise from fully enlightened Buddhas, which in turn arise from bodhisattvas. Bodhisattvas arise from compassion, a non-dual mind, and *bodhicitta*.

1:002 Compassion is essential for achieving Buddhahood in the beginning, middle, and end, like the seed, water, and fruit are in agriculture.

1:003 Sentient beings cling first to a self, then to what belongs to a self. They are bound to cyclic existence like buckets to a water-wheel. Candrakīrti pays homage to the first type of compassion, compassion directed at sentient beings.

1:004 Candrakīrti pays homage to the second and third types of compassion, compassion directed at phenomena, and compassion without object, seeing beings as impermanent and empty as the reflection of the moon in the water. Filled with compassion, the bodhisattva develops the intention to free all sentient beings from suffering.

Obtaining the 1st bodhisattva stage

1:005 Making the aspiration expressed in Samantabhadra's vow, the practitioner obtains the 1st bodhisattva stage and is now properly called a bodhisattva.

1:006 The bodhisattva has entered the lineage of the *tathāgata*. He has abandoned the three fetters, experiences great joy, and can make a hundred world-systems tremble.

1:007 The Bodhisattva advances to higher and higher stages, the paths to rebirth in the lower realms are closed to him, he is no longer an ordinary being, he is to be compared to a stream-enterer.

1:008 At the 1st bodhisattva stage the practitioner surpasses the *arhat*s and *pratyekabuddha*s in terms of his merit. Once he has reached the 7th bodhisattva stage he also surpasses them in terms of his insight into emptiness.

The perfection of generosity

1:009 At the 1st bodhisattva stage the practitioner masters the perfection of generosity. From his extraordinary ability to give away even his own body one may infer his other extraordinary qualities, which are not directly perceptible.

1:010 All beings long for happiness, but most cannot be happy without their basic needs being met. Seeing that generosity generates the karmic potential to fulfill these needs, the Buddha taught generosity at the very outset.

1:011 Generosity even produces results for those who pursue it for selfish ends, generating future wealth and alleviating suffering due to lack of material resources.

1:012 Those who practice generosity will quickly meet an enlightened teacher, and can then obtain liberation by following his instructions.

1:013 Bodhisattvas, who aim at the welfare of all, experience joy as a karmic result at the very moment of practicing generosity. Generosity is of fundamental importance for non-bodhisattvas as well as for bodhisattvas.

1:014 Even when just being asked to give, the joy the bodhisattvas feel exceeds that of attaining *nirvāṇa*. Even greater is the joy they feel when they give away all their possessions.

1:015 The bodhisattvas who feel physical pain when offering up their bodies will be reminded of how much greater the pain of beings in the lower realms is, and will be motivated to liberate all sentient beings from suffering in the quickest possible way.

1:016 The supramundane perfection of giving is distinguished from the mundane perfection by seeing the giver, the gift, and the recipient as empty, so that no attachment is developed toward them.

Metaphorical description of the 1st stage

1:017 The joy the bodhisattva experiences at the 1st bodhisattva stage is like the moonstone, dwelling in his mind, beautifying it, and clearing away the darkness of obscurations.

Chapter 2

Section 2. Obtaining the 2nd bodhisattva stage: The perfection of moral discipline

2:001 The bodhisattva does not carry out any non-virtuous actions even in a dream, but cultivates the ten virtues of body, speech, and mind.

2:002 The bodhisattva on the 2nd stage exceeds those on the 1st stage in terms of the perfection of moral discipline and becomes peaceful and radiant like the autumn moon.

2:003 The bodhisattva on the 2nd stage practices moral discipline without considering agent, action, or act to be intrinsically existent.

2:004 If one practices generosity without moral discipline, one will be reborn in an affluent state in the lower realms. Like spending capital and interest, rebirth there will make it difficult to generate further positive karma.

2:005 If one makes no effort to remain in the higher realms of rebirth when one is reborn in them, and therefore comparatively free, how will one escape the lower realms, as one is at the mercy of others when reborn there?

2:006 The Buddha taught moral discipline directly after generosity, for the fruits of generosity will not go to waste if, by moral discipline, one is born in a higher realm, and can thereby continuously cultivate generosity, producing further positive karma.

2:007 Moral discipline is a necessary precondition for attaining happiness in *saṃsāra*, for pursuing the goals of the *arhat* and *pratyekabuddha*, and for striving for complete enlightenment through the bodhisattva path.

2:008 The bodhisattva who has obtained the second stage does not mix with the unvirtuous.

2:009 Mundane moral perfection is based on the notion of the "three spheres" of abstainer, action abstained from, and object of the abstaining, while supramundane moral perfection is not based on these.

Metaphorical description of the 2nd stage

2:010 The 2nd bodhisattva stage is like the moon, an adornment of the world, yet transcending it, stainless, and removing the suffering of sentient beings by its light.

Chapter 3

Section 3. Obtaining the 3rd bodhisattva stage

3:001 On the 3rd, "luminous" stage, the fire of wisdom burns away objects of knowledge, producing a peaceful light. A copper-colored glow, similar to the sun, appears to the bodhisattva.

The perfection of patience

3:002 Even if someone cut the bodhisattva's body part by part, he would feel no anger, but only patience toward the perpetrator, out of his great compassion.

3:003 Realizing that all three spheres involved in the harmful act are like a reflection, the bodhisattva also develops patience out of his realization of emptiness.

3:004 Anger does not reduce the suffering we feel at present and is likely to lead to more suffering in the future.

3:005 The pain we feel when an enemy harms us is the karmic result of our angry mind-states in the past. When we have been harmed, their potential is exhausted, so why sow further seeds of suffering by anger toward the perpetrator?

3:006 Anger toward a bodhisattva undermines the positive karma accumulated by giving through many ages.

3:007 Anger leads to physical unattractiveness, to company with the non-virtuous, to the inability to tell right from wrong, and finally to a rebirth in the lower realms.

3:008 Patience leads to a beautiful appearance, esteem by the holy ones, proper moral discrimination, rebirth in a higher realm, and the elimination of negative karmic traces.

3:009 Realizing the benefits of patience and the disadvantages of anger, all beings, ordinary beings and bodhisattvas, should practice patience.

3:010 Even though dedicated to complete enlightenment, patience distinguishing between the three spheres is mundane patience, while supramundane patience is characterized by the absence of this distinction.

Further qualities of the 3rd bodhisattva stage

3:011 At the 3rd stage bodhisattvas also obtain absorptions and supernatural powers, they overcome attachment and aversion, and are able to remove attachment in the minds of others.

3:012 The first three perfections, generosity, moral discipline, and patience, are particularly recommended by the Buddhas to lay bodhisattvas. They generate the merit that produces the Buddha's physical body (*rūpakāya*).

Metaphorical description of the 3rd bodhisattva stage

3:013 Like the sun, the bodhisattva at the 3rd stage eliminates the darkness of his own defilements, then setting out to remove the defilements of others. Despite his intensity he is without anger, due to his accomplishment of patience.

Chapter 4

Section 4. Obtaining the 4th bodhisattva stage: The perfection of effort

4:001 The 4th bodhisattva stage is called "radiant" because it is characterized by the blazing forth of the perfection of effort. This is a cause of both the accumulations of merit and knowledge and brings about every good quality.

Further qualities of the 4th bodhisattva stage

4:002 A radiance even brighter than the copper-colored glow of the 3rd stage arises for the bodhisattva on the 4th stage, due to his practice of the 37 factors of enlightenment. As a result he fully abandons any sense of self.

Chapter 5

Section 5. Obtaining the 5th bodhisattva stage: The perfection of meditation

5:001 The bodhisattva on the 5th stage cannot be overcome by all Māras. Endowed with the perfection of meditation, he has mastered the subtle nature of the two truths.

Chapter 6

Section 6. Obtaining the 6th bodhisattva stage

6:001 Characteristics of the 6th bodhisattva stage

The perfection of wisdom

6:002 The other perfections need the perfection of wisdom.

The source and the recipients of the teachings on emptiness

6:003 The qualities of Nāgārjuna's thought, the basis of Candrakīrti's exposition.

6:004–6:005 The qualities of the student suited for the study of emptiness.

6:006–6:007 The ethical perfections practised by the student of emptiness.

6a. Refutation of the four ways of causal production

6:008a Negation of the four ways of causal production.

6a.1 Production from itself

6:008b–6:009 Self-causation is pointless since the effect already exists. Self-causation entails the non-arising of the effect and the eternal existence of the cause.

6:010 Change cannot be made sense of as a chain of self-causing moments. Nor could it be understood in terms of an underlying, indescribable entity that successively takes on different forms.

6:011 If cause and effect related by self-causation were to be understood as an underlying entity that takes on first the form of the cause, then that of the effect, we should always either perceive both of them, or neither.

6:012 According to the common-sense understanding of causality, when the effect exists, the cause has already disappeared. This does not cohere with self-causation, and hence self-causation is not even acceptable at the level of conventional reality.

6:013 If self-causation obtained, agent and action, and producer and produced would be identical. But they are distinct, and so self-causation cannot hold.

6a.2 Production from another

Refutation of production from another through reasoning

Refutation of production from another through reasoning with reference to an absurd consequence

6:014 If cause and effect were distinct, everything could arise from everything else.

6:015 No, only distinct things that form part of a single continuum could be cause and effect.

6:016 But being properly distinct and belonging to the same continuum are mutually contradictory.

6:017 Cause and effect do not exist at the same time, so one cannot be intrinsically other relative to another.

Refutation of production from another through reasoning with reference to time

6:018–6:019 Cessation of cause and arising of effect are simultaneous, like the sinking and rising of two ends of a scale. No—when the seed exists the sprout does not, unlike the two ends of a scale.

6:020 Could simultaneous cause and effect (e.g., an object perceived and its perception) be distinct? No, because if two things are simultaneous, how is one the *cause* of the other?

Refutation of production from another through reasoning with reference to four alternatives

6:021 An effect that is distinct from its cause should either be existent, nonexistent, both, or neither. But it cannot be any one of these four.

Refutation of production from another through experience

6:022 In fact there is no need to establish or defend self-causation inferentially, since ordinary, worldly perception establishes that cause and effect are distinct.

The two truths

6:023 Things have a double character: reality, when correctly seen, conventional truth when incorrectly seen.

6:024–6:025 Beliefs generated through internally or externally impaired sense-faculties are conventionally false, the others are conventionally true.

6:026 Mistaken philosophical views (a form of external impairment), like illusions, are not even conventionally true.

6:027 Ordinary perception (of cause and effect as distinct, etc.) can never undermine enlightened perceptions.

6:028 Delusion creates the conventional, concealing the nature of reality, and produces conventional truths and conventionally real objects.

6:029 Ordinary beings relate to Buddhas as sufferers from floaters seeing illusory hairs relate to those with healthy vision.

6:030 If ordinary perception saw the world correctly, there would be no need for the Buddha's path.

6:031 Conventional truth cannot refute ultimate truth, but mistaken conventional renderings of conventional truth can be refuted by other conventional truths.

6:032 People do not believe that cause and effect are distinct even at the level of conventional truth.

Implications of the theory of the two truths

Avoiding annihilationism and eternalism

6:033 Since distinctness of seed and sprout is negated, annihilationism is avoided, since identity of the two is negated, eternalism is avoided.

6:034 If things existed with intrinsic natures, the realization of emptiness would destroy these natures. This, however, is not the case.

Avoiding the view that intrinsic natures exist at the level of either truth

6:035 When things are analysed from the ultimate perspective only their empty nature remains. Hence ordinary things should not be subjected to ultimate analysis, expecting to find anything with intrinsic nature.

6:036 Things are not produced in any of the four ways ultimately or conventionally.

6:037–38 Empty things arise from empty things, like reflections in a mirror. In this way annihilationism and eternalism are avoided.

Accounting for karma

6:039 Karmic causality can be explained without recourse to structures like the foundational consciousness, etc.

6:040 Karmic results can be produced by a cause that is insubstantial and past, such as a woman in a dream after waking up.

6:041 Though a past cause is always past (and can still produce an effect) it will not continuously do so, but is subject to regularities, as floaters do regularly produce hairs, and not other illusions.

6:042 Wholesome actions produce pleasant effects, unwholesome actions unpleasant effects. Realizing the emptiness of karma means liberation, but mere analysis that might undermine our belief in karmic regularities is discouraged.

The Yogācāra position

Exposition of the Yogācāra position

6:043–6:044 The Buddha taught the foundational consciousness, the existence of selves, the aggregates, etc., provisionally for those disciples who would require such notions to aid their understanding.

6:045 Bodhisattvas know the world to be just consciousness, without a division into subjects and objects.

6:046 As waves arise from the ocean, so phenomena arise from the foundational consciousness.

6:047 The dependent nature is the source of all appearances, it does not depend on external objects, is fundamentally real, and beyond conceptual and linguistic constructions.

Refutation of the Yogācāra position through reasoning

Example 1: Dreams

6:048 Perceptions can arise without objects, like in a dream. However, for the Mādhyamika, dreamer and dream-object are equally unreal, so the Yogācāra example, where one is real, the other is not, is not accepted by both parties.

6:049 If being able to remember the dream makes the dreamer real, why does it not also make the object real, since both are part of what is remembered?

6:050 In dreams the sense-consciousnesses do not function, we experience exclusively mental objects, as we do in waking life.

6:051 In dreams sense-organs, sense-objects, and sense-perceptions are all equally false (it is not the case that the first two are unreal, and the last one is real).

6:052 In the waking state too there are no sense-organs, sense-objects, and sense-perceptions.

6:053 As the sense-organs, sense-objects, and sense-perceptions from a dream disappear when waking up, the sense-organs, sense-objects, and sense-perceptions of the waking state disappear upon enlightenment.

Example 2: Floaters

6:054 Hair-representations and the mind perceiving hairs are both real for the one suffering from floaters, and unreal for one with healthy vision.

6:055 If the floaters presented an example of perceiving nonexistent objects, the nonexistent hairs should also appear to one with healthy sight.

6:056 We cannot account for the appearance and non-appearance of hairs in terms of the presence or absence of karmic potentials for perceiving them, since such potentials are unreal.

The role of karmic potentials

6:057 There cannot be a potential for a present cognitive episode (it is already there) nor for a future one (something nonexistent cannot play a part in classifying existents).

6:058 In the absence of a *future* cognitive episode, a *present* potential cannot exist. Cognitive episode and potential must exist in an interdependent manner.

6:059 Does a *past* potential cause a *present* cognitive episode? No, because mind-moments are all intrinsically distinct. If one caused another, any one could cause any other.

6:060 It is not the case that any mental entity could cause any other one; causation is restricted to what happens in a single continuum.

6:061 But it makes no sense to assume that intrinsically different entities (such as one might consider two persons to be) belong to a single unified continuum.

6:062 A continuous stream of ripening karmic potentials is mistaken as the physical sense-faculty, even though this is wholly mental, not material.

6:063 Other cognitive episodes are misunderstood as being produced by external objects while cognitive episodes arise without such objects, through the relevant potentials.

6:064 As in a dream, perception arises from mind-internal potentials, not from external objects.

6:065 In this case, why can blind people not see when they are awake, simply because they, too, then have karmic potentials ripening, giving rise to visual cognitive episodes?

6:066 It cannot be the case that being asleep is responsible for the blind person's karmic potentials for visual experience to be activated.

6:067 Neither being asleep nor lacking eyes can be a cause for visual experiences. False experiences in a dream must have been caused by eyes and objects from the waking state.

The Yogācāra position is argumentatively and scripturally unsatisfactory

6:068 The Yogācāra arguments are unsatisfactory since they are merely repetitions of their mains claims. Also, there is no scriptural support for the Yogācāra view of ultimately real things.

Example 3: Meditative experience

6:069 Corpses observed as the result of meditative practice are also not an example of objectless perception, since this is an example of a cognitive episode based on the unreal (unlike in the Yogācāra case of perception).

6:070 If the observation of the corpses was not special in this way, the Yogācārin should accept that everybody, not just the meditatively trained, should see these corpses.

Common difficulties for all three examples

6:071 The examples of floaters, water seen as pus, etc., are all deficient because they presuppose that there could be representations without something represented. However, the two are mutually existentially dependent.

Dependent nature and reflexive awareness

6:072 The dependent nature could never be known, since it cannot be known by itself, and cannot be known by anything different from it.

6:073 The dependent nature cannot be known by reflexive awareness established from the existence of memory since there are alternative ways of accounting for memory.

6:074 Even if we accept reflexive awareness, it would not help us to explain memory, since for the opponent memory and remembered moment are intrinsically distinct.

6:075 Memory and what is remembered are not intrinsically distinct, and can hence be conventionally regarded as belonging to the same subject, in accordance with worldly convention.

6:076 If there is no reflexive awareness, nothing could observe the dependent nature, as actor, action, and object of action would be the same.

6:077 If the opponent accepts an unproduced, unknowable object like the dependent nature, he should also accept other unproduced, unknowable objects like the son of a barren woman.

6:078 If the dependent nature is shown to be nonexistent in this way, nothing can be based on it. The desire to introduce a fundamentally real entity finally undermines all of conventional reality.

Yogācāra and the two truths

6:079 There is no other path to liberation apart from the one taught by Nāgārjuna and his specification of the two truths.

6:080 Conventional truth is the means, ultimate truth the result. Those who do not understand these two truths correctly will not obtain liberation.

6:081 The dependent nature does not even exist at the level of conventional truth. The Mādhyamaka does, however, make assertions at the level of conventions in order to comply with the world.

6:082 For the *arhat*s who have entered *nirvāṇa* without remainder, conventional reality no longer exists. If this were the same for ordinary beings, the Mādhyamika would not assert its existence to them either.

6:083 If the Yogācārin can convince ordinary beings of his conception of the nonexistence of the imputed nature the Mādhyamika is happy to accept this as the conventional truth.

Why Yogācāra was taught

6:084 The reference to "merely mind" in the *sūtra*s is there in order to exclude other potential generating principles of the world, such as eternal agents.

6:085 The Buddha spoke about "merely mind" in the *Laṅkāvatārasūtra* in order to refute the mistaken views of other schools about the origin of the world.

6:086 A maker of the world such as is described in the other schools cannot be found, hence the Buddha declared that mind alone is the maker.

6:087 "Merely mind" like the term "Buddha", is an abbreviated phrasing and should be understood as expanded to "merely mind is the generating principle of the world."

6:088 If the mind was ultimately real, *sūtra*s deemed authoritative by the Yogācārin would not describe it as dependent on karma and ignorance.

6:089 All sentient beings and their environments are born from karma. This is why the mind is the primary generating principle of the world.

6:090 Matter exists, but unlike the mind it is not the generating principle of the world. Saying that there is no world-generator other than mind is not saying there is no matter.

6:091 At the level of conventional reality the five aggregates exist, but at the level of the highly realized meditative practitioner they no longer appear.

6:092 Mind and matter exist or fail to exist together. The Buddha taught the existence of both in the Abhidharma, and denied the existence of both in the Prajñāpāramitā.

6:093 The Yogācāra theory undermines the theory of the two truths. They should accept that things are ultimately non-produced, but conventionally produced.

Sūtras *teaching Yogācāra are* sūtras *with interpretable meaning*

6:094 The *sūtra* teachings that there are no external objects, but only mental phenomena, are interpretable, not definite teachings, and directed at those excessively attached to material things.

6:095 That these *sūtra*s are interpretable teachings follows from scripture and reasoning. Various *sūtra*s support the view that claims about "merely mind" cannot be regarded as definite teachings.

6:096 By negating the object of cognition, cognitions and cognizers can equally be shown to be insubstantial.

6:097 The texts that do not teach reality but lead one to an understanding of reality are interpretable. The texts that teach emptiness are definite.

6a.3 Production from itself and from another

6:098 Production from both itself and another combines the faults of each and therefore cannot obtain either at the level of conventional or ultimate truth.

6a.4 Production from no cause

6:099 If production came about without a cause, everything would arise from everything else, and nobody would make an effort to achieve a specific effect.

6:100 If there was no causation in the world, we could no more perceive things in the world than we can perceive sky-flowers.

6:101 The material elements do not have the natures the materialist ascribes to them. So if they are mistaken about the material world, how could they be trusted on more complex matters such as the existence of future lives?

6:102 For the materialist, demonstrably incorrect views (such as the view that the elements are substantially real) arise from the same basis (the body of the materialist) as views they deem to be correct (such as the denial of future lives). The latter should therefore be taken to be as false as the former.

6:103 The nonexistence of the elements has been demonstrated through the four ways of causal production. This refutation also applies to other supposed causal origins of the universe.

Intrinsic natures are mistaken projections

6:104 Because things are not produced in any of the four ways, they do not exist by intrinsic nature. Still, such natures are mistakenly perceived through the force of ignorance.

6:105 As an eye disease causes us to see things that are not there, ignorance causes us to see intrinsic natures that are not there.

6:106 Only the unwise hold that ignorance causes karma in any substantial manner. The wise realize the emptiness of dependent origination and are liberated.

Emptiness does not mean nonexistence

6:107 If all things are empty, everything is conventionally nonexistent, like a barren woman's son. Hence some things must be non-empty.

6:108 Hairs, but no other appearances, appear to sufferers from floaters. As the reason for this can be ascertained from sufferers from floaters, the reason why some things, but no others appear, though they are all empty, can be ascertained from beings deluded by ignorance.

6:109 In illusions, dreams, etc., specific perceptions appear to you, but not others. If all nonexistent objects are on a par, how would the opponent explain this difference?

6:110 That dreams, etc., are unreal does not preclude them from appearing, unlike a barren woman's son. Hence the argument from 6:107 fails.

6:111 A barren woman's son does not exist in conventional or in ultimate truth. In the same way, entities with intrinsic nature do not exist in conventional or in ultimate truth.

6:112 All phenomena are primordially peaceful and free from birth from the beginning. Hence nothing has ever arisen in any substantial manner.

6:113 Pots, etc., exist by worldly convention, though not substantially, like all things. Hence they differ from barren women's sons.

Benefits of realizing dependent origination

6:114 Things do not arise in the four ways of causal production, or from a creator god, but they are dependently originated.

6:115 The view of dependent origination undermines all mistaken metaphysical views.

6:116 Mistaken metaphysical views cannot be maintained in the face of dependent origination, as there cannot be fire without fuel.

6:117 Ordinary beings are trapped in cyclic existence by conceptualizations. Yogis are freed by the removal of these conceptualizations.

6:118 The aim of Madhyamaka arguments is not to refute others, but to help them to be liberated from conceptual constructions. The refutation of the systems of others is a side effect of this.

6:119 Attachment to one's own position and aversion to the position of others is a source of further suffering. Liberation is achieved through analysis without attachment and aversion.

6b. Refutation of intrinsically existent persons

6:120 All faults come from the mistaken view that the transitory collection of psycho-physical aggregates constitutes a self (*satkāyadṛṣṭi*). Since it has the self as its object, the practitioner sets out to refute the self.

6b.1 Refutation of the self and aggregates as different

6:121 The characterizations of the self in the different non-Buddhist schools are variants of the way in which it is described in the Sāṃkhya system.

6:122 The self-postulated by the non-Buddhists is nonexistent, because it is not causally produced, it cannot be the basis of our ordinary sense of self, and it is not even conventionally real.

6:123 A self that is causally unproduced cannot have any properties, like the ones ascribed to it by the Sāṃkhya system.

6:124 There is no self separate from the aggregates since it cannot be perceived without them. Worldly people do not have the Sāṃkhya conception of the self, hence their sense of self cannot be based on it.

6:125 Animals and beings born in other realms have not acquired their conception of the self by being habituated to the Sāṃkhya view, hence their sense of self cannot be based on it.

6b.2 Refutation of the self and aggregates as identical

6:126 Those who say that the self is not distinct from the aggregates, and claim, like the Saṃmitīya, that the aggregates are the support of the self, maintain that the self is all the aggregates, or just the consciousness-aggregate.

Refutation of the self and aggregates as identical by reasoning

6:127 If the aggregates were the self, the self would be multiple, substantial, and the mistaken view that the transitory collection of psycho-physical aggregates constitutes a self would be non-erroneous.

6:128 If the aggregates were the self, the self would be destroyed when *nirvāṇa* is obtained, the self would disappear and arise from one moment to the next, and the karmic fruit would be experienced by someone other than the one who sowed the seed.

6:129 If you reply that the mind-moments form a continuum, this has been addressed before. Also, that the self cannot be the same as the aggregates follows from the "unanswered questions" of the Buddha.

6:130 If the aggregates were the self, realizing selflessness would be realizing the nonexistence of the aggregates. If you respond that it is the nonexistence of the substantial self of the non-Buddhists that is realized, you are simply equivocating on the meaning of the term.

6:131 If the realization of selflessness was the realization of the absence of an *ātman* in the aggregates, this would not entail an understanding of the empty nature of the aggregates, and hence would not lead to liberation from *saṃsāra*.

Refutation of the self and aggregates as identical by scripture

6:132 The scriptural passage that the opponent takes to say that the aggregates are the self simply says that nothing other than the aggregates is identified with the self at the conventional level.

6:133 Elsewhere the Buddha denied of each one of the aggregates that it constitutes a self.

Refutation of the self as the collection of aggregates: the analogy of the chariot

6:134 If the self was simply all the aggregates collected together, how could a mere collection play the roles of protector, tamed, and witness that the Buddha says it plays?

6:135 If a chariot was all its parts collected together, just the parts could fulfill its function. The Buddha said that self depends on the aggregates, so it cannot just be all the aggregates collected together.

6:136 If the chariot is the shape of all the parts put together, this analogy cannot be extended to the self and the aggregates, since the parts of the chariot are all material, but the aggregates are not.

6:137 If the aggregates, as appropriated, and the self, as appropriator, were the same, object of action and agent would be identical, or there would be an object of action without an agent. Neither option is defensible.

6:138–6:139 The Buddha has said that the self is imputed on the aggregates, the sense-organs, and the different ways in which the mind relates to the objects of the sense-organs. It is therefore neither a different entity from the aggregates, nor is it identical with them.

Difficulties with mis-identifying the object of negation

6:140 If the opponent assumes that the realization of selflessness is the realization that there is no permanent self, such as postulated by the non-Buddhists, it remains unclear how this could lead to liberation, since it is not the belief in such a permanent self that keeps us bound to cyclic existence.

6:141 Negating a mistaken sense of self is as pointless as the attempt to dispel the fear of a snake hiding in the wall by pointing out that there is no elephant in the room.

Self and aggregates are not support and supported

6:142 The self and the aggregates do not stand in a supporter-supported relation, since this requires the two to be distinct.

The self does not possess the aggregates

6:143 The self does not possess the aggregates, since this would presuppose that the self and the aggregates are either distinct or identical.

The 20 wrong views of the self

6:144 There are 20 wrong views of the self: matter and self being identical, the self possessing matter, the self being contained in matter, and matter being contained in the self, and so for the remaining four aggregates.

6:145 The realization of selflessness destroys the mistaken view that the transitory collection of psycho-physical aggregates constitutes a self together with the twenty wrong views of the self that rest on it.

6b.3 Refutation of the self as neither identical with the aggregates, nor different from them

6:146 An alternative Saṃmitīya conception is that the self or person exists substantially, is the basis of our sense of self, and can be known by the six sense faculties, but that it is neither permanent nor impermanent, and neither identical with the aggregates, nor different from them.

6:147 The self cannot both be substantially real (as the mind is considered to be by the Saṃmitīya) and neither identical with nor distinct from the aggregates.

6:148 As a pot is neither identical with nor distinct from its parts, since it is a mere imputation, so the self, which the Saṃmitīya takes as being neither identical with nor distinct from the aggregates, cannot be substantially real.

6:149 What the Saṃmitīya considers substantially real, such as mind, is identical with itself, but different from matter. As the self stands outside of such relations, it cannot be a substantially real thing.

6b.4 Summarizing the view of the self

6:150 The self is not a substantially real basis of self-grasping, it is not identical with or different from the aggregates, it does not have the aggregates as a support and it does not possess them.

6b.5 The analogy of the chariot

The chariot does not exist in any of the seven ways

6:151 The chariot is neither the same as its parts nor different from it, it does not possess them, it neither depends on the parts, nor do the parts depend on it, it is not the mere collection of the parts, or the parts put together in a specific way.

6:152 If the mere collection of the parts of the chariot were the chariot, the unassembled collection would be the chariot. The assembled collection, on the other hand, depends on the chariot-parts which, however, cannot be made sense of without assuming the existence of the chariot.

6:153 If the parts of the chariot put together in a specific way, its shape, was the shape of the individual parts before assembly, then, since all the chariot-parts had the same shape prior to assembly, as there was no chariot then, there should not be one now.

6:154 And if the parts of the chariot put together in a specific way, its shape, was the shape of the individual parts after the assembly, then, since the shape of the chariot-parts does not change when they are arranged chariot-wise, the unassembled chariot should be the very same thing as the assembled chariot.

6:155 If the chariot being an arrangements of its parts means that the chariot is a property of the collection of its parts, this does not provide a foundation for chariot-hood, since the collection itself is only a superimposition (so we would have one superimposition based on another superimposition).

6:156 If instead the chariot, as an arrangement of parts, is superimposed on a basis, the collection of chariot-parts, that is itself deemed insubstantial we should understand that in fact all phenomena exist in this way, as a superimposition of something unreal on another unreal thing.

6:157 One cannot assume that a pot is superimposed on a collection of substantially real particles, because the particles, not being caused in any of the four ways of causal production, are themselves unreal.

6:158 The chariot does not exist in any of the seven ways either conventionally or ultimately. But without analysis we can still refer to the chariot; it is an entity that is dependently imputed on the basis of its parts.

The chariot exists as a mere dependent designation

6:159 From the worldly perspective the chariot is a part-possessor, a whole, an agent, and an appropriator. One should not undermine worldly conventions such as these.

6:160 The meditator realizes the nature of things by seeing that nothing exists when analyzed in terms of the seven possible relations. Nevertheless, this does not undermine the conventional existence of entities as long as they are not analyzed.

6:161 When the chariot does not exist anymore, its parts will not exist anymore, as once the whole of the chariot has been burnt, all of its parts will have been burnt too.

6:162 In accordance with worldly convention the self is based on the aggregates, elements, and sense spheres, it appropriates them as an appropriator, and acts on the appropriated as an agent.

6:163 Because the self is not substantially real, it is not permanent, impermanent, arising or ceasing, eternal, identical with the aggregates, or different from them.

6:164 Ignorance brings about a mistaken superimposition of the self deemed to be real onto the aggregates. This superimposition, which is experienced by all beings, is the object of the self-grasping mind.

6:165 Once he has realized that the self is a mere imputation the appearances of "I" and "mine" vanish and the meditator obtains liberation.

Other entities are similarly dependently designated

6:166 Other things should also be accepted to exist in the way ordinary worldly consensus considers them to exist, since the Buddha did not dispute with the way ordinary beings see the world.

6:167 Parts and whole, etc., do not exist in any of the seven ways, yet they exist in terms of worldly consensus.

6:168 Cause and effect are also mutually dependent, one cannot be established as prior to the other.

6:169 Cause and effect are not contiguous, else they would be one, nor are they distinct, else either the cause would not produce its effect, or the cause would produce any other distinct effect as well. There is no third possibility in which they could be related relative to contiguity.

6:170 As such, there is neither cause nor effect, but this is only a problem for the opponent, who conceives of them in terms of intrinsic nature, not for the Mādhyamika, who sees them as illusion-like appearances.

Is the Madhyamaka position self-refuting?

6:171 Is your argument contiguous or non-contiguous with what it sets out to refute? If neither is possible, you undermine your own argument and cannot refute any argument of another.

6:172 Moreover, non-contiguous things can stand in causal relations (like magnets and iron), and you, having no position of your own to defend, simply argue for the sake of arguing.

6:173 The problem of contiguity or non-contiguity only arises for those who believe in intrinsic natures. Since we do not think that arguments exist in this manner, the problem does not arise for us.

6:174 It makes no sense that the sun and its projection are either contiguous or non-contiguous, yet the projection can be used for studying an eclipse, as it is based on a framework of conventions.

6:175 As a reflection in a mirror is false, but can still be used to beautify our face, so the Mādhyamika arguments can be used to establish a claim, without assuming that they are grounded in the ultimate way things are.

6:176 The opponent's argument about contiguity presupposes that the Mādhyamika considers his arguments and what they establish as substantially real. This, however, is not the case.

6:177 It is easy to show by example how things are empty, but difficult to show what intrinsic natures could be like. What is the point of binding beings yet more to cyclic existence by conceptual constructions attempting to establish intrinsic natures?

6:178 Someone who objects to the argument from contiguity, or claims that the Mādhyamika is just debating for debating's sake, should be answered in light of the arguments for the emptiness of phenomena and persons presented earlier.

The 16 types of emptiness

6:179 For the purpose of liberation the Buddha differentiated the teaching of emptiness into two types—the emptiness of phenomena and the emptiness of persons—as well as classifying it in other ways.

6:180 According to the Mahāyāna understanding, emptiness is classified into 16 types, and into four types.

6:181 The eye is empty of the eye, etc., and so on for all the six sense organs, since that is their nature.

6:182 They are not permanent or perishing and hence have no intrinsic nature. This is emptiness of the internal.

6:183 Matter is empty of matter, etc., because that is how its nature is.

6:184 That is the emptiness of the external. That both are empty is the external-internal emptiness.

6:185 Everything is empty of intrinsic nature, including emptiness.

6:186 This emptiness of emptiness has been taught in order to stop the mind from clinging at emptiness as a real entity.

6:187 Space pervades all realms of existence, as the meditation on the immeasurables shows it is limitless in extent.

6:188 The emptiness of the great is taught in order to rule out misunderstanding space as substantially real.

6:189 *Nirvāṇa* is the ultimate since it is the highest goal. Its emptiness is the emptiness of the ultimate.

6:190 The emptiness of the ultimate has been taught to refute the view of *nirvāṇa* as substantially real.

6:191 The three realms are compounded phenomena. Their emptiness is the emptiness of the compounded.

6:192 Uncompounded phenomena do not arise, abide, or cease. Their emptiness is the emptiness of the uncompounded.

6:193 That which has gone beyond the two extremes is also empty of the nature of being gone beyond the two extremes.

6:194 Cyclic existence has no beginning or end, there is no coming and going in it, it is like a dream.

6:195 The emptiness of cyclic existence is called the emptiness of what has no beginning and no end and is clearly explained in the treatise.

6:196 There is one thing not eliminated.

6: 197 The emptiness of the thing not eliminated is the emptiness of non-elimination.

6:198 The nature of compounded things is not created by the Buddhas.

6:199 The emptiness of the nature of compounded things is called the emptiness of nature.

6:200–6:201 The eighteen sense spheres, contact and feelings that arise from them, material and immaterial things, compounded and uncompounded things are empty. The absence of their intrinsic characteristics in things is the emptiness of intrinsic characteristics.

6:202 Matter has the intrinsic characteristic of destructibility, feeling that of experience, perception that of grasping characteristic features, and dispositions that of intentional action.

6:203 Consciousness has the intrinsic characteristic of awareness with respect to its objects, the aggregates that of suffering, and the sense spheres that of a poisonous snake.

6:204 The sense spheres are the entrance-gate of suffering, and dependent origination is a collection of interlinked causes and conditions.

6:205 Generosity is characterized by patience, virtue by not being inflamed, patience by the absence of anger, effort by faultlessness.

6:206 Meditation is characterized by integration, and wisdom by the absence of attachment. These are the intrinsic characteristics of the six perfections.

6:207 The four absorptions, the four immeasurables, and the four formless absorptions have the intrinsic characteristic of dispassion.

6:208 The 37 factors of enlightenment have the intrinsic characteristic of leading to liberation. Of the three doors to liberation, the first, emptiness, is characterized as lacking the perception of substantially real entities.

6: 209 The second door, signlessness, is pacification, the third, desirelessness, suffering in the absence of ignorance. The eight liberations have the intrinsic characteristic of being conducive to liberation.

6: 210 The Buddha's ten powers have the intrinsic characteristic of being decisive in form. The Buddha's four fearlessnesses have the intrinsic characteristic of being well established in form.

6:211 The superlative individuating knowledges have the intrinsic characteristic of being uninterrupted. Great love has the intrinsic characteristic of bringing benefit to beings.

6:212 The intrinsic characteristic of great compassion is that it protects sentient beings from suffering, that of great joy the delight in the good fortune of others, that of great equanimity being unmixed with attraction and aversion.

6:213 The eighteen unique qualities of a Buddha have the intrinsic characteristic of being irremovable.

6:214 The Buddha's omniscience has the intrinsic characteristic of being perception. Cognitions of other beings are not to be understood as perceptions because they are limited in scope.

6:215 All compounded and uncompounded entities, with their associated intrinsic characteristics, are empty of intrinsic nature. This is the emptiness of intrinsic characteristics.

6:216 The past has ceased, the future has not yet arisen, the present does not abide, hence events in all three times are not apprehended.

6:217 Their non-apprehension neither persists nor ceases by its own nature; this is the emptiness of non-apprehension.

6:218 Things do not have the intrinsic nature of being causally produced, because they arise dependent on conditions. The emptiness of such nonexistents is the emptiness of the nonexistent.

Condensed classification into four types of emptiness

6:219 The five aggregates are empty, this is the emptiness of existence.

6:220 Unconditioned things like space are empty, this is the emptiness of nonexistence.

6:221 The nature of things is to be empty, and is unfabricated by realized beings. Its emptiness is the emptiness of intrinsic nature.

6:222 Emptiness remains whether or not the Buddhas appear in the world.

6:223 The emptiness of true reality and the limit of reality is the emptiness of intrinsic nature.

Conclusion

6:224 Through the preceding analysis the bodhisattva sees the three worlds as unborn, like a gooseberry in the palm of one's hand, and obtains cessation by means of conventional truth.

6:225 Though remaining in meditative absorption, the bodhisattva still practices compassion for the sake of all beings.

Having entered the 7th bodhisattva stage he outshines the *arhats* and *pratyekabuddhas* in terms of intelligence.

6:226 Like the king of wild geese the bodhisattva flies ahead of ordinary practitioners, carried by the wings of conventional and ultimate truth, and by the winds of his accumulated virtue, across the ocean of the Buddha's qualities.

Chapter 7

Section 7. Obtaining the 7th bodhisattva stage

7:001 At the 7th stage the bodhisattva can enter cessation at any moment, and he achieves the perfection of skillful means.

Chapter 8

Section 8. Obtaining the 8th bodhisattva stage

8:001 At the 8th stage the bodhisattva's aspirations are wholly pure, and, having entered cessation, he is raised from it by the Buddhas.

8:002 At the 8th stage bodhisattvas have removed all affliction from their minds and have gone beyond the three realms. Still, they have not yet attained the enlightenment of a fully awakened Buddha.

8:003 Although they are no longer reborn in cyclic existence, the bodhisattvas acquire ten powers that allow them to benefit sentient beings in *saṃsāra*.

Chapter 9

Section 9. Obtaining the 9th bodhisattva stage

9:001 At the 9th stage the perfection of power is fully purified and the bodhisattva attains the four superlative individuating knowledges.

Chapter 10

Section 10. Obtaining the 10th bodhisattva stage

10:001 At the 10th stage the bodhisattvas are empowered by all the Buddhas, perfect the perfection of knowledge, and issue forth a steady stream of teaching, benefiting all sentient beings.

Chapter 11

Explanation of the qualities of each bodhisattva stage in terms of its special enumerated features

11:001 At the 1st stage the bodhisattva can in an instant see a hundred Buddhas, know that he has been blessed by them, accomplish the progress of a hundred eons, and see a hundred eons into past and future.

11:002 At the 1st stage the bodhisattva can enter and exit a hundred meditative concentrations, shake a hundred worlds and fill them with light, bring a hundred beings to a direct realization of emptiness, and travel to a hundred pure realms.

11:003 At the 1st stage the bodhisattva can open a hundred doors of dharma, and manifest in a hundred forms, each accompanied by a retinue of a hundred bodhisattvas.

11:004 At the 2nd stage these twelve qualities apply to a thousand, not to a hundred.

11:005 At the 3rd to 7th stage these qualities apply to increasingly higher numbers.

11:006 At the 8th stage these qualities equal the number of atoms in one hundred thousand trichiliocosms.

11:007 At the 9th stage these qualities equal the number of atoms in one hundred thousand "countless" trichiliocosms.

11:008 At the 10th stage the number of these qualities is inexpressible, greater than the number of atoms in an inexpressible number of buddha-fields.

11:009 At the 10th stage the bodhisattva is also able to manifest at any instant as many manifestations as there are pores on his skin, of Buddhas, bodhisattvas, ordinary beings, gods, and so on, in order to help other sentient beings.

11:010 As the moon illuminates the night, so the bodhisattva at the 10th stage sees the path to Buddhahood clearly laid out before him and endeavors to obtain it, finally reaching enlightenment in Akaniṣṭha heaven.

Section 11. Explanation of the level of Buddhahood

The Buddha's knowledge

11:011 As the space enclosed by different jars always has the same nature, so the Buddha knows all phenomena to have the same nature in terms of being empty. Knowing the nature of all phenomena, he is omniscient.

11:012 If reality is completely pacified, the mind cannot know it. Hence there cannot be any knowledge of reality, nor any knower of reality.

11:013 Veridical perception happens when the mind correctly represents the form of an object. Since the Buddha's mind and reality have the same form, unborn, and without imputation, the former represents the latter correctly.

The Buddha's activity

11:014 Through his previously accumulated merit the Buddha can emanate animate and inanimate manifestations, teaching the way to liberation, free from any psychological states such as the desire to teach.

11:015 When a potter spins his wheel, it subsequently keeps on turning to produce pots without further effort.

11:016 In the same way the Buddhas can teach and benefit beings without further effort. All their activity manifests from the karma accumulated by them and by other sentient beings.

The three bodies of the Buddha

11:017 When the objects of knowledge are burned away by the fire of wisdom, the *dharmakāya* manifests. It is peaceful, beyond arising and ceasing, and without mental activity.

11:018 Like the wish-fulfilling tree and gem, the *saṃbhogakāya* benefits sentient beings without possessing mental states. It appears only to highly realized bodhisattvas.

11:019 In his *nirmāṇakāya* form the Buddha can demonstrate all of his past lives, in one instant and in their correct order.

11:020 The Buddhas can demonstrate in a single body the buddha-fields they were reborn in, their activities there, and their audiences.

11:021 They can show what bodhisattvas attended them, what they taught, their training, and what was offered to them.

11:022 Within a single pore the Buddhas can show all of these, and their practice of the six perfections.

11:023 In the same way the Buddhas can manifest all the Buddhas of the past, present, and future.

11:024 Knowing all phenomena to be illusory, they can demonstrate the entire spiritual development of a Buddha in a single pore of their bodies.

11:025 The Buddhas can also show all the actions of bodhisattvas, *pratyekabuddha*s, *arhat*s, and ordinary beings in a single pore of their bodies.

11:026 They can show the entire universe in a particle, without one decreasing, or the other increasing.

11:027 Though free from conceptual activity they can display as many actions in one instant as there are atoms in the earth.

The ten powers of the Buddha

11:028 The Buddhas have ten powers: the power of knowing what is the case and what is not, the power of knowing the consequences of actions, the power of knowing the dispositions of different beings, and the power of knowing the different elements.

11:029 The power of knowing which faculties are superior and which are not, the power of knowing the ways leading to all destinations, and the power of knowing the defilement and purification of all meditative states (*dhyāna*), liberated states (*vimokṣa*), absorptions (*samādhi*), and states of equilibrium (*samāpatti*).

11:030 The power of knowing how to remember previous lives, the power of knowing death and birth, and the power of knowledge of the eradication of the taints.

11:031 The power of knowing what is the case and what is not is to know that certain causes bring about certain results, and that other entities do not bring about these results.

11:032 The power of knowing the consequences of actions is the knowledge of specific actions and the effects they bring about.

11:033 The power of knowing the dispositions of different beings is to know afflictive and virtuous psychological states, and all the dispositions they give rise to.

11:034 The power of knowing the different elements is to know the nature of all the different elements that make up reality.

11:035 The power of knowing which faculties are superior and which are not is to know how conceptualizations are formed, how they lead to virtuous and non-virtuous states of different strengths, and how they interact with other epistemic faculties.

11:036 The power of knowing the ways leading to all destinations is the knowledge of where the path of each individual leads: to enlightenment, or to rebirth in one of the six realms of existence.

11:037 The power of knowing the defilement and purification of all meditative states, liberated states, absorptions, and states of equilibrium is the knowledge of the causes and nature of the various meditative states.

11:038 The power of knowing how to remember previous lives enables the Buddhas to know all the details of their own past lives, as well as those of all other sentient beings.

11:039 The power of knowing death and birth lets the Buddha know the death of every sentient being, and all the causes and conditions that lead to its future rebirth.

11:040 The power of knowledge of the eradication of the taints is the knowledge that all mental contaminants have been eliminated, leading to complete liberation from cyclic existence.

Describing the Buddha's qualities

11:041 The descriptions of the Buddha's qualities by bodhisattvas, *arhat*s, etc., are limited because of limitations of their expressive capacities.

11:042 Candrakīrti cannot give a complete account of the Buddha's qualities, hence he relies on the account provided by Nāgārjuna.

11:043 The Buddha's qualities are characterized as divided into the vast and the profound. Realizing these two leads to liberation.

The physical embodiment of the Buddha and its activity

11:044 Even though the Buddha has entered enlightenment, he manifests in cyclic existence in physical form and leads sentient beings to liberation through his teaching.

11:045 The nature of reality, its emptiness, is undifferentiated, and so is the Buddha's realization of it. For this reason he only taught a single vehicle expressing this realization.

11:046 The Buddha taught the lower vehicles to lead those beings to *nirvāṇa* who are, due to their afflictive obscurations, not yet ready to realize his teachings in their final form.

11:047 Like a guide manifests an imaginary city to a group of travelers so that they can rest on the way to the real goal, the Buddha has taught the *nirvāṇa* of the *arhat*s and of the *pratyekabuddha*s.

The continuity of the Buddha's teaching

11:048 It is a secret teaching that the Buddha manifests the obtaining of enlightenment in as many eons as there are atoms in all the buddha-fields.

11:049 As the Buddha has arisen from wisdom and compassion, he will continue his enlightened activities until the end of the world, until all beings have been liberated.

11:050 The pleasures of the five sense faculties are like poisoned food sentient beings consume. The Buddha, feeling greater compassion toward sentient beings than a mother seeing her child eat poison, will not pass into a state where he does not manifest his enlightened activities, until all beings have been liberated.

11:051 The suffering of cyclic existence, birth and death, being separated from what is pleasant and meeting the unpleasant is the result of considering things to be substantially real or substantially unreal. Seeing this, the Buddha will continue his enlightened activity until all beings are liberated.

Section 12. Origin and uniqueness of Candrakīrti's exposition of Madhyamaka

11:052 Candrakīrti composed this text in accordance with the *Mūlamadhyakakārikā*, the *sūtra*s, and oral commentaries.

11:053 No teaching other than Madhyamaka presents emptiness correctly. Candrakīrti's exposition of Madhyamaka differs from all other interpretations of emptiness.

11:054 Some thinkers are afraid by the brilliant color of the ocean of Nāgārjuna's thought. The nightly dew and rays of moonlight that are Candrakīrti's instruction will open the buds of the lotus flowers of their understanding.

11:055 Those who lack the relevant karmic potential will not understand the full truth of emptiness, even though they are very learned. Other traditions are the product of their author's own mind, not of the Buddha's enlightened wisdom. Hence one should not develop any enthusiasm for these traditions.

11:056 May the merit acquired from explaining Nāgārjuna's system fill all of space, may it shine like the autumn stars, and may it, like a mind-made serpent stone, lead all beings to liberation.

Index

Abhidharma, 2–3, 13–14, 15, 46n.10, 50n.1, 53n.5, 69, 74–75, 76, 99, 111, 116, 124, 127–28, 136, 137–38, 150, 154–55, 157, 158–59, 159n.140, 160–61, 162–63, 176–77, 179–80, 184–85, 186, 190, 203–4, 210, 216, 217. *See also* Sarvāstivāda; Sautrāntika; Saṃmitīya
  theories of causation, 50n.1, 69, 74–75, 111
  theory of perception, 99
Abhidharmakośabhāṣya, 46n.8
abhijñā. *See* supernatural powers
abhimukhī. *See* Turned toward
absences, 191–92
absorptions of the form realm, 31n.10, 46–47, 211
abstract objects, 83n.67, 167–68
acalā. *See* Immovable
accumulation of knowledge, 47–48, 49
accumulation of merit, 47–48, 49, 196, 205, 215
afflictive stains, 196
aggregates, physico-psychological, 15, 31–32, 111, 186
  relations to the self, 148–49, 161
  self as collection of, 142–46
  self as different from, 133–36
  self as identical with, 136–49, 161–62
  self as neither identical with nor different from, 149–52
ahaṃkāra, 61
akaniṣṭha, 202, 207, 215
ākāra. *See* representation, mental
Akutobhāya, 5n.12
ālayavijñāna. *See* foundational consciousness
Amshuverma, 1
anātman. *See* emptiness of persons
anger, 188
  as irrational response, 44
annihilation, 83, 87, 181
anti-foundationalism, 57–58
anti-reflexivity principle, 66n.39, 69–108, 116n.100
appearance/reality distinction, 84–85, 126
apramāṇa. *See* four immeasurables
arched gateway, 54
arciṣmatī. *See* Radiant
arguments as spatio-temporally located, 167–68
arhat, 15, 27–28, 32–33, 35, 111, 134n.112, 163, 192, 194, 208, 210, 212–15. See also *śrāvaka*
ārūpyadhātu, 17n.47
Āryadeva, 2–3, 38n.2, 40n.4, 137n.117
asaṃskṛta. *See* unconditioned things
Asaṅga, 46n.8
aṣṭavimokṣa. *See* eight liberations
aśubha-bhāvanā. *See* meditation on the impure
Aśvaghoṣa, 46n.7
Atīśa, 20–21

ātman, 104n.82, 141–42, 145–46, 147, 162–63
atoms, 113–14, 122–23, 177–78, 201, 208, 215
authority, scriptural, 18, 90–91, 101–2, 117, 140, 142
autumn stars, 217–18
Avalokitavṛata, 20
Avalokiteśvara, 16–17
Avataṃsakasūtra, 31, 30n.6, 33n.13
āveṇikabuddhadharma. *See* eighteen unique qualities of a Buddha
avidyā. *See* ignorance
avyākṛtavastu. *See* unanswered questions
awakening mind, 27–28, 194
āyatana. *See* sense spheres

barren woman, son of, 96, 108–9, 124–26, 127, 134, 191–92
basis of designation
  of the chariot, 143, 156–57
  of the self, 136, 137–38, 143, 149, 152, 162–63
blind men, example of, 55
blindness, Yogācāra view of, 100–1
Bhāviveka, 5–9, 8n.20, 9n.21, 16, 21, 46n.8, 49n.2, 68
bhūmi. *See* bodhisattva stages
Bodhicaryāvatāra, 20n.56, 29n.5, 46n.8, 54n.8, 143n.127
bodhisattva, 27–28, 29–34, 30n.7, 35, 36, 37–38, 39–41, 42–45, 46–48, 49, 50, 51, 52–54, 58–59, 91, 189, 194, 195, 196–97, 198, 199, 200–2, 205, 206–7, 208, 212–13
bodhicitta. *See* awakening mind
bodhipākṣikā dharma. *See* thirty-seven factors of enlightenment
bodhisattva stages, 11–13, 30–34, 30n.7, 35–36, 37–38, 39–41, 42–43, 44, 46–47, 48, 49, 50–51, 52–55, 56–57, 59–60, 90–91, 194, 195, 196, 198, 199, 207, 213
  special qualities acquired on each, 200–2
body of the Buddha, 47–48, 213–15
Brahmagupta, 1
brahmavihāra. *See* four immeasurables
Buddha, 27–28, 32, 33n.13, 39, 40–41, 42–43, 47–48, 52–53, 54, 62–63, 79, 80–81, 90–91, 101–2, 110, 112–14, 116, 117, 118, 123–24, 140, 142–43, 145, 163–64, 183, 184, 188–90, 192, 194, 196, 198, 199, 200–16
  activities of, 204–6
  as without cognitive activity, 22, 23, 57n.17, 79, 80, 204–5, 206
  fully enlightened Buddha, 201–16
  historical, 5, 46n.7, 50, 202, 207, 215
  knowledge of the, 188, 202–4, 206, 209–12
  lineage of the, 31–32
Buddhacarita, 46n.7
buddha-field, 28–29n.4, 31n.9, 201, 215. *See also* pure realm
buddhakṣetra. *See* buddha-field
Buddhapālita, 5–7, 5n.12, 8n.19, 9, 16, 49n.2
buddha-tattva, 114
buddhi
  Sāṃkhya notion of, 61

Candragomin, 4, 16–17
Candrakīrti
  contemporaries, 1
  dates, 1
  defending Buddhapālita, 8–9, 8n.19, 8n.20
  hagiography, 3–4

life, 3–4
name, 1
reception of his works in India, 18–20
reception of his works in Tibet, 20–24
and tantra, 2n.3
works, 2–3
and Yogācāra, 16–18
Cārvāka, 14–15, 79n.58, 79n.59, 141–42
Catuḥśataka. See *Four Hundred Verses*
causation, 4, 14–15
absence of, 120–23, 202–3
causal continua, 70–71, 139–40
causal production with intrinsic characteristics does not hold conventionally or ultimately, 85–86
causal regularity without ontological foundation, 86–87, 191
from another, 69–118
from another, incompatible with four alternatives, 75
from another, mistaken conventionally and ultimately, 82–83
causation from itself and another, 118–20
common sense view of, 67–69, 75–76, 78, 80–82
and epistemology, 120–21, 202–3
four ways of causal production, 14–15, 59–123
four ways of causal production as inconsistent, 85–86
four ways of causal production rejected conventionally and ultimately, 68
illusion-like, 167
mark of the real, 159n.139
potential/actualizer distinction, 119–20
self-causation, 60–69
self-causation subject to seven difficulties, 69
cause, productive and explanatory, 171
cause and effect
arising in dependence, 128, 164–65
contiguity of, 165–74
neither identical nor distinct, 83
not distinct conventionally, 82
as part of one continuum, 70–71
as simultaneous, 73
temporal relation between, 165–67
cessation, 36n.15, 52, 53–54, 193, 195–96
change and self-causation, 64–66
chariot, analogy of the, 142–64
as arrangements of its parts, 153–57
as a dependent designation, 157–63
seven possible relations of the chariot to its parts, 152–58, 159, 163–64
cittamātra. *See* merely mind
Clear Words, 2–3, 3n.4, 8n.20, 16, 21, 39n.3, 137n.117
Cloud of Dharma (10th bodhisattva stage), 30n.7, 199
cognitive obscurations, 27n.2
common sense, 67–68, 75–76, 78, 80–82
Buddhist skepticism toward, 67, 76, 78, 80–82
compassion, 42n.2, 195, 215
central role of, 28
directed at phenomena, 28–30
directed at sentient beings, 28–29
three types of, 28–30
compassionate mind, 27–28

compounded entities, 180, 184–85, 190, 210
computational theory of mind, 46n.9
conceptual construction, 127–28, 130–31, 191, 217–18
contiguity of cause and effect, 165–74
contradictory consequence, 6–7, 22
conventional reality. *See* truth, conventional
conventional truth. *See* truth, conventional
conventions, network of, 127–28
copper-like glow, 42–43
creation in Yogācāra, 91, 112–15
cyclic existence, 13–14, 17n.47, 23, 27, 28–29, 28–29n.4, 34, 35, 38–39, 40–41, 53–54, 58, 78–79, 81, 123–24, 130–31, 132, 141–42, 146, 163, 179–80, 182–84, 186–87, 188, 192–94, 196–97, 205–6, 207, 208, 209, 210, 212, 213, 216

darśanamārga. *See* Path of seeing
daśabala. *See* ten powers of the Buddha
daśabhūmi. *See* bodhisattva stages
Daśabhūmikasūtra, 11–12, 17–18, 33–34, 55–56, 59–60, 112, 114
debate
  Madhyamaka and philosophical debate, 130–31
  practice, 22–23
definite intent, 118
dependence
  existential, 154, 164
  mutual dependence of objects, 128, 145, 164–65
  notional, 154, 164
dependent nature, 91–92, 101–2, 110, 114, 116–17
  and reflexive awareness, 104–10
dependent origination, 45, 52–53, 55, 157–58, 173–74, 187
  benefits of realizing, 128–32
  and emptiness, 55–56
  as mark of definite intent, 118
  twelve links of, 29, 123–24
devaputra, 50
dharma, 13–14, 76, 116, 137, 138–39, 154–55, 157, 160–61, 176, 217
dharmakāya, 38n.2, 206, 207
Dharmakīrti, 1, 22, 23–24, 155n.136
dharmameghā. *See* Cloud of Dharma
dharmanairātmyā. *See* emptiness of phenomena
Dharmapāla, 217
dhātu. *See* elements; realm
Diṅnāga, 22, 23–24, 73n.45, 217
distinctness vs non-identity, 70, 72–73, 82
  strong distinctness, excluding the obtaining of relations, 70, 71–72, 73, 82, 106–7, 119, 139–40, 147, 151–52
divine eye, 211–12
divine realm, 216
doubt about the efficacy of the path, 31–32
doxography, 14–15, 62–63, 118, 130–31
dravya, 74
dreams, 37, 88–89, 173, 183
  perceptions in dreams, 93–94
  in Yogācāra, 92–94, 99–101
dūraṅgamā. *See* Far progressed
Dzogchen Pönlop Rinpoche, 10–11
Dzongsar Jamyang Khyentse Rinpoche, 10–11

effort, perfection of, 49, 187
eight liberations, 188, 211
eighteen unique qualities of a Buddha, 189–90
elements, 161

emergence, 121
emptiness, 11–12, 13–15, 27–28, 42, 180, 188, 191–92, 202, 210, 213–14
  and causal function, 110–11
  and dependent origination, 55–56
  different types of insight into, 32–33, 194, 196
  of emptiness, 177–78, 184, 192
  and ethics, 16, 30n.6, 36, 38, 43–44, 46, 58–59
  four types of, 191–93
  nihilistic misunderstanding of, 57, 124–28, 181
  of persons, 13–14, 15, 29–30, 32–33, 132–33, 173–74
  of phenomena, 13–16, 31n.9, 32–33, 80, 132–33, 173–74
  realization does not lead to a change in the world, 84, 159
  and realization of selflessness, 141–42
  realization vs rational assent, 53, 55, 193
  realized on the 1st bodhisattva stage, 56
  risks of misunderstanding, 57–58
  sixteen types of, 174–91
  typology of, 13–14, 15–16
epistemic instrument, 22, 23–24
epistemology, 22, 23, 76–77, 79n.59, 81–82, 104–5, 120–21, 186–87
  and causation, 120–21
  in Candrakīrti, 203–4
  and intrinsic nature, 185
equivalence of all things, 59–60
eternalism, 83
ethics, 22–23, 57, 187
  and conventional truth, 81
  synergy with moral discipline, 13–14, 15
  and virtual objects, 16, 30n.6, 36, 38, 43–44, 46, 58–59
extreme views, 181

falsity, conventional, 76–77
Far progressed (7th bodhisattva stage), 30n.7, 32–33, 194, 195
fire, 37, 42, 160–61, 176–77, 206
five aggregates, 30
  different from the self, 133–36
fivefold analysis, 15
five paths to enlightenment, 36n.15
formless absorptions, 46–47
foundational consciousness, 84, 90, 91n.7, 99–100, 116
foundationalism about collections, 156
four-dimensional space, 79–80
four fearlessnesses, 188–89
Four Hundred Verses, 2–3, 3n.4, 39n.3, 40n.4, 137n.117
four noble truths, 22, 53–54
  and two truths, 51
four immeasurables, 47, 188, 189
four superlative individuating knowledges, 189, 198
Fundamental Verses on the Middle Way, 2–3, 5–9, 12, 14–15, 27n.2, 39n.3, 50n.3, 60, 60n.26, 118n.101, 130–31, 137n.117, 138n.121, 161n.142, 216
  commentaries on, 5–6, 19n.50
future lives, knowledge of, 211–12

Gaṇḍavyūhasūtra, 31
dGe lugs pa, 23–24
generosity, perfection of, 33–36, 187
  and giving away one's body, 33–34, 36, 43
  and meeting teachers, 35
  of ordinary beings, 34–35, 36
  relation to negative karma produced by anger, 28–29n.4

resulting in wealth, 34–35
supramundane, 36
god
creator, 17–18, 112–14, 122–23
goose, 194
gooseberry, 193
Gorampa, 10–11
grammatical analysis of Sanskrit, 73n.46, 145

Hard to overcome (5th bodhisattva stage), 30n.7, 50–51
hermeneutics, Buddhist, 118
higher-order cognition, 105–6
Humean supervenience, 52–53
hypostatization
and dependent nature, 92

identity, 70, 72–73, 151–52, 202
identity and distinctness only holds between coexistent things, 72
identity and distinctness relations between substantially real things, 151–52
of indiscernibles, 137–38
ignorance, 123–24
Immaculate (2nd bodhisattva stage), 30n.7, 37–41
Immovable (8th bodhisattva stage), 30n.7, 196–97
impermanence, 29–30, 65–66, 135, 149–50, 161, 179–80, 186–87. *See also* momentariness
impredicative definitions, 154
imputed nature, 91–92, 101–2, 109, 111, 116–17
inconsistency of the four ways of causal production, 85–86
Indra's net, 30n.6
induction, proof by, 160–61
ineffable entities, 108–10, 150
inference, Indian theory of, 8
infinite regress, 105–6
of conventions, 81n.62, 111n.93, 127–28, 156–57
instrumental value of the Buddhist path, 183–84
interpretable meaning, 18, 90–91
and Yogācāra, 117–18
intersubjective agreement about perceptions, 103
intrinsic characteristics, 85, 86, 185–90
intrinsic nature. See *prakṛti*, *svabhāva*
Introduction to the Middle Way, 9–21, 59–60, 130–31, 216
commentaries on, 10–11
Indian reception of, 18–20
lineage of transmission, 19–20n.53
Sanskrit original, 9–10
structure, 11–16
Introduction to the Two Truths, 20–21
island of jewels, 214
Īśvarakṛṣṇa, 45n.5

Jainism, 14–15, 118
Jamgön Mipham, 10–11, 134n.112
jātaka tales, 208
Jayānanda, 19n.49, 21–24
jñāna and *jñeya*, 31n.8
jñeyāvaraṇa. *See* cognitive obscurations
Joyous (1st bodhisattva stage), 30–36, 37, 59, 194
and direct realization of emptiness, 56

kāmadhātu, 17n.47
Kamalabuddhi, 8n.19
Kamalaśīla, 19
Kapila, 61
kāraka, 73n.46

karma, 14–15, 29–30, 44–45, 55, 57, 89, 109–10, 114–15, 123–24, 209, 216
  collective karma, 76n.54, 114
  karmic seeds, 34–35, 38, 44–45, 46–47, 76n.54, 87–88, 90, 91, 95–101, 102–3, 139, 149, 186–87, 194, 196, 205–6, 209–10, 211, 212, 216, 217
  and time, 87–89, 139–40
  Vaiśeṣika notion of, 74
Karmapa
  8th, 10–11
  9th, 10–11
Geshe Kelsang Gyatso, 10–11
King Mind and King Matter, 114–15
knowledge
  of death and birth, 211–12
  of the eradication of the taints, 212
  perfection of, 199

Lakṣaṇaṭīkā, 19n.49
Lāṅkāvatārasūtra, 29n.5, 56, 113, 117
light, emanating from the Buddhas, 199
logic
  Indian, 22, 173
lotus pond, 217
lower realms, 14–15, 216
Luminous (3rd bodhisattva stage), 30n.7, 42–48

Madhyamaka, 1–2, 5–7
  debate with Yogācāra, 17–18, 181
  does not contribute to philosophical debate, 130–31
  illusionism, 4, 167, 173, 208
  origin, 5
  and science, 84–85
  self-refuting, 167–74
  theses held by, 7–9, 22, 82n.65, 129n.107
  uniqueness of, 216–18
  views of opponents of, 62–63
Madhyamakahṛdayakārikā, 46n.8
Madhyamakālaṃkāra, 77n.57
Madhyamakāvatāra. See *Introduction to the Middle Way*
magnetism, 168–69, 172
Mahāyāna, 1–3, 11–12, 14–15, 16, 27, 31n.9, 32–33, 36, 38n.2, 54, 174, 175, 183–84, 186, 187, 189–90, 194, 202, 206, 207, 214–15
manifestations, 201, 205–7, 208
Mañjuśrī, 16–17
Māra, 50
materialism, 121–23
  epistemology of, 121–22
material elements, four, 105n.84, 121–23, 145, 157, 184–85, 186–87, 210
material objects, Yogācāra denial of, 91, 111–12
meditation
  on the impure, 102–3, 117
  knowledge of meditative states, 211
  meditative states, sets of, 83, 188
  perfection of, 51, 53–54
  visual experiences during, 42–43
  and Yogācāra, 102–3
memory, 105–8, 139–40
mental activity in a Buddha's mind, 22, 23
mental body, 196–97
merely mind, 17–18, 112–17
mereology, 157–58, 160–61. *See also* part-whole relation
  dependence, 153, 158–59
  reductionism, 74, 81–82
metaphilosophy, 177–78
metaphysical views, 129–30, 131–32
middle point, absence in infinite sequences, 182

mind and matter
as equally real, 115–17
as interdependent, 77n.56, 116
mind as emergent phenomenon, 121
mirror, 169–71
as example for causation, 86–87
momentariness, 29, 67n.40, 87–88, 90, 129, 138–39, 176, 186–87, 190, 203–4
moon, 1, 29–30, 36, 37, 40–41, 201–2, 217
double moon illusion, 77
reflected in the water, 29–30
moonstone, 36
moral discipline, perfection of, 34, 37–41
necessary condition for liberation, 15
supramundane, 16, 38
synergy with generosity, 13–14, 15
Mūlamadhyamakakārikā. See *Fundamental Verses on the Middle Way*
mūlaprakṛti, 61

nāga, 5, 217–18
Nāgārjuna, 2–3, 5–7, 8–9, 11–12, 14–15, 18–21, 23–24, 27n.1, 36n.15, 38n.2, 46n.8, 50n.3, 55–57, 60, 60n.26, 68, 74n.50, 82n.65, 110, 118n.101, 128n.106, 130–31, 134n.113, 137n.117, 216, 217–18
as basis of Candrakīrti's exposition, 55–56, 212–13
Nag tsho tshul khrims rgyal ba, 21
Nālandā, 3–4, 8n.19, 16–17
neyārtha. *See* interpretable meaning
nihilism, 57, 83, 109–10
nimitta, 27n.1
nine attainments, 211
nirmāṇakāya, 31n.9, 207, 215
nirodha. *See* cessation
nirodhasamāpatti, 30n.7, 193, 196
nirodha-satya, 53–54
nirvāṇa, 35–36, 123–24, 138, 140, 141–42, 163, 179–80, 183, 190, 191–92, 194, 210, 214, 215
nītārtha. *See* definite intent
non-dual mind, 27–28
nonexistent objects, 83n.68, 121–22, 125–26, 135, 159n.140, 191, *See also* barren woman, son of
Nyāya, 18

ocean, 29–30, 165–66, 194, 217
expelling corpses, 15–16
Yogācāra metaphor, 91
omniscience, 185, 186, 190, 202, 211–12
ontology, ultimate, 129, 131–32, 171, 177–78, 179–80, 183–84, 192–93

pañcamārga. *See* five paths to enlightenment
Pañcaskandhaprakarāṇa. See *Treatise on the Five Aggregates*
parabhāva, 15–16, 50n.3, 161n.142
paratantra-svabhāva. *See* dependent nature
parikalpita-svabhāva. *See* imputed nature
pariniṣpanna-svabhāva. *See* perfected nature
part-whole relation, 143–44, 151, 152–56, 157–59, 160–61, 163–64. *See also* mereology
past lives, memory of, 31n.11, 209, 211
path of seeing, 16, 36
patience, perfection of, 43–48, 187
positive karmic consequences of, 45
supramundane, 46
Pa tshab nyi ma grags, 21

perception at a distance, 172
perceptual illusions, 77, 123, 125–26, 173
perceptual relation, 74–75, 190
  perception as the only epistemic instrument, 121–22
  perceptual processes as ripening of karmic seeds, 99–101
  perceptual processes in dreams, 93–94
  Sautrāntika theory of, 203–4
perfected nature, 91–92
Perfect Intellect (9th bodhisattva stage), 30n.7, 198
Perfection of Wisdom, 5, 12, 15–16, 33n.13, 55–56, 116, 175, 192, 193, 217–18
perfections
  six, 54, 187
  ten, 30n.7, 33–34
  for lay people and monastics, 47, 49
permanence of causes, 83, 87
permanent 61n.33, 83, 87, 112–13, 133, 134–36, 141, 146, 149–50, 161–62, 181, 186–87, 191, 192–93
perpetual motion machine, 28–29n.4
persons, refuting intrinsically existent, 132–67
philosophical positions, correct and incorrect, 77–78
Phya pa chos kyi seng ge, 21–24
poison, 186–87, 215, 217–18. *See also* three poisons
post-meditative state, 42–43, 46, 155–56, 195
potential/actualizer distinction, 119–20
potter, 118–19, 144–45, 205–6
power, perfection of, 198
prabhākarī. *See* Luminous
Prajñākaramati, 20, 20n.56
Prajñāpāramitā. See *Perfection of Wisdom*
Prajñāpāramitā-hṛdaya-sūtra, 76n.55
prakṛti
  as intrinsic nature, 15–16, 87
  Sāṃkhya notion of, 18, 47n.16, 61–63, 65, 113, 133
pramāṇa. *See* epistemic instrument
Pramāṇasamuccaya, 73n.45
pramuditā. *See* Joyous
prasaṅga. *See* contradictory consequence
Prāsaṅgika Madhyamaka, 9, 9n.21, 13, 16, 21, 20n.54, 68, 126, 217
  epistemology of, 81–82
Prasannapdā. See *Clear Words*
Pratibhāna, 27n.1, 189
pratisaṃvid. *See* four superlative individuating knowledges
pratītyasamutpāda. *See* dependent origination
pratyekabuddha, 15, 27–28, 31–33, 35, 194, 213–15
presentism, 49n.1, 72–73, 87–88, 190, 203–4
profound, 213
pudgalanairātmyā. *See* emptiness of persons
Pudgalavāda, 138
puruṣa, 18, 61, 133
pūrvanivāsānusmṛti. *See* past lives, memory of

quantum physics, metaphysical interpretation of, 61n.31, 82n.63
quartets of meditative states, 46–47, 188

Radiant (4th bodhisattva stage), 30n.7, 49

random succession of cause and effect, 83, 86–87, 89, 120–23, 129, 157
Ratnākaraśānti, 20
Ratnāvalī, 11–12, 27n.1, 36n.15
realm
  of existence, 28–29, 36, 38–39, 44–45, 50, 136, 180, 201, 216
  form realm, 46–47, 188, 202, 211
  heavenly realm (see *akaniṣṭha*)
  pure realm, 196–97, 200 (*see also* buddha-field)
  three realms, 17n.47, 180, 193, 196–97, 210
rebirth, 38–39, 45, 57, 58–59, 121–22, 180, 207, 210, 211–12, 216
reductionism
  about collections, 156
  about the self, 13–14
  mereological, 74, 81–82
reflection-like nature of phenomena, 54
reflexive action, 161–62
reflexive awareness, 20n.54, 104–10
regal succession, 199
relationism, 129–30
Rendawa, 10–11
Ṛenzong, 22
representation, mental, 203–4
revisionist metaphysics, 111–12
rituals, 31–32
rival views, 62–63
Rubik's color illusion, 29n.5
rūpadharma, 157, 186–87
rūpadhātu, 17n.47
rūpakāya, 31n.9
rūpāvacaradhyāna. *See* absorptions of the form realm

Saddharmapuṇḍarīkasūtra, 214
sādhumatī. *See* Perfect Intellect
Samantabhadra, 31
śamatha, 27n.1, 211
saṃbhogakāya, 31n.9, 207
Saṃdhinirmocanasūtra, 117
Sāṃkhya, 14–15, 17–18, 47n.16, 61, 63–64, 65–66, 78, 113, 133, 135
Sāṃkhyakārikā, 45n.5
Sāmmitīya, 15, 136–38, 140–41, 142, 143–44, 146, 147, 149, 150, 151–52
saṃsāra. *See* cyclic existence
saṃyojanatraya. *See* three fetters
Śāntarakṣita, 19, 77n.57
Śāntideva, 20, 20n.54, 20n.56, 29n.5, 46n.8, 54n.8, 116n.100, 143n.127
Sarvāstivāda, 50n.1, 53n.5, 74–75, 159n.140, 179–80, 216
śāstra, 33n.13
satkāryavāda, 62
satkāyadṛṣṭi, 31–32, 31n.11, 132, 137, 149
Satyadvayāvatāra. *See* Introduction to the Two Truths
Sautrāntika, 159n.140, 203–4, 216
scriptural support for Yogācāra, 101–2, 112–18
secret not commonly taught, 215
self
  basis of imputation of, 136, 137–38, 162–63
  belief in self vanishes at the 4th bodhisattva stage, 49
  belief in a substantial self, 28–29, 31–32
  as causally unproduced, 134
  and change, 161–62
  as collection of the aggregates, 142–46
  conceived as substantially real, 134–35
  as conventional designation, 152, 173–74
  different from aggregates, 133–36, 162

identical with the aggregates, 136–49
innate superimposition of, 133, 136
mis-identifying the self to be negated, 146
neither identical with or different from the aggregates, 149–52
ownership model, 147–48
realization of selflessness, 141–42
referent of the term, 136
transcendent, 134, 135, 146, 152, 162
twenty wrong views about, 148–49
view of the self as the result of bad philosophy, 133–36
self-grasping mind, 162–63
self-refutation, 167–74
self-reproduction, 47n.13
semantic insulation of the two truths, 57n.18
sense-faculties, 176, 177, 215
sense spheres, 161, 184–85, 186–87, 210
serpent-stone, 217–18
sevenfold analysis, 13–14, 15
Seventy Verses on the Three Refuges, 2–3, 3n.4
Seventy Verses on Emptiness, 2–3
ship, 196
simultaneity of cause and effect, 73, 96
Sixty Verses on Reasoning, 2–3, 3n.4, 20
skandha. *See* five aggregates
snake, 85–86, 146, 162–63, 186–87, 217–18. See also *nāga*, serpent-stone
solar eclipse, 169–71
Songtsen Gampo, 1
soteriology, 13–14, 22–24, 55, 58, 80–81, 82n.64, 109–10, 136–37
space, 105n.84, 167–68, 178–79, 180, 182, 190, 191–92, 202, 208, 210, 213–14, 217–18
four-dimensional, 79–80
śrāvaka, 27, 31–32. See also *arhat*
śrotāpanna. *See* stream-enterer
Strawson, Galen, 91n.77
stream-enterer, 32, 149
student
different kinds of, 176
suitable as a recipient of the teaching of emptiness, 56–57, 58
subjectivity of perception, 66n.38, 103–4
subject-object duality, 42–43, 91, 202–3, 204. *See also* three spheres
sudurjayā. *See* Hard to overcome
sun, 42–43, 48, 169–71
Śūnyatāsaptati. See *Seventy Verses on Emptiness*
superimpositions, 13–14, 27–28, 81–82, 84, 132–33, 137, 151, 157–59, 160, 162n.144, 163, 177–78, 182, 183, 203–4
innate superimposition of the self, 133
supernatural powers, 47, 196–97, 201, 208. *See also* manifestations
sūtra, 17–18, 24–25, 55–56, 91–92, 112–13, 114, 117, 142, 186, 189–90, 210, 216
svabhāva, 15–16, 29–30, 40, 42, 43–44, 46, 47n.16, 50n.3, 68, 70, 72–73, 76, 80, 82–83, 84, 87–88, 92, 94, 96–98, 106–10, 119–20, 120n.102, 123–24, 126–27, 128–30, 134n.113, 141–42, 151, 159, 160–61, 164–66, 167, 169, 171–72, 173–74, 176–78,

179–80, 182, 183, 185–89, 190, 191–92, 203, 216–17
as emptiness, 176–77
nonexistent ultimately and conventionally, 126–27, 216–17
svalakṣaṇa. *See* intrinsic characteristics
svasaṃvedana. *See* reflexive awareness
Svātantrika, 9n.21, 16, 20–21, 68
Śvetāśvara Upaniṣad, 61

Taizong, 1
Tāranātha, 16–17
tathatā, 180
tattva
Sāṃkhya notion of, 47n.14, 61–62, 63–64, 65–66
temporal relations, 63–64, 72–75, 165–66, 167–69, 171–72, 182, 206. *See also* time
ten
powers of the Buddha, 188, 209–12
virtuous actions, 15, 37
wrong actions, 15, 37
theses, held by Mādhyamikas, 7–9, 22, 82n.65, 129n.107
thirty-seven factors of enlightenment, 27n.1, 49, 188
three
bodies of the Buddha, 31n.9, 206–8
doors to liberation, 188
fetters, 31–32
knowledges of the Buddha, 207
mental qualities of the bodhisattva, 27–28
natures, 91–92
poisons, 47, 78, 183
spheres, 16, 36, 38, 43–44, 46
time, 72–75, 87–88, 90, 105n.84, 122–23, 127, 162, 164, 165–66, 176, 182–83, 190–91, 208. *See also* temporal relations
timira. *See* vitreous floaters
toraṇa. *See* arched gateway
Treatise on the Five Aggregates, 2–3, 3n.4
trichiliocosm, 201
trikāya. *See* three bodies of the Buddha
Triśaraṇasaptati. See *Seventy Verses on the Three Refuges*
Trisvabhāva. *See* three natures
truth
conventional, 4, 22, 23, 31n.8, 51, 53–54, 57, 68, 69, 76–79, 81–83, 84–86, 89, 94, 107–8, 109–10, 111–12, 116–17, 119, 120–21, 120n.102, 124, 125, 126, 127, 128–29, 134–35, 142–43, 145, 152, 156–58, 159, 161, 163–64, 169–71, 174, 176–77, 178–79, 184, 193, 194, 199, 203–5, 206, 213–14, 217
conventional truth as concealing, 78–79
conventional truth for facilitating communication, 111
two truths, 20–21, 51, 76–87, 109–10
two truths and four noble truths, 51
two truths, semantic insulation, 57n.18
two truths and Yogācāra, 110–12, 116–17
ultimate, 8–9, 22, 23, 38n.2, 51, 68, 74, 76, 79–80, 81–83, 84–86, 88, 91–92, 100–2, 107–8, 109–10, 112–14, 116–17, 119, 120n.102, 125, 126–28, 131–32, 134–35, 139–40, 145, 154–55, 156–59,

164–67, 170, 175, 177–78, 179–80, 181, 183, 185, 193, 194, 196, 199, 204–5, 206, 213–14, 216
ultimate truth as inexpressible, 79–80
Tsong kha pa, 10, 23–24, 52n.1, 111n.94, 139n.122, 181
Turned toward (6th bodhisattva stage), 12, 30n.7, 52–194

ultimate truth. *See* truth, ultimate
unanswered questions, 140
unconditioned things, 159n.140
unenlightened beings, 15, 22, 32, 46
universal set, 185

Vaidalyaprakaraṇa, 46n.8
vaiśāradya. *See* four fearlessnesses
Vaiśeṣika, 15, 74, 133–34, 178–79
vast, 213
Vasubhandu, 34n.14, 46n.8, 217
Vātsīputrīya, 137
Vedānta, 133–34
Vigrahavyāvartanī, 74n.50, 128n.106
vijñāna-skandha, 136–37
vimalā. *See* Immaculate
vimokṣamukha. *See* three doors to liberation
Visuddhimagga, 66n.37
vitaṇḍā, 174
vitreous floaters, 80, 89, 94–96, 102, 103–4, 123, 125–26, 130, 172
and Yogācāra, 94–96, 103–4

water-wheel, 28–29, 28–29n.4
wisdom, perfection of, 12, 39–40, 54–55, 187, 195, 199, 215
wish-fulfilling gem, 206–7
wish-fulfilling tree, 206–7

Xuanzang, 1

Yogācāra, 1–2, 4, 14–15, 16–18, 54n.10, 90–118, 130–31, 181
creation of the world, 91, 112–15, 122–23
debate with Madhyamaka, 17–18
denial of material objects, 91
scriptural support for, 101–2, 112–18
theory of perception, 99–101, 103
and two truths, 110–12, 116–17
Yogācārabhūmi, 46n.8
Yuktiṣāstikā. See *Seventy Verses on Emptiness*